The Pandemic and the People of God

Also by Gerald A. Arbuckle, SM

Strategies for Growth in Religious Life

*Out of Chaos**

*Earthing the Gospel**

Grieving for Change

*Refounding the Church**

From Chaos to Mission

*Healthcare Ministry**

Dealing with Bullies

Confronting the Demon

Violence, Society, and the Church

Crafting Catholic Identity in Postmodern Australia

A 'Preferential Option for the Poor'

Laughing with God

Culture, Inculturation, and Theologians

Humanizing Healthcare Reforms

*Catholic Identity or Identities?***

The Francis Factor and the People of God

Intentional Faith Communities in Catholic Education

*Fundamentalism at Home and Abroad**

*Loneliness****

*Abuse and Cover-Up*****

*USA Catholic Press Award
**USA Association of Catholic Publishers Award, 2014
***Spirituality & Practice, Top 50 Spiritual Books of 2018
****Book Authority, 7 Best New Social Abuse E-books of 2020

The Pandemic and the People of God

Cultural Impacts and Pastoral Responses

Gerald A. Arbuckle, SM

Maryknoll, New York 10545

Founded in 1970, Orbis Books endeavors to publish works that enlighten the mind, nourish the spirit, and challenge the conscience. The publishing arm of the Maryknoll Fathers and Brothers, Orbis seeks to explore the global dimensions of the Christian faith and mission, to invite dialogue with diverse cultures and religious traditions, and to serve the cause of reconciliation and peace. The books published reflect the views of their authors and do not represent the official position of the Maryknoll Society. To learn more about Maryknoll and Orbis Books, please visit our website at www.maryknollsociety.org.

Published by Orbis Books, Maryknoll, New York 10545-0302.

Manufactured in the United States of America

Library of Congress Cataloging-in-Publication Data

Names: Arbuckle, Gerald A., author.
Title: The pandemic and the people of God : cultural impacts and pastoral responses / Gerald A. Arbuckle, SM.
Description: Maryknoll, NY : Orbis Books, 2021. | Includes bibliographical references and index. | Summary: "Draws from anthropology and theology to provide an analysis of the role of the church in responding to the COVID-19 pandemic"— Provided by publisher.
Identifiers: LCCN 2021011102 (print) | LCCN 2021011103 (ebook) | ISBN 9781626984417 | ISBN 9781608339044 (epub)
Subjects: LCSH: Church work with the sick. | COVID-19 (Disease)—Religious aspects—Christianity. | Diseases—Religious aspects—Christianity.
Classification: LCC BV4335 .A73 2021 (print) | LCC BV4335 (ebook) | DDC 259/.41962414—dc23
LC record available at https://lccn.loc.gov/2021011102
LC ebook record available at https://lccn.loc.gov/2021011103

For Adolfo Nicolas, SJ (1936–2020),
friend and mentor

Contents

Acknowledgments

My particular thanks to Robert Ellsberg and Jill Brennan O'Brien for accepting this book for publication on behalf of Orbis Books; to Nicholas Curtis, AM, without whose encouragement, business insights, and concern for international justice this book would never have been written; and to Thomas Ryan, SM, Brian Cummings, SM, and Anthony Corcoran, SM, for their astute comments on the text. These people, however, are in no way responsible for any deficiencies of the book. My gratitude also to the following for permission to adapt material I have originally published: Michael Goonan, SSP, St. Paul's Publications, Sydney, in *Intentional Faith Communities in Catholic Education* (2016): 71–74, 141–60; Hans Christoffersen, Liturgical Press, in *Catholic Identity or Identities? Refounding Ministries in Chaotic Times* (2013): 179–96, 223–25; Betty Crosby, in *Health Progress: Journal of the Catholic Health Association of the United States*, "Mission and Business: Resolving the Tension" (September–October 1999: 22–24), "Retelling 'The Good Samaritan'" (July–August 2007: 20–24), "The People of God: Healing through Mourning" (March–April 2020: 47–50), and "The Pandemic: Enduring Human Costs of Poverty" (May 18, 2020:1–4).

The book is dedicated to Adolfo Nicolas, SJ, the late Jesuit superior general. When we first met at the East Asian Pastoral Institute in Manila in 1978, he said: "I, a theologian, need the ongoing help of your cultural anthropology. A theology that loses touch with culture is a dead theology!" I valued his warm friendship and gift of sharing our different disciplines for forty years. His attitude toward anthropology mirrored the advice of the master theologian, Karl Rahner: Theology may discover "its most significant dialogical partner not in philosophy but in the natural, psychological, and social sciences, which shape people's self-understanding in the present."[1]

[1] Karl Rahner, cited by Anne Carr, "Theology and Experience in the Thought of Karl Rahner," *The Journal of Religion* 53, no. 3 (1973): 373.

Introduction

Solidarity is the road to take towards a post-pandemic world, towards the healing of our interpersonal and social sicknesses. There is no other path.

—Pope Francis, General Audience, September 22, 2020

[Solidarity] means thinking and acting in terms of community . . . [of] combatting the structural causes of poverty, inequality.

—Pope Francis, *Fratelli Tutti*, 2020

The coronavirus is not the only disease to be fought, but rather, the pandemic has shed light on broader social ills. One of these is a distorted view of the person. . . . At times we look at others as objects, to be used and discarded. . . . [This] fosters an individualistic and aggressive throw-away culture, which transforms the human being into a consumer good.

—Pope Francis, General Audience, August 12, 2020

The world is in chaos. It is grappling with the most severe health and economic emergency of modern times as a consequence of COVID-19, the disease caused by a virus a thousand times tinier than a dust speck. An untold number of people have died.[1] The enduring human suffering, especially among society's most vulnerable—the poor and the elderly—is incalculable. It is estimated that the pandemic could cast 490 million people in seventy countries into extreme poverty, reversing almost a decade of advances.[2] Many societies have the means to control the disease, but it is here in the fundamentals of public health that too many governments have miserably failed their people.[3] Business institutions worldwide have encountered disruptions at a rate and scale without precedence since the Great Depression. World order is further endangered. "It is not yet multipolar," declares António Guterres, secretary general of the United Nations, "it's essentially chaotic."[4] Only international cooperation can end the pandemic's medical, social, and economic consequences. But the signs are not good.[5]

This book focuses on the enduring national and international human costs of this chaos; the injustices suffered by the vulnerable; and the human values of solidarity, compassion, and justice that must infuse the decision-making of individuals and governments in their efforts to respond to the pandemic and its aftermath. The obstacles are not minimized (see Chapters 1, 4, and 5).

---

[1] At the end of September 2020, "The United States saw its official covid-19 death toll—higher than that of all western Europe put together—break the 200,000 barrier. India . . . will soon take America's unenviable laurels as the country with the largest official case count. The world looks set to see its millionth officially recorded death from covid-19." "Grim Tallies," *The Economist* (September 26, 2020), 17. By late October 2020, the third surge of the pandemic was under way.

[2] See "Failing the Poor," *The Economist* (September 26, 2020), 10. The pandemic led "to a labour-market implosion in which the equivalent of nearly 500 million full-time jobs disappeared almost overnight." "Winners and Losers," *The Economist* (October 10, 2020), 14.

[3] Richard Horton, editor of *The Lancet,* writes: "The response of governments to COVID-19 represents the greatest political failure of Western democracies since the Second World War. A government's first responsibility is its duty of care to citizens. Early government inaction led to the avoidable deaths of thousands of those citizens. The failures were legion." *The COVID-19 Catastrophe* (Cambridge: Polity Press, 2020), 84.

[4] António Guterres, cited in "Missing in Action," *The Economist* (June 20, 2020), 4.

[5] See Thomas J. Bollyky and Chad P. Bown, "The Tragedy of Vaccine Nationalism," *Foreign Affairs* 99, no. 5 (2020): 96–108.

There is a yearning for the "normality" of the pre–COVID-19 times, but it cannot be. When an event as huge and globally significant as the pandemic happens, the political, social, and economic reverberations take years and even generations to play out, and they spin off in unpredictable directions (see Chapters 1 and 3). Moreover, an experience of such traumatic severity leaves physical and mental marks that are indelible. There is a difference between a felled tree and a felled human being. The tree is doomed. Uprooted human beings may be equally powerless, but they are conscious of their fate.

No single crisis since the Second World War has left so many people in so many nations traumatized, overwhelmed by grief, and stunned by the cultural and economic consequences of the disease. Globally, an untold number of people have died, many without funerals or memorials to honor them. There is also the massive escalation of world poverty and inequalities, millions of people without jobs, and the surge of nationalism and racism fueled by authoritarian populist leaders, who further add to the trauma by ignoring the ongoing ecological crisis. No one is certain how best to move forward to protect lives while struggling to overcome the devastating impact of these social and economic problems (see Chapters 4 and 5).[6] The pandemic reminds us that contemporary human sciences are not infallible.

World Order Threatened

Before the pandemic, economic and social inequalities—the breeding ground of violence and racial tensions both within and between nations—had been on the rise (see Chapters 3 and 4).[7] Yascha Mounk cogently argued in 2018 that three big happenings are driving the

---

[6] See "Starting Over Again: The Pandemic Has Accelerated a Rethink of Macroeconomics. It Is Not Yet Clear Where It Will Lead," *The Economist* (July 25, 2020), 13–15.

[7] See Gerald A. Arbuckle, *Fundamentalism at Home and Abroad: Analysis and Pastoral Responses* (Collegeville, MN: Liturgical Press, 2017); Martin Sandbu, *The Economics of Belonging* (Princeton, NJ: Princeton University Press, 2020), 17–18, 28–29, 56–62; Jack Kelly, "US Lost Over 60 Million Jobs—Now Robots, Tech and Artificial Intelligence Will Take Millions More," *Forbes* (October 27, 2020); and Robert D. Putnam and Shaylyn Romney Garrett, *The Upswing: How America Came Together a Century Ago and How We Can Do It Again* (New York: Simon and Schuster, 2020), 186–99.

instability of democracies.[8] First and most important, there is the slow economic growth and the widening gap between the rich and poor; people in industrial areas destroyed by economic failures become avid supporters of the enticing unreality of populist leaders such as Donald Trump and others.[9] Second, the recent surge in immigration in most prominent democracies is fueling a backlash against ethnic and cultural pluralism. Third, the expansion of social media is providing an opportunity for autocratic and fundamentalist voices to circumvent traditional media gatekeepers. The rise of digital technology "has favoured the spread of hate speech and conspiracy theory."[10]

The pandemic has dramatically intensified these realities. The consequences? The more unequal a society, the more the political and social upheaval. Democracy is experiencing its worst crisis since the tragic explosion of nationalism in the 1930s that ended with the Second World War, with millions of people killed and millions of others displaced from their homelands. Political polarizations, nationalisms, and severe economic depressions are socially and politically dangerous mixes.[11] "In a world of increasing fundamentalist movements, of wall-builders, door-slammers, and drawbridge raisers,"[12] the dangers to world peace are again rapidly becoming evident (see Chapters 2 and 3). Pope Francis in *Fratelli Tutti* calls this a rebirth of nationalistic

---

[8] See Yascha Mounk, *The People vs. Democracy: Why Our Freedom Is in Danger and How to Save It* (Cambridge, MA: Harvard University Press, 2018).

[9] See Sandbu, *The Economics of Belonging*, 17–36, 192; Harriet Bradley, *Fractured Identities: Changing Patterns of Inequality* (Cambridge: Polity, 2016), 260–78; and Simon Winlow, Steve Hall, and James Treadwell, *The Rise of the Right: English Nationalism and the Transformation of Working-Class Politics* (Bristol: Policy Press, 2017), 197–208.

[10] Mounk, *The People vs. Democracy*, 237; also see Cynthia Miller-Idriss, *Hate in the Homeland: The New Global Far Right* (Princeton, NJ: Princeton University Press, 2020), 7–8, 20–22, 56–62. Mounk emphasizes the disturbing fact of "mainstreaming extremism," which is the spread of hateful and violent attitudes so that ever more people share and promote them.

[11] See Pippa Norris and Ronald Inglehart, *Cultural Backlash: Trump, Brexit and Authoritarian Populism* (Cambridge: Cambridge University Press, 2019), 464.

[12] Madelaine Drohan. "Liberty Moves North," *The Economist* (October 29, 2016), 8.

"narcissism . . . born of a certain insecurity and fear of the other that leads to rejection and the desire to erect walls for self-defence. . . . The sense of belonging to a single human family is fading" (nos. 146, 30). Little wonder that populist leaders, with their simplistic solutions to economic and social problems, are in the ascendancy.[13]

It is a cliché of management-speak that culture is set at the top. The contribution of Donald Trump's term as president to the enduring human costs of the pandemic both internationally and locally is immense (see Chapter 3). To overcome the long-term consequences of COVID-19 there must be international cooperation, but President Trump did his best to prevent this happening by his frequent attacks on NATO and the United Nations. He praised autocrats and denigrated allies. He abandoned the World Health Organization (WHO), a body dedicated to tackling the pandemic especially in the most vulnerable nations. He formally withdrew from the 2015 Paris Agreement on climate-change mitigation.

When Donald Trump first began to campaign for the US presidency with the slogan "Make America Great Again," the nation was divided. For liberals, the major worry for the previous thirty-five years had been the injustice of the economy—virtual wage inertia for most workers, enormous increases for the top 1 percent, and the negligent regulatory and enforcement regimes that have allowed these results, along with slow recovery from the most recent recession of 2008.[14] For conservatives, for about the same period, the main anxiety was about what is generally called the nation's "culture," by which is really meant the anger felt by mainly older white Americans that the nation is no longer "theirs." Their former status and authority, they claimed, had vanished. The "culture" that they now despised and

[13] David Goodhart comments: "Populists . . . tend not to be interested in the complexities of policy and . . . usually offer merely simple solutions to complex problems. The problem with simple solutions [of populist leaders] is that they raise expectations that are almost always disappointing, which then encourages even simpler or more radical solutions in a downward spiral of anger and denunciation." *The Road to Somewhere: The Populist Revolt and the Future of Politics* (London: Hurst, 2027), 74.

[14] In the United States, while "American GDP per person grew by 14% in 2001–15, median wages grew by only 2%." "The Politics of Anger," *The Economist* (July 2, 2016), 9. See Arbuckle, *Fundamentalism at Home and Abroad*, 78–81.

feared encompassed a number of concerns—immigration, especially illegal immigration; same-sex marriage; a black president in the White House; and all the things that conservatives package together under the detested category of political correctness. According to them, it is some kind of disease that has infected every institution in their once-great nation and is corrupting it daily before their eyes.[15] Trump tapped into this anger during his campaign leading up to the 2016 presidential election.

Not surprisingly, therefore, his election "stoked fears, incited hatreds, and sowed doubts about American leadership in the world, and about the future of democracy itself."[16] The fears proved justified. Trump spent four years exacerbating this national division, with global consequences. His xenophobic right-wing populism reached a new level of vicious cultic fundamentalism. As a fundamentalist populist,[17] Trump became a "rage machine,"[18] striking out at whatever his followers felt angry and resentful about even if this meant scores of false statements, boasting, and scapegoating. The more vulgar and xenophobic he became, the more his widespread following increased.

Trump's popularity was built on fostering ever-increasing fear, hatred, and violence in his audiences. He vowed to overturn Obamacare legislation that ensures the poor have medical insurance,[19] thus making them more vulnerable to the pandemic infection. His lack of national leadership during the crisis encouraged the spread of the virus at the cost of countless lives and livelihoods. His followers could not get enough of his unrestrained conspiracy accusations and anger.[20] For

---

[15] See Michael Tomasky, "The Dangerous Election," *The New York Review of Books* (March 24, 2016).

[16] Jill Lepore, *These Truths: A History of the United States* (New York: W. W. Norton, 2018), 782.

[17] See Gerald A. Arbuckle, *Loneliness: Insights for Healing in a Fragmented World* (Maryknoll, NY: Orbis Books, 2018), 67–68.

[18] See Michael Tomasky, "Trump," *The New York Review of Books* (September 24, 2015).

[19] David M. Craig correctly comments: "The Affordable Care Act [Obamacare] and the Tea Party can be thought of as fratricidal twins. They grew up together. . . . The conflict is over America's values and their role in reforming US health care." *Health Care as a Social Good: Religious Values and American Democracy* (Washington, DC: Georgetown University Press, 2014), 183.

[20] See Arlie Russell Hochschild, *Strangers in Their Own Land: Anger and Mourning on the American Right* (New York: New Press, 2016); Nancy

four years, by his constant attack on presidential norms and conventions of government, including his refusal to accept the legitimacy of the election process and provoking the mob assault on the Capitol, Trump has helped to undermine the trust that is the foundation of democracy and an essential condition for collective action against the enduring human costs of COVID-19. Sadly, his anti-democratic actions and refusal to acknowledge the human costs of the pandemic encouraged autocratic leaders of other nations to grab more power for themselves at the cost of their citizens. And Trump's political party did not sleep through all this. Members of the Republican Party colluded with, even at times openly encouraged, Trump's autocratic behavior.

However, the failures to address the pandemic crisis point to individualism, not the authoritarianism of one man, as the ultimate cause of America's contemporary calamity. Trump is not the most distressing reality in America's cultural trauma. He is no longer president, but the culture of narcissistic individualism remains significantly present. It gravely hampers collective action for national healing (see Chapters 4 and 5).[21] Social researcher Jean Twenge concludes: "No single event initiated the narcissism epidemic; instead, Americans' core ideals slowly became more focused on self-admiration and self-expression. At the same time, Americans' faith in the power of collective action of the government was lost."[22]

All this is making it difficult for Trump's successor, President Joe Biden, to foster national and international solidarity in order to combat the human costs of the pandemic. The cultural narcissism, racial divide, cultural conflict, and political polarization Trump fostered and intensified will be hard to heal. It will take far more than one presidential election to unite a profoundly divided nation, a "nation whose political cleavages run so deep that the polity cannot even agree to wear masks during a deadly pandemic."[23]

Isenberg, *White Trash: The 400–Year Untold History of Class in America* (New York: Penguin Books, 2017), xiii–xxiv, 310–21.

[21] See Don Watson, "American Carnage: Donald Trump and the Collapse of the Union," *The Monthly* (July 2020), 19.

[22] Jean M. Twenge and W. Keith Campbell, *The Narcissism Epidemic* (New York: Simon and Schuster, 2020), 67.

[23] Mark Danner, "The Con He Rode in On," *The New York Review of Books* 67, no. 18 (2020): 37.

COVID-19 and Aftermath: Options

Vaccines alone will not resolve the chaos. Individually and collectively, therefore, we are confronted with a choice: to let the world drift further into global divisions and conflict, or to find ways to cooperate in refounding institutions on moral values of justice and compassion, no matter how difficult that sounds. International solidarity and strengthened multilateral institutions have never been so vital. Pope Francis, a truly global leader, is right when he says: "If the struggle against COVID-19 is a war . . . [we are] an army whose only weapons are solidarity, hope, and community spirit, all revitalizing at a time when no one can save themselves alone."[24]

Ultimately, the repercussions of the pandemic can only be resolved through global cooperation, but the possibility of such international solidarity appears increasingly remote. The United Nations, established in 1945 "to save humanity from hell,"[25] now looks shaky as a guardian of international peace. There is a global crisis of leadership today.[26] Relevant here are the words of the late political philosopher Tony Judt, bemoaning the poverty of political leadership in the world and the failure to make decisions based on moral values:

> Whatever their political affinities, Leon Blum and Winston Churchill, Luigi Einandi and Willy Brandt, David Lloyd George and Franklin Roosevelt represented a political class deeply sensitive to its moral and social responsibilities. . . . Today, neither incentive is at work. Politically speaking, ours is an age of pygmies. . . . The institutions of the republic have been degraded, above all by money. Worse, the language of politics itself has been vacated of substance and meaning.[27]

---

[24] Pope Francis, cited in Antonio Spadaro, SJ, "'A New Imagination of the Possible': Seven Images from Francis for Post-Covid-19," *La Civiltà Cattolica* (July 14, 2010).

[25] Dag Hammarskjöld, cited in "The New World Disorder," *The Economist* (June 20, 2020), 7.

[26] See Special Report, "Global Leadership Is Missing in Action," *The Economist* (June 20, 2020), 3–12.

[27] Tony Judt, *Ill Fares the Land: A Treatise on Our Present Discontents* (London: Allen Lane, 2010), 164–65.

He is right.[28] Nothing has changed since Judt wrote this in 2010 (see Chapter 3).

However, we cannot wait for the right political leaders to emerge. Regardless of our position in society, each of us can act to build social relations on moral values. We have to reconnect social relations with morals (see Chapter 1).[29] In order to move forward in a transforming manner, we need to be steered by a mythology or narrative, not of individualism powered by "dog-eat-dog" behavior, but of solidarity, respect for human dignity, and participation—all the values inherent in the Good Samaritan parable, as expounded by Pope Francis in *Fratelli Tutti* (FT, nos. 56–86). The encyclical is a clarion call for the refounding of the capitalist system. Together, in solidarity, we can creatively manage the enduring chaos, if we wish. However, "The word 'solidarity' is a little worn and at times poorly understood, but it refers," writes Pope Francis in *Evangelii Gaudium*, "to something more than a few sporadic acts of generosity. It presumes the creation of a new mindset which thinks in terms of community and the priority of the life of all over the appropriation of goods by a few" (no. 188).[30] Solidarity means compassion, suffering with others, and bearing burdens together. On the other hand, if we struggle to emerge from the pandemic to embrace individualism, with its egotistical grasping, this will lead to more chaos. We are again in danger of falling victim to the seductive lures of authoritarian and populist leaders (see Chapter 3).

Rites of Passage

This book argues that nations, institutions, and individuals, when motivated by the values of solidarity, compassion, and justice, are

---

[28] James F. Keenan, SJ, wrote in 2018 that the three most urgent issues today in ethics are the climate crisis and its impact on the poor and marginalized; the tragic banality of contemporary leadership; and racism and antiblackness. See "Prophetic Pragmatism and Descending to Matters of Detail," *Theological Studies* 79, no. 1 (2018): 128–45.

[29] See Michael J. Sandel, *What Money Can't Buy: The Moral Limits of Markets* (New York: Farrar, Straus and Giroux, 2012), 3–15.

[30] See comments by Conor M. Kelly, "Everyday Solidarity: A Framework for Integrating Theological Ethics and Ordinary Life," *Theological Studies* 81, no. 2 (2020): 415–37.

called in the threatening world of the pandemic and its consequences to participate in rites of passage (see Chapters 2, 3, and 6). With value-based leaders, these rites aim to guide people individually and collectively through chaotic times to a new life of integration. They are rites of initiation into a different way of living.

Formal and informal initiation rituals are common in everyday life to mark a change of status; for example, we ritualize marriage engagements, the first day at school, graduation from school and university, and retirement from employment. Such rites pilot initiates through the chaos of uncertainties to a new life and status, reminding them that they have to learn new behaviors and abandon former ones. In the process there is always a liminal period of ambiguity and risk. Initiates must grapple with a threefold tension: the urge to escape nostalgically to a past status, or to remain paralyzed by doubts, or to move forward into the unknown to obtain a fresh status. Initiates need the guidance of a new transforming narrative that contains values which form the foundation of the new status.[31] Will initiates choose to accept advice? Will they give up their old ways of acting? If not, they fail the initiation.

There are many rites of passage in the Bible, such as the Exodus and the return of the banished Israelites from Babylon in the Old Testament and the anointing of Christ as Savior in the New Testament (see Chapters 2, 3, and 6). These rites teach us strategic contemporary lessons. Ritual leaders make concrete, by their inner conversion and conviction, the idea that a new world of integration is possible. Mythologist Joseph Campbell describes the ritual leader in this way: he or she is a "hero" who "ventures forth from the world of common day into a region of supernatural wonder; fabulous forces are encountered and a decisive victory is won. The hero comes back from this mysterious adventure with the power to bestow boons on his fellow man."[32] The ritual leader is a hero who has visited this "region of supernatural wonder" and has been converted to the founding narrative of the group and the vision of a new world of integration. The hero's behavior mirrors this interior transformation. Initiates in groups, recognizing that their leaders carry within themselves the vision of

---

[31] See Jean Holm and John Bowker, eds., *Rites of Passage* (London: Pinter, 1994).

[32] Joseph Campbell, *The Hero with a Thousand Faces* (Princeton, NJ: Princeton University Press, 1949), 30.

their journey's end, are drawn to experience the same action-oriented conversion.

Reactions of Nations

The effectiveness of individual nations' responses to the pandemic is being calculated in the number of people who have died. It is a heartless bookkeeping process that tells us nothing about the reactions of individual national leaders. Are political leaders effectively acting as ritual guides of national rites of passage to shape a new order of justice? The answer to the question lies in the cultures of the different countries. Following the Second World War, Western capitalist nations—with the notable exception of the United States—fostered liberal values of solidarity, egalitarianism, and compromise that led to welfare-state policies. With the demise of communism in the late 1980s, governments began increasingly to undermine these values with neoliberal policies leading to more and more individualism and to social and economic inequalities.[33]

When COVID-19 struck, democratic governments had to make a decision: either they could discard neoliberal policies and reembrace solidarity; or they could reinforce neoliberal strategies, thereby increasing the wealth of a few and intensifying inequalities. Leaders of governments that choose the latter may turn to populism and nationalism to divert the attention of citizens from what is really happening. As Pope Francis notes in *Fratelli Tutti*, "lack of concern for the vulnerable can hide behind a populism that exploits them demagogically for its own purposes" (no. 155). He forthrightly confronts the political leaders and governments that embrace neoliberalism: "The notion of 'every man for himself' will rapidly degenerate into a free-for-all that would prove worse than any pandemic. . . . The marketplace, by itself, cannot resolve every problem, however much we are asked to believe this dogma of neoliberal faith" (FT, nos. 36, 168).

This book particularly examines the response of the political leaders of New Zealand, Australia, United States, Britain, China, Brazil, and Russia (see Chapter 3). The leaders of countries giving priority to solidarity and transparency, such as in Australia and New Zealand,

---

[33] See Branko Milanović, *Capitalism, Alone: The Future of the System That Rules the World* (Cambridge, MA: Harvard University Press, 2020).

have been more successful in controlling the spread of the virus and moving forward with justice and compassion than those overemphasizing individual rights and neoliberal values, such as in the United States, Britain, and Brazil. Leaders of autocratic countries such as China and Russia, which suffer from pervasive corruption and lack of transparency and trustworthiness, are more concerned with protecting their own power base. The pandemic may not have spread globally if local officials in China had not attempted to conceal its first appearance in Wuhan. I assert that chaos can be the catalyst for new life, but only if we are prepared to recognize that solid cultural change is slow and at times filled with uncertainty, thus demanding tolerance, patience, and the willingness to work in solidarity. In the process we become open to imaginative and alternative ways of doing things.

The People of God, COVID-19, and Hope

> Despite these dark clouds . . . I invite everyone to renewed hope. . . . Hope speaks to us of a thirst, an aspiration, a longing for a life of fulfilment, a desire to achieve great things. . . . Hope is bold. . . . It can open us to grand ideals. (FT, no. 55)

The Catholic Church is deeply affected by the pandemic (see Chapter 6). Already struggling to heal from the global chaos of the cover-up of sexual abuses by the clergy, it has been pushed further into cultural trauma by COVID-19. Churches were closed or attendance at services restricted, and financial support has been significantly reduced for schools and social services. What are we to make of all this trauma? How can we cope?

In our experience of chaos we can rediscover with God's energizing help our human powerlessness. Ponder the emphasis of chaos in the Book of Job, a relevant text about the human struggle for meaning within a bleak world: "the land of gloom and chaos where light is like darkness" (Job 10:22). When Job suffers afflictions, he contemplates the vulnerability and powerlessness of humankind. As God so exquisitely explains to Job, when God's face turns away from us and we encounter the fear-evoking force of darkness and uncertainty, then as creatures of God we come into contact with the chaos—out of which we were shaped—and the lessons it symbolizes. That is, we confront anew, if we freely choose to do so, the narrative foundations of our being, our own vulnerability, and at the same time the saving, recreative, and energizing power of God in Christ. We relearn to detach ourselves from an overconfidence in our abilities to act without God:

> But I am poor and needy;
>   hasten to me, O God!
> You are my help and my deliverer;
> O LORD, do not delay! (Ps 70:5)

The sufferings caused by the pandemic and its aftermath can be viewed very appropriately through the eyes of St. Paul. Almighty God's loving concern for us reaches unimaginable heights when Christ dies that we may live:

> who, though he was in the form of God
>   did not regard equality with God
>   as something to be exploited,
> but emptied himself,
>   taking the form of a slave . . .
>   even [to] death on the cross.
> Therefore God also highly exalted him.
> (Phil 2:6–9)

And we, as God's adopted children, are called to share in Christ's suffering, dying, and the glory of his resurrection: "For you did not receive a spirit of slavery to fall back into fear, but you have received a spirit of adoption . . . and if children [of God], then heirs, heirs of God and joint heirs with Christ—if, in fact, we suffer with him so that we may also be glorified with him" (Rom 8:15, 17). St. Paul continues:

> We know that the whole creation has been groaning in labor pains until now; and not only the creation, but we ourselves, who have the first fruits of the Spirit, groan inwardly while we wait for adoption, the redemption of our bodies. For in hope we were saved. . . . Likewise the Spirit helps us in our weakness; for we do not know how to pray as we ought, but that very Spirit intercedes with the sighs too deep for words. And God,

> who searches the heart, knows what is the mind of the Spirit, because the Spirit intercedes for the saints according to the will of God. (Rom 8:22–27)

Using the analogy of a woman giving birth, St. Paul describes the whole of creation, including humanity, struggling perilously forward with groans and travails, yearning for the final transformation. We are already sharing, however imperfectly, the transformed world born through the resurrection in Christ: "The sufferings of this present time are not worth comparing with the glory about to be revealed to us" (Rom 8:18). We are in the liminal stage of a rite of passage,[34] the in-between time in which we have received the "first fruits" of our redemption as God's children, but its completeness has yet to be fully embraced. Then "death will be no more; mourning and crying and pain will be no more, for the first things have passed away" (Rev 21:4)—and we will see "the new heavens and the new earth where righteousness is at home" (2 Peter 3:13).

This rite of passage is an enigmatic or paradoxical mixture—simultaneously a taste of the transcendent and an experience of belonging in the here and now. Hope keeps us moving forward on track. We are not lost. God is present in the midst of the pain. God, indeed, is groaning in labor also. The pandemic reminds us that we are in the midst of this rite of passage, and that our ritual guide, and one with us, is the Spirit of Jesus. The Spirit of Jesus, our journey's companion, is *with* us, groaning *with* us, interceding *for* us;[35] the rite of passage is a cooperative action of the praying Christian with the revitalizing

---

[34] In anthropology, the liminal stage is the precarious point in a journey of change when travelers have forsaken the past and strain forward to reach their journey's end, inspired by an interiorized vision of the future. See Chapter 2 for a fuller explanation.

[35] This text does not support providentialism, which is the belief that all events are controlled by God. Providentialists assert that the pandemic is retribution for sins. Earlier, Reverend Jerry Falwell interpreted the 9/11 attack on the World Trade Center in New York City as divine retribution for America's sins. See Michael J. Sandel, *The Tyranny of Merit: What's Become of the Common Good* (London: Allen Lane, 2020), 45. Providentialism is particularly popular among evangelical Christians, but it has supporters among American Catholic groups. See Rebecca Bratten Weiss, "COVID-19 Pandemic Has Revealed a Dangerous Providentialism among Catholics," *National Catholic Reporter* (September 3, 2020).

encouragements of the Spirit.[36] A central task in this in-between time is to pray—in the presence of the Spirit and in the midst of the world's pains.[37] It is a time for lamentation, for prayer amid the chaos of the pandemic (see Chapter 2):

> How long must I bear pain in my soul,
> and have sorrow in my heart all day long? . . .
> Consider and answer me, O Lord my God! . . . .
> But I trusted in your steadfast love;
> my heart shall rejoice in your salvation.
> (Ps 13:2, 3, 5)

Lamentation is inspired by hope.

Overview of the Book

This book of practical theology, written for the general reader, views the impact of COVID-19 on the lives of people and the options for moving forward through the lenses of cultural anthropology, scripture, and the writings of Pope Francis. Why turn to cultural anthropology? Economists can offer advice, as can epidemiologists and other medical experts, but ultimately cultures influence how people choose to act (see Chapter 1). In their studies of crises anthropologists explore changing social networks, while economists commonly focus on trade and investment flows. As Gillian Tett of the *Financial Times* writes: "Humans have psychological biases, cultural assumptions and inconsistent incentives. When these are ignored—as they often have been by financiers—they can derail forecasts and risk analyses. Culture matters."[38] The axiom "culture eats strategies for lunch" bespeaks profound truth.

---

[36] See Sarah Coakley, *God, Sexuality, and the Self: An Essay "On the Trinity"* (Cambridge: Cambridge University Press, 2013), 112.

[37] See N. T. Wright, "The Letter to the Romans," in *The Interpreter's Bible,* vol. 10 (Nashville, TN: Abingdon Press, 2002), 597–608, idem, *God and the Pandemic: A Christian Reflection on the Coronavirus and Its Aftermath* (London: SPCK, 2020), 38–51; and Robert Jewett, *Romans: A Commentary* (Minneapolis: Fortress Press, 2007), 508–28.

[38] Gillian Tett, "How Will We Weigh the Threats When We leave Lockdown?" *Financial Times* (May 8, 2020); see also Mary Douglas, *Risk:*

What is cultural anthropology? Veteran anthropologist Raymond Firth calls cultural anthropology "an inquisitive, challenging, uncomfortable discipline, questioning established positions . . . peering into underlying interests, if not destroying established positions and empty phrases . . . at least exposing them."[39] Anthropological fieldwork is a method "of studying *with* people, rather than simply the study *of* people."[40] It has two stages. The first stage is called participant observation, in which anthropologists strive to obtain an in-depth and holistic understanding of the contexts from which observations about human activities, behaviors, and values are derived. They delve beneath the surface of social life in order to uncover its underlying dynamics. Anthropologists aim to immerse themselves totally in the lives of the people they study by listening, observing what they say and do, and at times questioning everything; the purpose is to uncover the biases and assumptions by which people order their lives. Notetaking must be as extensive as possible to ensure accuracy. In the second stage, anthropologists systematize their findings by constructing a cultural model of what they have found. The model aims to illuminate reality by highlighting emphases and downplaying details that might obstruct the clarity of the process; the model is then modified or discarded in light of the data being reviewed. A model is simply a way of helping people to comprehend the main strands of very complex processes, and we should expect no more from it.

For this book I became a fieldworker (participant observer) for several months, listening to the extensive reactions of people to the pandemic as recorded in a wide range of national and international media and academic reports. Having amassed and filed the data, I gradually modified my Cultural Trauma: Grief-overload Model[41] (see Chapter 2) and continued to update it as more information emerged

---

Acceptability according to the Social Sciences (London: Routledge and Kegan Paul, 1985), 53–64.

[39] Raymond Firth, "Engagement and Detachment: Reflections on Applying Social Anthropology to Social Affairs," *Human Organization*, no. 40 (1981): 200.

[40] Tim Ingold, cited in Alan Barnard, *Social Anthropology: Investigating Human Social Life* (Abergele: Studymates, 2006), x.

[41] This model updates the one I first published in the following volumes: *The Francis Factor and the People of God: New Life for the Church* (Maryknoll, NY: Orbis Books, 2015), 126–98; and *Fundamentalism at Home and*

about the ways different political leaders reacted to the ongoing pandemic emergency. Some readers may find that the model further enlightens their own observations and experience, while others may see the need to modify it.

While I am aware that the world is complex and that no data-based academic model can definitively anticipate future developments, I conclude from the data amassed that national and international frictions will continue to escalate. Tensions are mounting, exacerbated by COVID-19, as they did before the two world wars, with deepening rivalries among the great powers, especially between China and the United States, and with regional conflicts threatening to pull in other nations. Memories of the outcome of the Great Depression and nationalisms of the 1930s give reality to our fears. It would be foolish to ignore them. History has a habit of repeating itself, at times even more dramatically and catastrophically.[42]

There are relevant scriptural reflections near the end of each chapter. Traditional pedagogical methods of evangelizing in the church have overstressed cognitive conversion or coercion, but this approach runs contrary to the preferred inductive pedagogical manner of the prophets of the Old Testament and Jesus Christ.[43] All four Gospels are narratives about the person of Christ; the focus is on the experience of Christ, the revelation of God. People are called repeatedly to remember and retell the story of Jesus Christ and in so doing to develop a deep personal relationship with him. The more the early Christians contemplated the story of Jesus in light of their own particular social, political, and economic circumstances, the more they could believe in Christ's loving concern for them as individuals and communities.

Abroad: Analysis and Pastoral Responses (Collegeville, MN: Liturgical Press, 2017), 73–93.

[42] Francis Fukuyama is not overly pessimistic on this point: "[Just] as the Great Depression not only produced fascism but also reinvigorated liberal democracy, so the pandemic may produce some positive political outcomes, too. . . . With the most urgent and tragic phase of the crisis past, the world is moving into a long, depressing slog. It will come out of it eventually, some parts faster than others." "The Pandemic and Political Order," *Foreign Affairs* 99, no. 4 (2020): 29, 32.

[43] See Gerald A. Arbuckle, *Catholic Identity or Identities? Refounding Ministries in Chaotic Times* (Collegeville, MN: Liturgical Press, 2013), 121–42.

In repeating his parables and rereading what he said and did, they discovered the values and narratives that should shape their lives. It was not an abstract or academic knowledge of Christ but a belief in a person who intimately cared for and loved them. To know Christ was for them "a dynamic, experiential, relational activity involving the whole person and finding expression in a lived response of loving obedience to God's will."[44]

This scriptural pedagogical method is followed in this book. It is the same process that Pope Francis commonly uses in his encyclicals and homilies, the see-judge-act mode of learning. The reader is invited, after reading the first descriptive section of each chapter, to then ponder the scriptural texts that follow, asking questions such as:

- What feelings do the scriptural passages evoke in me?
- What values in the scriptural texts are especially relevant to shaping my reactions to the crisis?
- Do the scriptural passages inspire courage in me to do something, however small, to assist others?
- What can I do in solidarity with others to plan and implement actions, based on gospel values, which help people who are poor?

Each chapter concludes with further questions that focus on the material presented therein.

Chapter 1: Shining Light on the Pandemic's Cultural Complexities

When large-scale dramatic events such as COVID-19 happen, the culturally distressing repercussions take years, even generations, to play out. This foundational chapter has two aims. The first is to clarify in a series of axioms significant anthropological terms used throughout the book's text, such as *culture, cultural chaos and trauma, the meaning and power of mythologies, conspiracy thinking and scapegoating, moral panics, the power of ritual,* and *grieving and mourning.* The second is to emphasize values such as solidarity, compassion, and justice that

---

[44] Thomas H. Groome, *Christian Religious Education: Sharing Our Story and Vision* (Melbourne: Dove, 1980), 144.

must guide all decisions and actions in the struggle to recover from the pandemic trauma. As Pope Francis advises in *Fratelli Tutti*, the parable of the Good Samaritan graphically articulates these values, which are contrary to the free-market fundamentalism of neoliberal economics.

Chapter 2: Journeying through Traumatic Times: Rites of Passage

A cultural trauma occurs when people are collectively subjected to a distressing event, such as the COVID-19 pandemic, that leaves indelible and paralyzing marks upon their group consciousness. In this chapter the Cultural Trauma: Grief-overload Model is formulated. Societies and individuals, as a consequence of cultural trauma such as COVID-19, need to enter a tripartite journey: separation, liminality, and reentry. This journey is a rite of passage, an initiation into a new status. The second or liminal stage of the rite is especially dangerous, as normal cultural constraints are suspended. In this stage, as historic examples illustrate, people can experience a strong emotional bonding called communitas during which they challenge injustices. The rite of passage fails unless ritual guides have effective leadership qualities. Experiences of chaos, liminality, cultural traumas, and rites of passage are frequently evident in the scriptures, which contain a multitude of lessons to guide societies and individuals through their own rites of passage.

Chapter 3: Successes and Failures of the Pandemic Rite of Passage

The Cultural Trauma: Grief-overload Model is applied to the pandemic and its consequences. The ways governments react to the pandemic are influenced by their political leaders and the operative mythologies of their countries. In the nations analyzed we find that political leaders—serving as "ritual guides"—who emphasize the democratic value of solidarity over individualism are more likely to lead their countries successfully through the tough tripartite rite of passage of the pandemic. Autocratic leaders are taking advantage of a world distracted by the pandemic to grab more oppressive power. At the same time, people freed from the regular cultural constraints in the liminal chaos stage are collectively claiming their authority to protest social abuses such as institutional racism and poverty. Prophetic leaders in the crisis relive Christ's initiation as Savior.

Chapter 4: The Enduring Impact of Poverty

The most enduring and devastating consequence of the pandemic is the increase of world poverty. People who are poor face a higher risk of contracting and subsequently spreading COVID-19 due to the lack of resources to prepare and protect them against the coronavirus and/or the unwillingness of governments to act appropriately. Moreover, the pandemic has increased existing poverty, suddenly casting millions more people into its appalling grip. This chapter aims to highlight (1) the global impact of the pandemic on poverty levels, and (2) the need to define poverty not only statistically but especially in terms of its human costs.[45] The scriptures call for holistic healing, which today includes physical and mental healthcare services along with the removal of social and economic inequalities.

Chapter 5: Racism and Institutional Racism Exposed

During the liminal stage of the pandemic the tragic death of George Floyd at the hands of police in America inspired local and global protests from Brazil to Indonesia and France to Australia, as the world reacted to graphic video images of deep-rooted racial inequalities in the United States and elsewhere. This chapter defines terms such as *prejudice, racism, ethnic group, ethnicity,* and *institutional racism*, using examples to illustrate their meaning. Racism is a persistent evil that flourishes in the midst of social and economic inequalities. Tragically, in the wake of the pandemic these inequalities are increasing and reinforcing institutional racism. At the time of Jesus Christ there were also wide gaps between the rich and the poor, much institutional bullying, and racist-like cultural customs that degraded people.[46] Jesus, by his methods of evangelizing and his teachings, neither tolerated nor turned a blind eye to these realities.

---

[45] A fuller development of the meaning of poverty and its impact on people is to be found in Arbuckle, *Loneliness*, 89–115.

[46] See John Stambaugh and David Balch, *The Social World of the First Christians* (London: SPCK, 1986).

Chapter 6: The Call to Refocus on Christ and His Mission

The people of God are stunned by two liminal traumatic experiences: the trauma of the church muddied by the sexual abuse and cover-up crises, and now the trauma of the global pandemic and its aftermath. Following the advice of Pope Francis, now is the time for the people of God to refocus on Christ, the Good Samaritan, and Christ's mission of holistic healing. The time is right for imaginative and creative pastoral responses such as fostering intentional faith communities in parishes and ministries, challenging institutional injustices, avoiding fundamentalist attitudes and actions, and ensuring that it is the mission of Christ, rather than neoliberal values, driving ministries.

1

Shining Light on the Pandemic's Cultural Complexities

> *COVID-19 attacks our physical bodies, but also the cultural foundations of our lives, the toolbox of community and connectivity that is for the human what claws and teeth represent to the tiger.*
>
> —Wade Davis, "The Unraveling of America"

> *Culture hides much more than it reveals, and strangely enough what it hides, it hides most effectively from its own participants.*
>
> —Edward T. Hall, *The Silent Language*

This chapter explains that:

- Mythologies bind people collectively together.
- Culture provides security and a feeling of normality.
- Cultural traumas destroy security, causing chaos and fear.
- The COVID-19 pandemic evokes global cultural trauma.
- Conspiracy thinking and scapegoating are attempts to cope with fear.
- Good Samaritan values guide the way forward.

A primary determinant of the response to difficult life situations is culture. The pandemic and its aftermath have affected not only the health of individuals but also the cultural foundations of their lives.

The fact is that chaos, disorder, and sudden profound cultural changes such as those caused by the pandemic "invalidate the conceptions of self and world that serve as guides by which new experience acquires meaning and life gains coherence."[1] But what is *culture*? What is the meaning of *cultural foundations*? *Culture* is surely a slippery, promiscuous word to define. The first part of the chapter seeks to answer these questions; the second, a scriptural reflection, focuses on the moral truths and values, evident in the Good Samaritan parable, which should guide the cultural rebuilding of the post-pandemic world.

Culture is a "silent language"[2] that gives us a sense of belonging and normality. This is so because a culture influences how we feel, think, and act without our being aware that this is happening. A culture tells us what is sacred and profane, right and wrong. It stipulates "guardrails" that hold us in line to ensure we do what is expected of us. Long-established cultures can be said to have lives of their own that are independent of the individuals that belong to them. I am born into an existing culture; when I die, it remains. The incontrovertible fact is that culture is very much about power; it has the capacity to make or break the best of us. And that power is often hidden. For example, we can rightly claim not to be racist but be totally unaware that we are colluding with institutional cultures of oppression and racism (see Chapter 5).

However, there is considerable disagreement about ways to further refine the meaning of culture.[3] Academics have tried to pin this down for decades. For example, writers researching management offer a popular definition—culture is "what we do around here"—but the meaning of culture is far more complicated than this. Others define

---

[1] Ervin Staub, *The Roots of Evil: The Origins of Genocide and Other Group Violence* (Cambridge: Cambridge University Press, 1989), 41.

[2] See Edward Hall, *The Silent Language* (New York: Doubleday, 1959).

[3] See Boris Groysberg et al., "The Leader's Guide to Corporate Culture," *Harvard Business Review* 96 (January–February 2018): 46. Two anthropologists—Kluckhohn and Kroeber—in 1952 gathered 156 different definitions of culture! Almost seventy years later, in view of the mushrooming interest in culture in many different disciplines, the number of definitions has dramatically increased. See Alfred Kroeber and Clyde Kluckhohn "Culture: A Critical Review of Concepts and Definitions," in *Papers of the Peabody Museum of American Archaeology and Ethnology*, no. 47 (Cambridge, MA: Harvard University Press, 1952), 5.

culture by detailing its characteristics: "culture is learned; culture is transmissible; culture is dynamic; culture is selective; the facets of culture are interrelated, and culture is ethnocentric."[4] The word is applied extensively to vastly different situations. Pope Francis in his encyclical *Fratelli Tutti* speaks of "popular culture, university culture, youth culture, artistic culture, technological culture, economic culture, family culture and media culture" (FT, no. 199). Given this widespread and random use of the term *culture*, Raymond Williams, British cultural historian, expressed the frustration of many people when he wrote: "I don't know how many times I've wished that I'd never heard the damned word."[5]

Because of the confusion surrounding the meaning and use of the word *culture* and related terms, and because cultural anthropological literature is not readily accessible to the general reader, my aim is to clarify in a series of axioms what I mean by culture and to begin to describe ways in which the pandemic is having an impact on cultures.[6] In subsequent chapters readers are directed back to these axioms.

COVID-19 Evokes Cultural Trauma

Axiom 1. We fear chaos because culture responds to our need for normality, that is, consistency and felt order;[7] COVID-19 evoked cultural trauma, that is, the sudden, collective breakdown of order.

---

[4] Richard E. Porter and Larry A. Samovar, "An Introduction to Intercultural Communication," in *Intercultural Communication: A Reader*, 7th ed., ed. Larry A. Samovar and Richard E. Porter (Belmont, CA: Wadsworth, 1994), 12.

[5] Raymond Williams, *Politics and Letters: Interviews with New Left Review* (London: New Left Books, 1979), 125.

[6] Some of these axioms were first listed in Gerald A. Arbuckle, *Abuse and Cover-Up: Refounding the Catholic Church in Trauma* (Maryknoll, NY: Orbis Books, 2019), 5–48. They are revised and adapted here. A fuller background to the meaning of culture is available in Gerald A. Arbuckle, *Culture, Inculturation, and Theologians: A Postmodern Critique* (Collegeville, MN: Liturgical Press, 2010).

[7] Dianne Waddell and Amrik S. Sohal caution that resistance in certain circumstances is necessary. It can have an essential role in emphasizing inappropriate aspects in what is proposed, thus acting as a catalyst for new alternatives to emerge. "Resistance: A Constructive Tool for Change," *Management Decisions* 36, no. 8 (1998): 543–48.

C. Fred Alford points out that "one can neither work nor play nor theorize with chaos. Chaos is pure terror. One must find forms and frames within which to contain it."[8] When lockdown ended in Sydney I was able again to enjoy an afternoon walk and visit my favorite cafe for a cup of green tea. What a relief to escape the confines of my living quarters! I turned to another cafe regular I had not seen for three months and asked him what it was like to be back at the cafe. "I cannot adequately describe what I feel! To be able to sit at the same table where I have sat for several years, to have my beloved cup of coffee, to be able to see my friends here again—what heaven this is! I feel normal again! My afternoons during the lockdown were chaos. I could not get used to going without my regular cafe visits." Ponder the experience of my friend in the cafe. The pandemic had interrupted an important daily routine. He felt lost. He yearned for life to return to normality.

This simple incident, possibly repeated globally in millions of different ways by people following the relaxation of lockdown restrictions, speaks volumes about the power of culture. People resist changing the familiar. For example, without a vaccine the virus can be contained with three tactics: changes in behavior, such as social distancing; testing, tracing, and isolation; and, if they fail, lockdowns. The worse a country is at testing—and many governments failed to build enough capacity—the more it has to resort to the other two tactics. However, because people are apt to resist change, governments face one of the most challenging problems—how to convince people to change their long-established ways of behaving in order to prevent new outbreaks of COVID-19. The new and needed behaviors include social distancing, wearing masks, and self-isolating when necessary. The wearing of masks is to protect both oneself and others. Yet there is resistance despite the urgency. Recall that the world has been aware for decades that AIDS can be prevented only by safe sex and the use of clean needles, yet in 2018 "1.7 million were newly infected with HIV, the virus that causes it."[9] After lockdown regulations were first relaxed in England, people flocked to the familiar beaches and pubs, ignoring the norms and dangers. Consequently, the country was hit

---

[8] C. Fred Alford, "The Group as a Whole or Acting Out the Missing Leader," *International Journal of Group Psychotherapy* 45, no. 1 (1995): 133.

[9] "COVID-19 Is Here to Stay: People Will Have to Adapt," *The Economist* (July 2, 2020).

by a second wave of COVID-19. Change, in brief—sometimes even just the faintest whisper of it—substitutes ambiguity and uncertainty for the familiar. We hanker after the predictable, longing for order.

The pandemic illustrates a profound lesson about culture. Within each human person there is an unlimited yearning for liberty, but this desire competes with a longing for normality, order, and the familiar. Ultimately, this last desire most often wins. We may even put up with persecution, provided it is predictable! As Peter Berger writes, culture protects people from the awesome insecurities and meaninglessness of chaos (*anomy*). Culture (*nomos*) is "an area of meaning carved out of a vast mass of meaninglessness, a small clearing of lucidity in a formless, dark, almost ominous jungle. . . . Every *nomos* is an edifice erected in the face of the potent and alien forces of chaos. This chaos must be kept at bay at all costs."[10] Chaos is feared. Order must prevail. Anthropologist Clifford Geertz agrees: "Man depends upon symbols and symbol systems with a dependence so great as to be decisive for his creatural viability and, as a result, his sensitivity to even the remotest indication that they may prove unable to cope with one or another aspect of experience raises within him the gravest sort of anxiety."[11]

These comments by Berger and Geertz help to explain the overwhelming power of cultural trauma caused globally by the pandemic. In the space of a few weeks order and predictability were destroyed, throwing cultures into the awesome insecurities and numbness of chaos, with long-term human consequences. "[Cultural trauma occurs when] members of a collectivity feel they have been subjected to a horrendous event that leaves indelible marks upon their group consciousness, marking their memories forever, and changing their future identity in fundamental and irrevocable ways."[12] In summary, changes substitute ambiguity and uncertainty for the known, the normal. In her conclusion to her study of cultures Shirley P. Lowry writes: "Most mythic systems agree on this basic point: What

---

[10] Peter Berger, *The Sacred Canopy: Elements of a Sociological Theory of Religion* (New York: Doubleday, 1969), 23.

[11] Clifford Geertz, *The Interpretation of Cultures* (New York: Basic Books, 1973), 99.

[12] Jeffrey Alexander, quoted in Neil J. Smelser, "September 11, 2001, as Cultural Trauma," in *Cultural Trauma and Collective Identity*, ed. Jeffrey C. Alexander et al. (Berkeley and Los Angeles: University of California Press, 2004), 265.

promotes cosmic order, harmony, and life is good, and what promotes chaos, disintegration . . . is evil."[13] The trauma of the pandemic left us with the numbness of chaos, a collective evil with enduring and indeterminate consequences.

Defining Culture

Axiom 2: A culture more or less coheres because of symbols, myths, and rituals.

Pope Francis addresses this in *Querida Amazonia,* written in 2020:

> For centuries, the Amazonian people passed down their cultural wisdom orally, with myths, legends and tales, as in the case of "those primitive storytellers who traversed the forests bringing stories from town to town, keeping alive a community which, without the umbilical cord of these stories, distance and lack of communication would have fragmented and dissolved." (QA, no. 34)

COVID-19 dramatically undermined the mythological foundations of our culture. What do we mean by *mythological foundations,* and why are they so imperative for our collective and individual recovery? Pope Francis in the above quotation tenderly goes to the heart of the meaning of culture when he reflects on what binds Amazonian people together—their mythology. Consistent with this, culture is defined in this book as

> a pattern of meanings, encased in a network of symbols, myths and rituals, created over time by dominant groups, subcultures and individuals, as they struggle to achieve their identities in the midst of the competitive pressures of power and limited resources in a rapidly globalizing and fragmenting postmodern world, and instructing its adherents about what

[13] Shirley P. Lowry, *Familiar Mysteries: The Truth in Myth* (New York: Oxford University Press, 1982), 131.

> is considered to be the correct and orderly way to *feel*, *think*, and *behave*.[14]

The impact of a culture on individuals is never uniform; some will be strongly influenced, and others less so.

The definition highlights the fact that, as described in Axiom 1, a culture (and its subcultures) through its symbols, myths, and rituals shapes its people's emotional responses to the world around them.[15] Through a culture people feel an affective sense of belonging, but also, depending on the context, other emotions, such as shame or anger when cultural norms are broken. During the lockdown in Sydney there were angry voices in my local supermarket when some patrons ignored the rules restricting the purchase quantity of some items. "Don't you feel ashamed that you are trying to buy more than the rules decree?" cried one shopper. An observation by psychoanalyst Erich Fromm is particularly incisive—the "fact that ideas have an emotional matrix" is "of the utmost importance" as this is "the key to the understanding . . . the spirit of a culture."[16]

A symbol "is any reality that by its very dynamism or power leads to (that is, makes one think about, imagine, get into contact with, or reach out to) another deeper (and often mysterious) reality through a sharing in the dynamism that the symbol itself offers (and not merely by verbal or additional explanations)."[17] There are three essential elements to any symbol: the meaning, the emotive, and the directive. The meaning aspect is its thought element; the symbol makes a statement about something that the mind is able to grasp. One example is that

---

[14] Gerald A. Arbuckle, *Culture, Inculturation, and Theologians: A Postmodern Critique* (Collegeville, MN: Liturgical Press, 2010), 17. See also Geertz, *The Interpretation of Cultures*, 5.

[15] The UNESCO Declaration of Cultural Diversity (2001) describes culture as "the set of distinctive spiritual, material, intellectual and emotional features of society or a social group, and that . . . encompasses, in addition to art and literature, lifestyles, ways of living together, value systems, traditions and beliefs." The positive value of this definition is that it includes the emotional and spiritual aspects of culture.

[16] Erich Fromm, *The Fear of Freedom* (London: Routledge and Kegan Paul, 1960), 240.

[17] Definition by Adolfo Nicolas, SJ (personal communication, July 7, 1987).

care homes (also called nursing homes) are for older people who can no longer care for themselves.

A symbol also has an emotive element that affects the hearts and imaginations of people, evoking positive or negative feelings in them. For example, on the one hand I feel comforted that in the future I may benefit from the services of a care home. On the other hand I am deeply saddened that during the pandemic in Italy, the United States, England, and other countries many elderly people and their caregivers have died in these facilities. The emotive aspect of a symbol represents the object: an image of a care home down the street.

A symbol has a directive quality as well. As a result of its cognitive and emotional impact, I am directed to act in a certain way.[18] I joyfully think what it will be like to join a care home in the future, or I feel anxiety about becoming a member of a care home because many deaths have occurred in these homes.

Of the three elements of a symbol the emotive power is the most significant. When I think of care homes, I also recall that a dear friend of mine died recently in one. I feel deep sadness. All this illustrates that a symbol can have simultaneous, multiple meanings. Consider, for example, the campaign to remove statues of Confederate and racist leaders in the United States. Symbolically the statues evoke anger in people overwhelmed by existing racism; others feel sadness that their ancestors lost the Civil War. Consider also the global emotive power of the word *mask* during the epidemic. For some Americans the word evokes feelings of security and protection but also anger because of those who refuse to wear them; for others, the word evokes anger because state governments insist that they be worn. Thus symbols are cultural constructs, and most do not have universally recognized meanings.

Distinguishing Mythos and Logos

Myths

Myths[19] as narrative symbols shape the heart of every culture, providing meaning to people's lives; emotionally embedded in myths are a

---

[18] For a fuller explanation see Arbuckle, *Culture, Inculturation, and Theologians*, 22–29.

[19] Some claim—for example, Carl Jung—that primordial images of the collective unconscious, or archetypes, are expressed in myths. This view,

culture's fundamental values and assumptions about life.[20] Contrary to popular understanding, myths are not fairytales. They reveal to people in an imaginative and symbolic way essential truths about the world and human life;[21] they explain what usually is beyond empirical observation. No matter how hard we seek to deepen our grasp of the meaning of myths, they still remain ambiguous and mysterious because they attempt to articulate what cannot be fully articulated. Because they are stories shaping people's behavior, they can inspire people and energize them to act, to make sacrifices. I think of healthcare workers I know who daily risk their life, often working hours beyond their normal schedule, to care for patients suffering from COVID-19. If I ask them why they do this, it is not uncommon for them to reply: "Our duty is to be Good Samaritans to the most vulnerable!" Thus, the Good Samaritan mythology inspires them to act heroically.

There are two important ways of knowing: through *logos* and *mythos*. *Logos* is the rational, pragmatic, objective, and scientific knowledge that permits people to function in the world. This "is rationalistic language. This is specific and empirical, and eventuates in logic." However, a myth "does not attempt to be 'factual' or rational, and so it cannot be demonstrated or verified."[22] Myths (*mythos*) answer the issues of ultimate meaning; they respond to the need we all have for the sense of purpose in our lives. *Logos,* with its emphasis

---

however, is too exclusive because it denies to culture any formative role. For Freud, myths and dreams are the projections of frustrated desires that the conscious mind represses, so that they eventually surface in distorted imagery. But the source of myth for Freud is far too dependent on the individual; the role of cultures is ignored. Myths are the result of both conscious and unconscious elements, but Claude Lévi-Strauss overstresses an unconscious element that can occur in myths. Like Carl Jung, he underestimates the visible role of cultures in the evolution of myths. See G. S. Kirk, *Myth: Its Meaning and Functions in Ancient and Other Cultures* (Cambridge: Cambridge University Press, 1970), 275–80; and Percy S. Cohen, "Theories of Myth," *Man: Journal of the Royal Anthropological Institute* 4, no. 3 (1969): 340–41.

[20] See Cohen, "Theories of Myth," 337–53; William G. Dotty, *Mythography: The Study of Myths and Rituals* (Montgomery: University of Alabama Press, 1986), 41–71.

[21] See Gerald A. Arbuckle, *Earthing the Gospel: An Inculturation Handbook for Pastoral Workers* (Maryknoll, NY: Orbis Books, 1990), 26–43; and Arbuckle, *Culture, Inculturation, and Theologians*, 19–42.

[22] Rollo May, *The Cry for Myth* (New York: Delta, 1991), 26, 79.

on rational thinking alone, cannot possibly address issues of ultimate meaning.[23] Rollo May writes: "Whereas empirical language refers to objective facts, *myth refers to the quintessence of human experience, the meaning and significance of human life.* The whole person speaks to *us*, not just to our brain."[24] Given the universal mythological rebirth of nationalism, racism, religion, and fundamentalism, so evident in the pandemic crisis, any claim that we do not need *mythos* has again proved a hazardous delusion.

Myths are not unfinished or muddled histories.[25] The purposes of myth and history differ; myth is concerned not so much with a series of events as with the moral significance of these happenings. A myth is a "religious" commentary on the beliefs and values of a culture. May describes it this way: "The myth is a drama which begins as a historical event and takes on its special character as a way of orienting people to reality."[26] Franklin Roosevelt can be viewed in historical or mythological terms. As seen from the historical perspective, he is portrayed as belonging to a definite time period, influencing and being influenced by events around him. If, however, he is assessed as one who exemplifies virtues of compassionate and courageous leadership in establishing the New Deal to help the United States move more humanely out of the Great Depression, then we are measuring him by a moral benchmark, and perhaps even by a gospel mythology (see Chapter 2).

In brief, myths are the emotional adhesive that affectively cements people together at the most profound level of their collective life; myths exude power because every "society is held together by a myth system, a complex of dominating forms that determines and sustains all its activities."[27] Myths are like invisible designs shaping the way people view the world. May says that "myths are like the beams in a house: not exposed to outside view, they are the structure which holds

---

[23] See Karen Armstrong, *The Battle for God: Fundamentalism in Judaism, Christianity, and Islam* (London: HarperCollins, 2001), 365.

[24] May, *The Cry for Myth,* 26; see also Gerald A. Arbuckle, *Fundamentalism at Home and Abroad: Analysis and Pastoral Responses* (Collegeville, MN: Liturgical Press, 2017), 31–32.

[25] See Arbuckle, *Culture, Inculturation, and Theologians*, 29–30.

[26] May, *The Cry for Myth*, 26.

[27] Robert M. MacIver, *The Web of Government* (London: Macmillan, 1947), 4.

the house together so people can live in it."[28] Myths can be likened to knowledge hidden in the DNA of a cell or the programming technology of a computer; myths are the cultural templates or invisible blueprints of the heart and mind, the programs that frame the way we interpret the world and how we must act.[29] Hence, another way of defining culture is: "*the collective programming of the heart and mind that distinguishes the members of one group or category of people from another.*"[30] When this collective programming is destroyed for whatever reason, we are in chaos. I appreciate the way Pope Francis describes culture in *Laudato Si' (On Care for Our Common Home)*: "Culture is more than what we have inherited from the past; it is also, and above all, a living, dynamic and participatory present reality, which cannot be excluded as we rethink the relationship between human beings and the environment" (LS, no. 143).

An example illustrates the binding power of mythology and what happens when it is undermined. The Great Seal of the United States, which is copied on one side of the one-dollar bill, contains these words articulating the fundamental quality of collective unity in the nation's founding mythology: *E pluribus unum* (out of many, one). However, in recent decades this shared unity has gravely fractured. The democracy is polarized "not just by policy differences but by deeper sources of resentment, including racial and religious differences."[31] The result? Chaos. The founding story is ceasing to operate, making a united response to the enduring human costs of COVID-19 nearly impossible. The democracy has no future unless both polarized sides collectively reclaim this narrative. Former president Barack Obama

---

[28] May, *The Cry for Myth,* 15.

[29] See description by Sam Keen, "The Stories We Live By," *Psychology Today* (December, 1988): 10; Geertz, *The Interpretation of Cultures*, 216–18.

[30] Geert Hofstede, *Cultures and Organizations* (London: HarperCollins, 1994), 5. Hofstede notes that this emphasis on "collective programming" resembles the notion of *habitus,* an insight of the French sociologist Pierre Bourdieu: "Certain conditions of existence produce a *habitus*, a system of permanent and transferable dispositions. A habitus . . . functions as the basis for practices and images . . . collectively orchestrated without an actual conductor." Pierre Bourdieu, *Le sens practique* (Paris: Editions de Minuit, 1980), translation by Hofstede in *Cultures and Organizations*, 18.

[31] Steven Levitsky and Daniel Ziblatt, *How Democracies Die* (New York: Crown, 2018), 220.

fears for the American future: "Our democracy seems to be teetering on the brink of crisis—a crisis rooted in a fundamental contest between two opposing visions of what America is and what it should be."[32] His fears seem well grounded (see Chapter 3).

Myths Change

Fresh myths are formed and old ones retained, persistently modified, or totally lost due to different forces, changing needs, and new ways of viewing society. When myths are lost because they no longer serve a purpose, they become powerless legends. Myths may change through extension, substitution, drift, or revitalization.

- *Myth extension* occurs, for example, when the meaning, not the words, changes. In the founding myth of the United States the words "all men are created equal . . . [and] are endowed with unalienable Rights" originally excluded all women, African Americans, and Native Indians (see Chapters 3 and 5). Only later were such groups given the political right to vote.
- *Myth substitution* occurs when there is a deliberate effort to radically change a myth. For example, Gorbachev tried unsuccessfully to substitute the Marxist autocratic system for the mythology of democracy; Donald Trump attempted to replace the founding mythology of the United States with a racist one (see Chapter 3).
- *Myth drift* happens when myths change, degenerate, or disappear without conscious decision-making on the part of individuals or groups. Sometimes the dominant myth is distorted because a secondary myth takes on an exaggerated role. This has happened to the Genesis creation story—extreme capitalism, with its emphasis on individualism, displaces the original stress on the myth of solidarity and on our responsibility to be

---

[32] Barack Obama, *A Promised Land* (New York: Viking, 2020), xv. Elsewhere he comments: "I . . . [am] very worried about the degree to which we do not have a common baseline of fact and a common story. . . . Without this common narrative, democracy becomes very tough." Jeffrey Goldberg, "Why Obama Fears for Our Democracy," *Atlantic*, November 16, 2020.

co-creators with God in this world. Social consciousness is then so moderated that it becomes a distorted myth.[33]

- *Myth revitalization* happens when a people's culture is threatened with disintegration or experiences cultural trauma and subsequently feels the urge to reclaim and relive their original creation myth. When this happens, people experience renewed energy (see Chapters 2, 6).

Axiom 3: Among the many types of myths, the creation, public, operative, and residual myths are particularly relevant to the themes of this book.

Not only are *creation* myths the most all-embracing of mythic proclamations, addressing themselves to the wide range of questions of meaning, but they are also the most profound. Creation myths speak about first causes; in them people express their primary understanding of humankind, the world, time, and space. Consider the creation story in the Book of Genesis. In highly symbolic language we are told that God created the world out of chaos, that our first parents sinned, and that we are called to cooperate with God in continuing creation (see Chapter 2).

On a far less exalted level are the creation stories telling how nations were formed. Australia legally became a nation in 1901 when existing separate colonies united into a federation, but its creation myth grew out of the defeat of its soldiers by the Turks at the battle of Gallipoli in 1915; it is the spirit of "mateship," of caring for one another, especially for the "underdogs" of society (see Chapter 3).[34] The creation mythology of the United States reminds Americans that

---

[33] There has likewise been myth drift concerning the American Revolution and the founding of the nation. The popular romanticized mythology says that it was an orderly, restrained rebellion, with brave patriots defending their noble ideals against an oppressive empire. In fact, it was violent and divisive. For example, writes historian Holger Hoock, African Americans suffered disproportionately, and George Washington's army waged a genocidal campaign against the Iroquois Indians (see Chapter 5). See Holger Hoock, *Scars of Independence: America's Violent Birth* (New York: Crown, 2017), 281–83.

[34] See Bruce Kapferer, *Legends of People: Myths of State* (Washington, DC: Smithsonian Institution Press, 1988), 151–82.

God, or some extraordinary destiny, calls them to participate in a new Exodus, a new journey from the poverty and oppression of other nations, in order to build a new promised land. It is made concrete in the lives of cultural heroes such as George Washington, Abraham Lincoln, and Martin Luther King Jr. When there is disagreement about who has the right to share a founding story, then we can expect social unrest and even violence (see Chapters 3, 5). For example, many of former president Donald Trump's supporters feel that their unemployment has so marginalized them that they are unable to benefit from America's founding story; they yearn for someone to put things right.

A *public* myth is a set of stated ideals that people openly claim bind them together, such as the mission statement of an organization; in practice these ideals may have little or no cohesive force. An *operative* myth is what actually gives people their felt sense of identity; the operative myth can and often does differ dramatically from the public myth (see Chapter 6). A *residual* myth is one with little or no daily impact on a group's life but one that at times can become a powerful operative myth. Residual myths lurk in the culture's unconscious, always ready to reemerge. For example, the racist mythology that oppressed African Americans and Native Americans in the founding of the United States has resurfaced in recent years (see Chapters 3 and 5).[35]

Axiom 4: Myths are able to be manipulated in ways that exploit and oppress people without them being aware of what is happening.

Myths tell those who believe them what reality is and what it should be.[36] However, myths can be a mixture of remembering, forgetting, interpreting, and inventing historical events. That is, myths can discard historical facts, particularly if they may be detrimental to the dominant social group in power. This is the reason Erica Schoenberger warns

---

[35] See Gerald A. Arbuckle, *Loneliness: Insights for Healing in a Fragmented World* (Maryknoll, NY: Orbis Books, 2018), 70–82.

[36] See Bruce Lincoln, *Discourse and the Construction of Society: Comparative Studies of Myth, Ritual, and Classification* (Oxford: Oxford University Press, 1989), 24.

that myths can "provide a comforting—if false—sense of continuity and stability in the face of uncertainty and external turmoil. . . . They tend to blind people."[37] For example, the American Indians living from the Atlantic seaboard to the eastern parts of Louisiana were decimated and displaced, year after year, between 1790 and 1803, as the result of warfare with white settlers, famine, disease, coercive land turnovers, and sheer exhaustion.[38] This tragedy is not recorded as such in American mythology; instead, the winning settlers manipulated the nation's founding story in their favor.

The manipulation of myth is also visible in the contemporary United States. The nation has long accepted that the mythology of democracy ultimately depends on an honest election system. However, throughout his presidency Donald Trump sought to implant an alternative mythology without any proof. Consequently, "four in every five Republican voters say [the recent presidential] vote was 'stolen' [and that] trust in the fairness of [the election system] has been shaken."[39]

Recall that in our daily lives we do many things without conscious deliberation; for example, we sit automatically, as it were, at a particular place at table (see Axiom 1). Anthropologist Edward Hall thus cautions: "The cultural unconscious, like Freud's unconscious, not only controls man's actions but can be understood only by painstaking processes of detailed analysis."[40] Hence the importance of ongoing individual and collective cultural reflection. Prior to the pandemic, neoliberal economic mythology with its reliance on market forces unquestionably assumed that it could control any emergency without governmental interference. It had become so much a part of the Western cultural unconscious that few doubted it. The onslaught of the pandemic proved the mythology wrong (see Chapter 3).

---

[37] Erica Schoenberger, *The Cultural Crisis of the Firm* (Oxford: Basil Blackwell, 1997), 132.

[38] See Peter Nabokov, "The Intent Was Genocide," *New York Review of Books* 67, no. 11 (July 2, 2020): 51–52; Jeffrey Ostler, *Surviving Genocide: Native Nations and the United States from the American Revolution to Bleeding Kansas* (New Haven, CT: Yale University Press, 2019).

[39] "The Resilience of Democracy," *The Economist* (November 28, 2020), 11.

[40] Edward Hall, *Beyond Culture* (Garden City, NY: Anchor Press/Doubleday, 1977), 43.

Ritual Power and COVID-19

Axiom 5: Ritual is the repetitive spontaneous or prescribed symbolic use of bodily movement and gesture to express and articulate meaning within a social context in which there is possible or real tension/conflict and a need to resolve or hide it.[41] Restrictions imposed by COVID-19 are rituals.

Rituals, whether religious or secular, structure orderly roles and boundaries for ourselves and for society. Rituals reassure us that we are in control in the midst of a chaotic world; for example, traffic laws decreeing whether we drive on the left or right give us a sense of safety. Rituals allay anxieties. They stabilize life; they encode and enforce behavior, socializing people into culturally acceptable ways of relating.[42] Rituals reveal values at their deepest level. That is, through rituals we articulate the values and goals expressed in our cultural myths (see Chapter 2). But when the pandemic hit, the avoidance of certain social and political rituals became crucial for maintaining life. For example, the ritual of shaking hands as a form of greeting ceased; shaking hands became an open act of civil defiance and disregard for health. Rituals defined new boundaries. People suspected of having COVID-19 had to be rigidly quarantined and were punished for breaking corresponding rules. There was to be no room for ambiguity. Government officials, such as those in South Korea, Australia, and New Zealand, regularly and publicly reminded citizens of the new rituals both to dispel anxieties and to reinforce new behavior patterns (see Chapter 3).

Two types of rituals need to be distinguished: models *for* and models *of*.[43] The purpose of models-for rituals is to impose, reaffirm, and strengthen public conformity to the status quo. For example, signposts reminding drivers to stop at certain intersections are such rituals because public safety demands that people conform to the

---

[41] See Robert Bocock, *Ritual in Industrial Society: A Sociological Analysis of Ritualism in Modern England* (London: George Allen and Unwin, 1974), 35–59; see also Arbuckle, *Fundamentalism at Home and Abroad,* 55–56; and Arbuckle, *Earthing the Gospel*, 96–112.

[42] See Byung-Chul Han, *The Disappearance of Rituals*: *A Topology of the Present* (Cambridge: Polity, 2020), 1–15.

[43] See Arbuckle, *Earthing the Gospel*, 102.

rules of the road to prevent deaths. Models-of rituals exist where consensus does not have to be imposed but needs to be reaffirmed or celebrated. For Americans, the flag is a symbol of national unity. Its raising, especially in times of national tragedy or celebration, carries enormous symbolic meaning as a sign of collective unity. However, if a model-of ritual is disrespected in any way—such as burning the flag—there can be chaotic social consequences.

Another example is the debate between American presidential candidates, which is traditionally a globally respected institution. The aim of the ritual is to celebrate the fact that while two people can disagree on key policy issues, they nonetheless accept and respect the norms of democracy binding the nation in unity. Significant failure to abide by the ritual would result in chaos. That is precisely what happened in the first debate between Donald Trump and Joseph Biden in 2020. It became an epic and demoralizing disaster due to the constant refusal of Trump to adhere to the rules of the ritual. Instead of a ritual celebrating unity in diversity, it became a ritual symbolizing a radically divided nation. Likewise, the traditional counting of the Electoral College ballots during a joint session of Congress on January 6, 2021, should have been a crucial model of ritual hailing national unity in diversity in the presidential transfer of power, but the mob attack on the Capitol sought to negate this celebration.

Scapegoating and Conspiracy Thinking

Axiom 6: People are apt to see their own culture as clean or pure, while people of other cultures are viewed as "barbarian" (FT, no. 27),[44] dirty, polluting, or impure, and therefore threatening—people thus seek to exclude or eliminate these other cultures.[45]

This axiom helps to explain the tragic, widespread, and sometimes violent reaction to immigrants, minority groups, and people in poverty, a reaction that was often seen in contemporary Western countries in the time of the pandemic and its aftermath (see Chapters 3, 4, 5).

---

[44] See also Ernest Becker, *Escape from Evil* (New York: Free Press, 1975), 108–14.

[45] This axiom is more fully developed in Arbuckle, *Fundamentalism at Home and Abroad,* 43–48.

Pope Francis writes with deep sadness about the current world scene, with its "temptation to build a culture of walls, to raise walls, walls of the heart, walls on the land, in order to prevent . . . encounter with other cultures, with other people." He continues, "[The] outside world ceases to exist and leaves only 'my' world, to the point that others . . . become only 'them'" (FT, no. 27). Why is this so? Anthropologist Mary Douglas writes, "In short, our pollution behaviour is the reaction which condemns any object or idea likely to confuse or contradict cherished classifications."[46] Remember: culture is about order; whatever endangers or "pollutes" established order threatens what we most like, that is, a world of the familiar and predictable.

Douglas's definition does not denote the intrinsic hygienic qualities of things but rather their symbolic aspects. The more tribal or closed-in cultures become, the more they fear the socially contaminating threats of other cultures. Each tribal group takes the position of "thinking and feeling that anyone whose behaviour is not predictable or is peculiar in any way is slightly out of his mind, improperly brought up, irresponsible, psychopathic, politically motivated to a point beyond redemption, or just plain inferior."[47] Ethnocentrism—the belief that one's culture is *the* culture—reaches extremes when victims are dehumanized (see Chapter 5). Once people are declared nonhuman, their tormenters have no restraints. Nazis, for example, stripped their victims of all protective dignity.[48]

The rhetoric of Donald Trump's first presidential campaign frequently dehumanized and marginalized whole groups of people.[49] He degraded women, categorizing them as objects for the enjoyment of men. He maligned Muslims and African Americans, performed a mocking impression of a disabled journalist, and encouraged his followers to beat up protesters.[50] At his hate-charged rallies, at which his followers screamed, "Burn her at the stake" (of Hillary Clinton), and "Kill Obama," he portrayed illegal immigrants as rapists and

---

[46] Mary Douglas, *Purity and Danger: An Analysis of the Concepts of Pollution and Taboo* (London: Routledge and Kegan Paul, 1966), 36.

[47] Hall, *Beyond Culture*, 43.

[48] See Jonathan Glover, *Humanity: A Moral History of the Twentieth Century* (London: Jonathan Cape, 1999), 338–39.

[49] See David Frum, *Trumpocracy: The Corruption of the American People* (New York: Harper, 2018), 103–23.

[50] See "The Trump Era," *The Economist* (November 12, 2016), 31.

murderers. He exemplified many of the nastiest qualities of a scapegoating populist leader, for example, giving simplistic solutions to complex issues and in the process claiming his opponents were dangerous and corrupt elites who were "immoral . . . illegitimate, unfit, contemptible, un-American or . . . 'disgusting.'"[51] Many of his followers colluded in this dehumanizing rhetoric (see Chapter 3).

Axiom 7: Conspiracy theories and scapegoating, as seen in the COVID-19 pandemic and its aftermath, marginalize people believed to be causing harm to individuals and groups; by transferring the blame for their afflictions onto others, people are able to distract themselves from the real causes.[52]

"Conspiracy theories have traditionally functioned either to bolster a sense of an 'us' threatened by a sinister 'them,' or to justify the scapegoating of often blameless victims."[53] Conspiracy theories flourish in chaotic times. Individuals and groups displace their aggression and fears of the unknown onto groups or individuals that are visible and relatively powerless. In conspiracy thinking, agents perceived as threatening are commonly identified, ridiculed, gossiped about, persecuted, or eliminated. Scapegoats are usually chosen from groups that are already devalued. Devaluation gives a sense of superiority to the one doing the scapegoating. In the United States, for example, some poor southern whites who led underprivileged and degrading lives could raise their self-esteem whenever they scapegoated African Americans as the cause of their troubles (see Chapter 5).

In conspiracies, truth and objectivity lose out. As long as the group is protected from the assumed source of evil, nothing else matters, regardless of what moral or physical violence the innocent experience

[51] Ibid., 37.

[52] See Gerald A. Arbuckle, *Violence, Society, and the Church: A Cultural Approach* (Collegeville, MN: Liturgical Press, 2004), 136–51.

[53] Peter Knight, *Conspiracy Culture: From Kennedy to the X Files* (London: Routledge, 2000), 3. For a comprehensive analysis of reasons for the rise of contemporary conspiracy thinking, see Michael Butter, *The Nature of Conspiracy Theories* (Cambridge: Polity, 2020), 9–32, 121–50. Also see Russell Muirhead and Nancy L. Rosenblum, *A Lot of People Are Saying: The New Conspiracism and the Assault on Democracy* (Princeton, NJ: Princeton University Press, 2019), 19–78.

as a consequence. The preservation or the restoration of the status quo must be achieved at all costs.[54] As conspiracy theories provide their devotees with a much-needed mythological sense of identity and security in the midst of chaos, they are not easily debunked by rational presentation of facts.[55]

In pandemics throughout history, some groups are regularly made scapegoats. In medieval Europe during the Black Death plague, Jews were accused for spreading contagion and poisoning wells; at the peak of the plague from 1348 to 1351, more than two hundred Jewish communities were destroyed.[56] Following the First World War, Adolf Hitler and other anti-Semites blamed the Spanish flu pandemic, the defeat of Germany in World War I, and the subsequent economic depression on the machinations of international Jewry. Hitler and his supporters turned their rage on the vulnerable Jews.[57] In May 2009, during the swine flu outbreak, Mexicans became the target, with American politicians calling for the closure of the border. President Trump blamed immigrants for introducing the coronavirus into the United States in 2019.[58] In Australia the pandemic sparked racist attacks on Asian-looking residents, who were accused by their attackers of spreading the disease.

Michael Butter lists the three foremost ways that conspiracy theories can be dangerous during the COVID-19 pandemic: "They can lead to radicalization and violence; they can make people disregard medical knowledge and, as a consequence, endanger themselves and others; and they can undermine trust in elected politicians and the democratic process as such."[59] Vulnerable people such as migrants, minority groups, and people who are poor or elderly are in constant danger of being wrongfully blamed, stigmatized, and further

---

[54] See Daniel Pipes, *Conspiracy: How the Paranoid Style Flourishes and Where It Comes From* (New York: Free Press, 1997); Arbuckle, *Violence, Society, and the Church,* 140–41.

[55] See Butter, *The Nature of Conspiracy Theories,* 150–63.

[56] See Keith Thomas, *Religion and the Decline of Magic* (New York: Charles Scribner's Sons, 1971), 560.

[57] See George M. Fredrickson, *Racism* (Melbourne: Scribe, 2002), 106; Arbuckle, *Violence, Society, and the Church,* 136–40.

[58] See Cynthia Miller-Idriss, *Hate in the Homeland: The New Global Far Right* (Princeton, NJ: Princeton University Press, 2020), 56, 59–60.

[59] Butter, *The Nature of Conspiracy Theories*, 152.

marginalized for causing the virus or the resultant unemployment. In India the Muslim minority has become a scapegoat for COVID-19.[60]

Soon after the outbreak of COVID-19, the World Health Association (WHO) coined the word *infoepidemic* to name the spread of misleading or fabricated news, images, and videos about the virus. One particularly blatant example of American conspiracy thinking is a video watched by more than eight million people across social media before it was removed. In the video Dr. Anthony Fauci, a notable American contagious disease authority, is falsely accused of making the virus and forwarding it to China.[61] The same video deceitfully claims that wearing masks will cause self-infection. President Trump fostered this and other conspiracies by refusing to wear a mask. Thousands of his followers followed his behavior and an unknown number were infected by COVID-19 and possibly died in consequence.

Americans are particularly susceptible to global conspiracy thinking whenever their world moves from relative stability to widespread turmoil with its accompanying uncertainties and fears. For example, recall the conspiracy-inspired anti-Catholic, racist Know-Nothing Party in the mid-nineteenth century, and the anti-communist witch hunts led by Joseph McCarthy in the late 1940s and early 1950s.[62] Trump simply tapped into this tradition. His technique, when first campaigning for the presidency, was to tell his devoted and angry followers that they were casualties of a plot to destroy the strength of the United States. In his narrative, conspiring foreign governments outsmarted a selfish political elite in Washington. As president, he claimed, he would stop this. He based his reelection campaign on several different conspiracy narratives, for example, blaming the rapid spread of COVID-19 in the United States on China and the WHO. He also did not condemn the QAnon theory that inspired many of his followers to storm the US Capitol on January 6, 2021.[63] The QAnon narrative asserts that there is a global ring of Satan-worshipping

---

[60] See "COVID-19 and Autocracy," *The Economist* (April 25, 2020), 50.

[61] See World Health Organization, "Immunizing the Public against Misinformation" (August 5, 2020); "Fake News: Return of the Paranoid Style," *The Economist* (June 6, 2020), 50–51.

[62] See Arbuckle, *Fundamentalism at Home and Abroad,* 11–12, 16–17.

[63] For an analysis of President Trump's encouragement of conspiracies see Butter, *The Nature of Conspiracy Theories,* 5, 39, 70, 82, 85–87, 144–50.

pedophiles who seek to rule America, and that Trump alone has the necessary autocratic and military power to destroy it.

Pandemic Chaos and Creative Potential

Axiom 8: There are two poles in tension within a culture—order (the default pole) and chaos. An experience of chaos, such as the COVID-19 pandemic, contains potential for significant creativity; individuals or groups have the chance to rediscover, and be reenergized by, their mythological roots or, alternatively, to become paralyzed by the chaos.

Cultural myths provide people with the comforting support of identity, a feeling of belonging. Chaos, however, is the frightening experience of mythlessness: "*The loneliness of mythlessness is the deepest and least assuageable of all.* Unrelated to the past, unconnected with the future, we hang as it were in mid-air."[64] Significant interference with or destruction of the inner mythological scaffolding of cultures, even when there is acceptance of the changes, can devastate the stable feeling of a people's identity and sense of belonging. However, chaos can also be a liberating or subversive experience (see Chapter 2), for it disrupts the constraining crust of custom or habit, allowing the imagination to dream of alternative or profoundly different ways of doing things.[65] For example, the chaos of the pandemic has evoked remarkable innovation in healthcare, as seen by increased access to telemedicine and rapid vaccine development. As noted in *The Economist*:

> Vast, bureaucratic and amorphous, health care has long been cautious about change. However, the biggest emergency in decades has caused a revolution. From laboratories to operating theatres, the industry's metabolism has soared. . . . [Medical

---

[64] May, *The Cry for Myth,* 99.

[65] Anthropologist Mircea Eliade asserts that cultures are apt to experience cyclic regression to chaos as a prelude to a new creation. *Myth and Reality* (London: Allen and Unwin, 1964), 187–93.

workers'] creativity holds the promise of a new era of innovation that will boost access for the poor and improve treatment.[66]

When people own their own chaos, admitting their powerlessness and vulnerability, they return to the sacred time of the founding of the group. There they are challenged to ask fundamental questions about the group's origins, about what is essential to the founding mythology and should be kept, and what is accidental and should be allowed to fade away (see Chapters 2 and 6). If the positive possibilities of chaos are ignored, disaster results. We can deny chaos or embrace it, but it cannot be ignored. Mary Douglas describes the creative potential of chaos or disorder, a key theme in cultural anthropological discourse: "Though we seek to create order, we do not simply condemn disorder. We recognise that it is destructive of existing patterns; also that it has potentiality. It symbolizes both danger and power."[67]

From Grieving to Mourning

Axiom 9: COVID-19 has caused thousands of deaths, mass unemployment, and a lack of physical connections with others. These losses have not been evenly distributed; the poor suffer the most.[68] Loss evokes the sadness of grief in individuals and cultures, and unless this grief can be openly named in mourning rituals, it will haunt the living and lead to dysfunctional behavior.[69]

A clear distinction must be made between *grieving* and *mourning*. Grieving refers to the internal feelings of sadness, sorrow, anger,

---

[66] "Health Care: The World's Most Complex and Immovable Industry Has Been Reinventing Itself," *The Economist* (December 5, 2020), 14; see "The Plague Year," *The Economist* (December 19, 2020), 15.

[67] Douglas, *Purity and Danger*, 2.

[68] The death rate of African Americans from COVID-19 is up to ten times higher than that of white individuals. See Marissa Evans, "The Relentlessness of Black Grief," *Atlantic* (September 27, 2020).

[69] For a fuller explanation of grief and mourning, see Gerald A. Arbuckle, *The Francis Factor and the People of God: New Life for the Church* (Maryknoll, NY: Orbis Books, 2015), 59–124.

loneliness, anguish, confusion, shame, guilt, and fear as consequences of experiencing loss. Grief can go beyond individuals and institutions to embrace an entire culture.[70] Recall how Americans were overcome by collective grief after the 9/11 terrorist disasters. People were collectively traumatized. Mourning, on the other hand, enables us to respond to grief or cultural trauma so that healing can occur. Mourning embraces two simultaneous and complementary dynamics. First, it refers to the cultural rituals that publicly acknowledge that the bereaved experience grief. These rituals can take many forms, such as religious services, protest movements, or public inquiries that allow injustices to be named and resolved.[71] Second, mourning connotes the agonizing inner journey that the bereaved must make to let go what is lost in order to be able to move forward. Unless grief can be overtly voiced in mourning rituals, it will haunt the living, evoking untold heartache and anxiety.[72] As the Roman poet Ovid wrote centuries ago: "Suppressed grief suffocates."[73] It is of overriding importance for people to say that grief hurts and to be able to express this freely and unashamedly. Tennyson simply articulates this crucial advice: "Ring out the grief that saps the mind."[74] True, we must not forget the past and its lessons. But we must be released from excessive attachment to it (see Chapters 2, 3, 5, and 6).

Scriptural Reflection: Moral Foundations of Society

> A theology of neighbor is a call to accompany neighbors in need. It is a proactive, place-changing love for God and the poor . . . As the Samaritan shows, it is a love that is not content to stay "on its own front porch."[75]

---

[70] See Ron Eyerman, "Cultural Trauma: Emotion and Narration," in *The Oxford Handbook of Cultural Sociology*, ed. Jeffrey C. Alexander, Ronald Jacobs, and Philip Smith (Oxford: Oxford University Press, 2012), 564–82.

[71] See Kenneth J. Doka and Terry L. Martin, *Grieving beyond Gender: Understanding the Ways Men and Women Mourn* (New York: Routledge, 2010), 28–30.

[72] See ibid., 18–25. See also Therese A. Rando, *Treatment of Complicated Mourning* (Champaign, IL: Research Press, 1993), 146–47, 177–78, 185–240, 380–81, 584.

[73] Ovid, *Tristia* V.1.63.

[74] Alfred Tennyson, *In Memoriam* cvi.st.3.

[75] Marcus Mescher, *The Ethics of Encounter (*Maryknoll, NY: Orbis Books, 2020).

Thus far in this first chapter the aim has been to clarify key anthropological terms that will be used in the remaining chapters, such as *culture, mythology, cultural chaos and trauma, the pandemic as cultural trauma, conspiracy thinking and scapegoating,* and *grief and mourning.* There are no clear-cut road maps for rebuilding global and national societies, but whatever economic and social plans are devised and implemented, they must be based on sound moral values.[76] These values are evident in the Good Samaritan parable (Lk 10:25–37), so central to Pope Francis's encyclical *Fratelli Tutti.*

Philosopher Charles Taylor, when reflecting on the foundations of Western civilization, concludes that the parable of the Good Samaritan "can be seen as one of the original building blocks out of which our modern universalist moral consciousness has been built."[77] Paul Ricoeur asserts that the parable is "a fiction capable of redescribing life."[78] For St. John Paul II the parable that best articulates the heart of the mission and ministry of Jesus Christ is that of the Good Samaritan.[79] And in Pope Benedict XVI's first encyclical, *Deus Caritas Est (God Is Love)*, he points four times to the significance of the parable of the Good Samaritan as the model for holistic care. The parable, he writes, "remains as a standard which imposes universal love towards the needy . . . whoever they may be" (no. 31a).

The Good Samaritan Parable: Cultural Analysis

Over time the parable has been misinterpreted or misused by politicians and others in ways that hide its radical lessons.[80] Without an exploration of the cultural background to the story, the parable will remain so domesticated in the popular imagination that its extensive relevance can be missed. Therefore, to understand its relevance to

---

[76] A value is an action-oriented priority, an internal compass or catalyst for action.

[77] Charles Taylor, *The Secular Age* (Cambridge: Cambridge University Press, 2007), 738.

[78] Paul Ricoeur, "Biblical Hermeneutics," *Semeia* (1975), 89.

[79] John Paul II, "Contemplate the Face of Christ in the Sick," message for the World Day of the Sick, no. 8.

[80] See Nick Spencer, *The Political Samaritan: How Power Hijacked a Parable* (London: Bloomsbury, 2017), 31–82; Tony Keddie, *Republican Jesus: How the Right Has Rewritten the Gospels* (Oakland: University of California Press, 2020), 125–32, 165–91.

the pandemic chaos we are experiencing, we must first appreciate the general cultural environment at the time in which the parable was told. This will be followed by an analysis of the truths inherent in the parable.

Disease and Illness

To appreciate the depth of suffering of the injured man in the parable, a distinction is made in the Hebraic culture between two types of sickness: disease and illness.[81] Today's medical anthropologists make the same distinction.[82] Disease—cancer, leprosy, a severe injury—is visible. Illness, however, cannot be seen. It is the inner pain of the heart that accompanies significant disease. Or it can occur by itself, with no disease being present, such as the grief over the loss of good health or the death of a friend. It is summed up in questions such as, If I survive the cancer, will I have a job? If I die, who will look after my family?

In the culture of the ancient Hebrews certain diseases automatically marginalized the sufferers, isolating them from all human contact. Socially they became nonpersons and were considered worthless, even dangerous to society. The chief Hebraic concern about leprosy, for example, was not that it was primarily contagious but ritually polluting (see Axiom 6).[83] In Psalm 88, "A Despairing Lament," the sufferer beseeches God: "I cry out to you in the night" (Ps 88:1). He has a disease that has exiled him from society, and the anguish in his heart is devastating. He is, he says, being consigned to "the brink of Sheol" (Ps 88:4) and being "left among the dead" (Ps 88:6). The inner pain is personally crushing. The reader can still feel the sufferer's torment. "You have deprived me of my friends," he cries. "You have made me repulsive to them" (Ps 88:9). The sufferer is not asking for physical healing of his disease but rather for God to hear and feel with him the pain of abandonment by his former friends. This is the illness. When God responds with his compassionate touch, the sufferer's heart will

---

[81] See Gerald A. Arbuckle, *Healthcare Ministry: Refounding the Mission in Tumultuous Times* (Collegeville, MN: Liturgical Press, 2000), 219–22.

[82] See Cecil G. Helman, *Culture, Health, and Illness: An Introduction for Health Professionals* (Oxford: Butterworth, 1994), 101–45.

[83] See Bruce Malina, *The New Testament World: Insights from Cultural Anthropology* (Louisville, KY: Westminster/John Knox Press, 1993), 165–66.

be healed. The disease needs healing for sure. But the first priority is the healing of the heart through empathy.

This distinction between disease and illness and the priority given to the latter are carried over into the New Testament, as we see in Pope Benedict's *Deus Caritas Est*. He says that although professional competence for healing physical sickness is necessary, "it is not of itself sufficient. . . . We are dealing with human beings . . . [who] . . . need heartfelt concern" (DC, no. 31a). This is the reason Benedict gives such importance to the parable of the Good Samaritan, in which the theme of healing of the heart is given central importance. In the parable the caregiver seeks to heal the body of the victim, but above all, he seeks to respond to the sufferer's innermost pain of rejection. The late Cardinal Joseph Bernardin highlights this quality of Christian healing ministries:

> Our distinctive vocation in Christian health care is not so much to heal [the sickness] better or more efficiently than anyone else; it is to bring comfort to people by giving them an experience that will strengthen their confidence in life. The ultimate goal of our care is to give those who are ill . . . a reason to hope. . . . In this we find the Christian vocation that makes our health care truly distinctive.[84]

The distinction between disease and illness is always important, but it is especially so in this pandemic crisis. COVID-19 has affected the mental health of millions of people globally within a short period of time. It has caused anxiety, stress, and worry, arising both from the disease itself and from its ongoing social and economic consequences. There is fear of falling sick and dying, fear of losing employment, fear that social distancing will isolate people from loved ones and friends, fear of starvation, fear of being unable to cope with powerlessness and loneliness, and an all-embracing fear about the uncertain future. The mental-health consequences of these fears will endure for generations (see Chapter 4).

Now let us ponder the Good Samaritan parable. What moral lessons does it contain to guide our response to the pandemic and its

---

[84] Cardinal Joseph Bernardin, *A Sign of Hope: A Pastoral Letter on Healthcare* (October 18, 1995), 5, 7.

multifarious effects? First, we shall describe the scene and the persons involved.[85]

Types of Violence

Violence, we must remember, is not always physical; it is whatever is insensitive to and oppressive of a person's dignity. The parable includes six types of violence: verbal, physical, ritual, social, racial, and occupational. The story itself and the way Jesus tells it provide insightful lessons on how to relate to violence with compassion and justice.

The story begins with a Torah scholar or religious lawyer who questions Jesus in a verbally aggressive and polemical manner.[86] "And who is my neighbour?" he asks (Lk 10:29). Evangelist Luke states that the lawyer's intention is to "test" Jesus; in Hebraic culture, questions phrased in this way are public challenges to personal honor. The lawyer hopes that Jesus will be unable to answer the question appropriately, for failing to do so will cause Jesus public shame. This is what is meant by the words "but the man was anxious to justify himself" (Lk 10:29).[87]

The second act of violence is physical: an innocent man is assaulted by bandits (Lk 10:30). The victim may have been a wealthy man; in those days it was common for gangs of thugs to rob well-off travelers, and then to give the proceeds to the poor.[88] The third act of violence is ritual. Because the victim is covered in blood, he is automatically stigmatized as impure, untouchable, and, therefore, a social outcast. This branding would have caused the victim intense

---

[85] See Brad H. Young, *The Parables: Jewish Tradition and Christian Interpretation* (Peabody, MA: Hendrickson, 1998), 101–18; Bruce J. Malina and Richard L. Rohrbaugh, *Social Commentary on the Synoptic Gospels* (Minneapolis: Fortress Press,1992), 346–48; Joseph A. Fitzmyer, *The Gospel according to Luke X–XXIV* (New York: Doubleday, 1985), 228–30; Klyne R. Snodgrass, *Stories of Intent: A Comprehensive Guide to the Parables of Jesus* (Grand Rapids, MI: Eerdmans, 2008), 338–62.

[86] See R. Alan Culpepper, "The Gospel of Luke," *The New Interpreter's Bible,* vol. 9 (Nashville, TN: Abingdon Press, 1995), 229–30.

[87] This negative interpretation of the scholar's question is queried by Luis Schottroff, *The Parables of Jesus* (Minneapolis: Fortress Press, 2006), 132.

[88] See Malina and Rohrbaugh, *Social Commentary on the Synoptic Gospels,* 270.

inner pain. People would hesitate to touch him because doing so would render them ritually impure, thereby necessitating lengthy rituals of purification.

The victim has also been stripped of his clothing (Lk 10:3). This is the fourth act of violence. In those days it was customary to strip prisoners naked before scourging them, "and death suffered as much from the shame of involuntary nakedness as from the lash" (Mt 27:28, 31).[89] To strip a person naked, as Jesus was stripped before being hung on the cross, was the ultimate act of subjugation and social marginalization.

The priest and the Levite, two pillars of biblical Jewish culture mentioned in the parable, represent the religious fundamentalism of their time. The Israelite tradition required that people must show compassion, especially to those who are poor and marginalized (Isa 58:6–8), but Hebrew fundamentalists discarded this obligation, developing instead a religion that focused on external conformity to rituals of incidental importance. The priest returning from the Temple in Jerusalem to his home in the country refuses to help the robbery victim for two reasons. He fears being attacked by bandits himself, but more important, he is not prepared to be defiled by touching the victim (Lk 10:31). The Levite belongs to an order of cultic officials "devoted to the LORD" (Ex 32:28); they were inferior to the priests but nonetheless a privileged group in Hebrew society. But the Levite declines to help for the same reasons, although he is portrayed as hesitating slightly before making his decision (Lk 10:32).[90]

The figure of the Samaritan traveler symbolizes a fifth form of violence. The Hebrews regarded the heretical Samaritans as racially inferior, and the Samaritans had a similar view of their Hebrew neighbors; their mutual hatreds led to bitter feuding and marginalization.[91] The story also contains a sixth example of violence: occupational prejudice

---

[89] See John J. Pilch and Bruce J. Malina, eds., *Biblical Social Values and Their Meaning* (Peabody, MA: Hendrickson, 1993), 121.

[90] See Marcus Mescher, *The Ethics of Encounter: Christian Neighbor Love as a Practice of Solidarity* (Maryknoll, NY: Orbis Books, 2020), 46.

[91] John McKenzie comments: "To the Jews the Samaritans were a heretical and schismatic group of spurious worshippers of the God of Israel, who were detested even more than pagans. The origins of the schism between Jews and Samaritans lie deep in early Israelite history. . . . There was no deeper breach of human relations than the feud of Jews and Samaritans." *Dictionary of the Bible* (London: Geoffrey Chapman, 1968), 765, 766.

and discrimination. Traders in oil and wine, such as the Samaritan, were stigmatized because both Hebrews and Samaritans saw them as having become rich through shady dealings. The Samaritan, like the victim, knows the pain of social rejection and loneliness.

The Samaritan's Qualities

The crux of the story, which must have shocked the Hebrews, is that it is a Samaritan—a person considered a religious heretic, and racially and occupationally inferior—who spontaneously aids the robbery victim. Marcus Mescher writes, "It is difficult to translate what a 'Samaritan' would be for us today, but one has to imagine the kind of person who would make your stomach turn and skin crawl."[92] By contrast, those who should have acted—the priest and the Levite—turn their back on the injured and marginalized victim. Through compassion, the Samaritan breaks through the many layers of violence. The story details the qualities of the Samaritan. He is courageous, because he risks his own life by dismounting from his donkey, his only form of protection, thereby becoming himself vulnerable to attack by bandits. Every moment he is off of his mount, the physical danger to him intensifies. His courage is further tested when he walks the donkey to avoid exacerbating the sufferings of the victim, thus further risking an attack. The story's listeners would have known that the road from Jericho to Jerusalem, with its tortuous bends and rocky sides, was ideal for robbers.

In addition to the physical risks there are the ritual and social costs of touching the victim. We read that the caregiver "bandaged his wounds, pouring oil and wine on them" (Lk 10:34). To bandage the victim, the Samaritan must touch him, and since the Samaritans had similar laws to Jews about ritual impurity, the caregiver himself becomes ritually unclean. This willingness to go to the margins of society in his ministry of healing defines the depth of his compassion. The victim is deeply comforted by this touch. At last there is someone who feels with him in his anguish of ritual and social marginalization. We are not told whether the victim survives, but we know with certainty that, through the Samaritan's touch, the victim's inner pain is healed. That is the priority Jesus wishes to emphasize.

---

[92] Mescher, *The Ethics of Encounter,* 47.

The Samaritan exercises the gift of hospitality. He gives of his substance, or capital—the oil and wine—that he intended to sell at the market. In biblical cultures hospitality was never restricted to one's friends or family members; rather, it referred primarily to receiving strangers and being willing to share one's capital goods with them without the expectation of reciprocation. Outsiders were invited to cease being strangers and become instead honored guests.[93] The law required this because the Israelites, having been strangers in Egypt, should themselves show hospitality to strangers (Ex 23:9). The Book of Leviticus says, "The alien who resides with you shall be to you as the citizen among you; you shall love the alien as yourself" (Lev 19:34). "You will treat resident aliens as though they were native-born and love them as yourself" (Lev 19:34). Jesus would develop this further, not only in this parable but through his example and teachings. People who receive the disciples of Jesus would, he said, be in fact receiving Jesus himself (Mt 10:40–42). To offer or refuse hospitality meant that the gospel had been accepted or rejected.[94]

The fifth character in the story, the innkeeper, has a significant role as well. At the time of Christ inns were not welcoming havens but dens of thieves led by roguish innkeepers. But the Samaritan seeks to build a relationship with the innkeeper in this story. Knowing from his own trading experience what to expect from the innkeeper, the Samaritan bribes him to guarantee the patient will be looked after. He leaves the innkeeper a certain amount but promises more when he returns (Lk 10:35). In other words, the Samaritan was just as "street smart" as the innkeeper and would keep tabs on him by promising to return and check that the innkeeper had complied with his requests.

Foundational Truths

In his efforts to address the different types of violence shown in the incident, the Good Samaritan exemplifies the following truths that form the moral foundations of Catholic social teaching and the values that must guide the recovery from the pandemic crisis.

---

[93] See Pilch and Malina, *Biblical Social Values,* 104–7.

[94] See A. J. Malherbe, "Hospitality," in *The Oxford Companion to the Bible*, ed. B. M. Metzger and M. D. Coogan (New York: Oxford University Press, 1993), 292–93.

1. Creation is a gift of God.

All life must be respected as coming from God. Human persons mirror God's power in the sense that they think and act freely, but this freedom must be exercised in ways that respect the purpose of the Creator. Respect for human dignity is a value from which other values flow. Racism is an evil, a denial of God's gift of creation; poverty is an evil, the deprivation of the social structures and personal opportunities to live out God's plan (see Chapters 4 and 5). Every person should expect from society equitable access to what is necessary to live with dignity, such as education and healthcare, allocated in ways that respect the rights of others. This is the meaning of justice. Hospitality is another value that flows from this truth; when we are hospitable to a stranger, we are only sharing what belongs to God. Above all, however, the Samaritan is motivated by love of God and neighbor.

2. We must make a commitment to stewardship.

We are called to co-create with God, that is, to continue God's creation in the world in ways that mirror the dignity of God. This truth contains the core values of justice, mercy, compassion, empathy, excellence, and simplicity. Because all creation comes from God, we must use it as stewards of God. Pope Francis writes in *Laudato Si'*:

> The created things of this world are not free of ownership: "For they are yours, O Lord, who love the living" (Wis 11:26). This is the basis of our conviction that, as part of the universe, called into being by the one Father, all of us are linked by unseen bonds and together form a kind of universal family. . . . An inadequate presentation of Christian anthropology gave rise to a wrong understanding of the relationship between human beings and the world. . . . Instead, our "dominion" over the universe should be understood more properly in the sense of responsible stewardship. (LS, nos. 89, 116)

Compassion has an interesting origin. The Samaritan traveler "was moved with pity" (Lk 10:33). Compassion is a value originally founded on kinship obligations, whether natural or symbolic.[95] The Hebrew word for "compassion" is derived from the word for "womb," implying the need of one person to sympathize for another because they are born of the same mother. God is that mother, and we are all children of that womb and must accordingly feel with, and care for, one another as brothers and sisters. The Samaritan feels the inner pain of marginalization that the victim—his brother—is experiencing.

We exercise the value of excellence when we recognize that our gifts come from God and are to be used in God's service. Excellence in this sense covers all human endeavors, including research that is at the service of God and humankind. It allows for no selfishness, mediocrity, or laziness in the use of one's talents. The Samaritan exercises this value when he uses his experience concerning human nature in relating to the innkeeper. Simplicity is not synonymous with an ignorance that causes people to act imprudently. On the contrary, people act with nothing in mind other than the will of God. Out of love God gives creation to us to be used as God wishes, namely, with a single-minded commitment to justice and love in the service of others. There is to be no holding back, fuss, pretense, or double dealing as stewards of God's gifts. Such is the example of the Good Samaritan.

3. We must strive for solidarity.

There is no support for individualism in the parable. In the Jewish tradition people are expected to work together for the good of all in imitation of God's desire to build community with the Israelites: "I will place my dwelling in your midst . . . and I will walk among you, and will be your God, and you shall be my people" (Lev 26:11–12). The values of solidarity, unity, collaboration, dialogue, and mutuality are marks of an authentic community. The victim's pain of marginalization reminds the Samaritan of his own similar experience and his need for community.[96] Mescher writes: "Solidarity is equality and mutuality expressed in an inclusive community of belonging in

---

[95] See David K. Urion, *Compassion as a Subversive Activity* (Cambridge, MA: Cowley Publications, 2006), 48; John Swinton, *Raging with Compassion: Pastoral Responses to the Problem of Evil* (London: SCM Press, 2018).

[96] See comments by Conor M. Kelly, "Everyday Solidarity: A Framework for Integrating Theological Ethics and Ordinary Life," *Theological Studies* 81, no. 2 (2020): 415–37.

partnership for just social, economic and political structures."[97] He cites ethicist David Hollenbach, SJ, who writes: "Solidarity is not only a virtue to be enacted by persons one at a time. It must be expressed in the economic, cultural, political, and religious institutions that shape society. Solidarity is a virtue of communities as well as individuals."[98] Pope Francis in *Evangelii Gaudium* reminds us that solidarity demands of us sustained conversion: "Solidarity . . . refers to something more than a few sporadic acts of generosity. It presumes the creation of a new mindset which thinks in terms of community and the priority of the life of all over the appropriation of goods by a few" (EG, no. 188).

Fundamentalist neoliberal economics,[99] that is, blind faith in the efficiency of deregulated markets to maintain order in society, ignores the moral implications of the truth that creation is a gift of God and that we must work for the common good of all. It is an economic philosophy that privileges and promotes the capitalist market system, assessing states of affairs in terms of economic productivity alone. Its ideological assumption is that monetary profit is the sole measure of value and that we should favor unrestrained competition over collaboration for the common good. The rights of the individual, not the well-being of the community, have priority.[100] This creates a culture of violence in which the poor and vulnerable in society are the first

---

[97] Mescher, *The Ethics of Encounter*, 94–95.

[98] David Hollenbach, *The Common Good and Christian Ethics* (Cambridge: Cambridge University Press, 2002), 189. St. John Paul II writes in *Sollicitudo Rei Socialis* that solidarity "is not a feeling of vague compassion or shallow distress at the misfortunes of so many people. . . . On the contrary, it is *a firm and persevering determination* to commit oneself to the *common good*; that is to say to the good of all and of each individual, because we are all really responsible *for all*" (SR, no. 38).

[99] Pope Francis writes in *Fratelli Tutti*: "The marketplace, by itself, cannot resolve every problem, however much we are asked to believe this dogma of neoliberal faith. . . . Neoliberalism simply reproduces itself by resorting to the magic theories of 'spillover' or 'trickle'—without using the name—as the only solution to societal problems. There is little appreciation of the fact that the alleged 'spillover' does not resolve the inequality that gives rise to new forms of violence threatening the fabric of society" (FT, no. 168).

[100] See Robert N. Bellah et al., *Habits of the Heart: Individualism and Commitment in American Life* (San Francisco: Harper and Row, 1985), 275–96.

to suffer.[101] Pope Francis will have none of this: "Everything comes under the laws of competition and the survival of the fittest, where the powerful feed upon the powerless. . . . Masses of people find themselves excluded . . . without work, without possibilities" (EG, no. 53).

4. We have a commitment to maintain a preferential option for the poor.

In the scriptures the phrases "people who are poor" and "the little ones" commonly refer to those who, through no fault of their own, are powerless in society. Structures of oppression such as institutional racism condemn them to economic, social, and political poverty (see Chapter 5). In the parable Jesus identifies with the actions of the Samaritan. His primary concern in his ministry is to be with those who are marginalized in society. By his actions and words Jesus frequently repeats this message: "I was hungry and you gave me food . . . I was a stranger and you welcomed me" (Mt 25:35). Jesus becomes so closely identified with people who are poor that, when we refuse them justice, we are refusing Jesus himself (Mt 25:40, 45). The ultimate test of our concern for human dignity is the priority we give to people who are especially disadvantaged, people society considers worthless. The relentless pursuit of profit is devoid of compassionate feelings toward strangers, motivated solely by self-interest, and is cold and callous toward fellow human beings, seeing them only as means to one's own ends.

5. We must make a commitment to holistic healing.

The mission of the healing Jesus Christ, the Good Shepherd, commits us to a holistic understanding of health: "See, I am making all things new" (Rev 21:5). Healing is a process whereby humankind individually and collectively struggles to be restored to the divine image in which it was originally formed. Where there is injustice, there is ill-health; where there is suffering without meaning, there is ill-health; where there is oppression of the poor, there is ill-health. St. John Paul II writes that this parable "not only spurs one to help the sick, but also to do all one can to reintegrate them into society.

---

[101] For a fuller development of the relationship between postmodernity and violence, see Arbuckle, *Violence, Society, and the Church*, 153–214.

For Christ, in fact, healing is also this reintegration: just as sickness excludes persons from the community, so healing must bring them to rediscover their place in the family, in the Church and society" (SR, no. 15).

6. Commitment to a prophetic role is required.

In the parable, to be a prophet is to remind people of foundational truths when they ignore them: "The task of prophetic imagination is to cut through the numbness, to penetrate the self-deception."[102] But we must be prepared to accept the consequences of doing so. On the bandit-infested road the Samaritan not only risks his life for the victim but also, because of his actions, suffers further marginalization from both the Hebrew people and those of his own culture. Christ, the ultimate Good Samaritan, will, of course, give his life in the service of others, no matter the cost.

Summary

- COVID-19 attacked the cultural foundations of our lives—international, national, and local.
- A culture consisting of symbols, myths, and rituals binds people together with varying degrees of intensity. It provides people with a feeling of order and normality. Myths are stories that express hidden truths by which people chart their lives.
- Cultural trauma, a collective overwhelming and haunting experience of disaster, occurs when a people's culture suddenly disintegrates, as happened when COVID-19 spread across the globe. Chaos results; normality is destroyed. The long-term human consequences of cultural trauma can last for generations.
- Because chaos is so frightening, people are prone to accept conspiracy theories that falsely blame vulnerable groups for their plight. Conspiracy beliefs respond to a pressing need for people who cannot maintain their self-esteem or identity unless they view themselves as victims of a plot. "If no conspiracy were

[102] Walter Brueggemann, *The Prophetic Imagination* (Minneapolis: Fortress Press, 1978), 49.

available to them, such persons would have to re-examine their assumptions with the foreknowledge that these were invalid."[103]

- The Good Samaritan parable highlights the truths and values of solidarity, compassion, and justice that must infuse the decision-making of individuals and governments in their efforts to respond to the pandemic and its aftermath.

Reflection Questions

1. What points in this chapter relate to your experience?
2. In what ways has the pandemic affected your life, family, and close friends?
3. The values and truths in the Good Samaritan parable should guide the actions of governments as they seek to lead the recovery from COVID-19. Why is this so? Has your government adhered to these values and truths in reacting to the pandemic? In your experience of the pandemic and its aftermath, can you identify people or groups who have lived these values and truths?

---

[103] Hans Toch, *The Social Psychology of Social Movements* (London: Methuen, 1966), 70.

2

Journeying through Traumatic Times: Rites of Passage

Rites of passage are rituals that accompany a change of place, state, social position, and age. . . . [They] enable societies to effect an orderly, meaningful transition for individuals and groups.

—Meredith B. McGuire, *Religion: The Social Context*

Liminality . . . breaks, as it were, the cake of custom and enfranchises speculation.

—Victor Turner, *The Ritual Process*

This chapter explains that:

- Cultural traumas leave people collectively benumbed.
- Rites of passage mark status changes and manage tensions.
- The three stages in rites of passage are separation, liminality, and reentry.
- Cultural traumas can be rites of passage to new life.
- Biblically, rites of passage initiate people into conversion.
- The response to COVID-19 grief calls for lamentation.

A fundamental theme of this book is that the interference with, or destruction of, the inner mythological framework of cultures, even when there is conscious and intellectual assent to what is happening, destroys the stable, deep-rooted sense of people's felt belonging. Traumatic events such as the pandemic shatter the mythological assumptions about the world and one's place in it. People's lives and livelihoods are devastated. The world is seen as less controllable and predictable, less safe, and less benevolent.

This chapter focuses on developing a model of cultural trauma, that is, what can happen to cultures when traumatic events occur, such as a pandemic, that destroy or seriously threaten the acceptable order. It will be seen that when people and cultures are traumatized, their movement forward into new life through chaos can be a rite of passage with three identifiable stages: separation, liminality, and reentry. Leadership is required at each stage. The scriptures are filled with rites of passage, traumatic periods of transition and transformation, as this chapter explains. The next chapter applies the model to the COVID-19 pandemic and its aftereffects.

Cultural Rites of Passage

This section describes rites of passage as a preface for understanding the Cultural Trauma: Grief-overload Model. Ritual is "a performance, planned or improvised, that effects a transition from everyday life to an alternative context within which the everyday is transformed" (see Axiom 5, Chapter 1).[1] To lose ritual is to lose direction. It is a situation that is not only pitiable but also dangerous: "As for the whole society, sooner or later it will find rituals again, but they may be of an oppressive rather than a liberating kind. Rituals have much to do with our fate."[2] This is especially true of rites of passage.

Rites of passage is a term first used by anthropologist Arnold van Gennep (1873–1957) to describe particular transformative rituals that assist people or groups to transition from one social status to

---

[1] Bobby C. Alexander, "Ritual and Current Studies of Ritual: Overview," in *Anthropology of Religion: A Handbook*, ed. Stephen D. Glazier (Westport, CT: Greenwood Press, 1997), 139.

[2] Tom F. Driver, *The Magic of Ritual: Our Need for Liberating Rites That Transform Our Lives and Our Communities* (New York: HarperSanFrancisco: 1991), 4.

another.[3] The crossing over to a new status can be full of uncertainty and tensions. Hence the name rites of passage. They are *initiation* rituals because they assist individuals or groups to make the transition from one social status to a new identity, as well as assisting society to accept significant changes in the status of members. Examples of life-crisis rituals are those accompanying birth, marriage, initiation into adulthood, employment and retirement, and appointment to or departure from political or religious offices.

Van Gennep found that all processual rituals have three stages: separation, transition or liminality, and re-aggregation or incorporation. Between the stages there are clear symbolic demarcations. There is first a rite to mark the separation from the former status. Then there is a period of transition or liminal stage when the person or group has left the old status but has not yet reached the new status. For example, a person entering a new job may require an initial period of testing before the employment is approved and the new role is formally assumed. Finally, there is the rite of reentry in which the new status is confirmed. Van Gennep notes that the middle or liminal stage is normally lengthy because the letting-go of attachment to former status—the grieving dimension of the ritual and the birthing of the new—can be slow, hesitant, and painful. It is also dangerous because rights and roles are temporarily ambiguous and disordered.

Anthropologist Victor Turner further refined van Gennep's insights by emphasizing the relevance of his model for cultural change, not only for individual transitions. He distinguishes two types of cultures. First, there is what he calls *societas,* a type of culture in which there is role differentiation, structure, segmentation, and a hierarchical system of institutionalized positions. Most people live most of their lives in cultures like this.[4] The second cultural type is called *liminal* or *liminality*, that is, a homogenous type of culture in which individuals relate to one another integrally or as one human being to another; they are not segmented into status and roles. Such is the case, for example, when people go to a baseball game. All distinguishing

---

[3] See Arnold van Gennep, *The Rites of Passage*, trans. M. Vizedom and G. Caffee (Chicago: University of Chicago Press, 1960).

[4] For a fuller development of this subject see Gerald A. Arbuckle, *From Chaos to Mission: The Refounding of Religious Life Formation* (London: Geoffrey Chapman, 1995), 113–37; and idem, *Intentional Faith Communities in Catholic Education* (Strathfield: St. Pauls Publications, 2016), 71–83.

statuses are left behind at the gate; in the stadium patrons have only one status, namely, they are spectators. Turner argues that life is a process whereby individuals and cultures pass from societas through liminality (the "betwixt and between" stage) to societas, having been enlivened by the experience.[5] The moment the ball game is over and the spectators pass through the gates, they return refreshed to their usual statuses in life.

Liminality Stage: Dangers and Hopes

Initiation rituals require leaders to be deeply imbued with the mythology of the culture into which the initiate is to enter. Following van Gennep, Turner recognizes that the first stage of initiation rituals for individuals and cultures is short and dramatic. Turner highlights the ritual leveling at the following liminal stage. To illustrate this point he uses examples from the initiation rituals in traditional cultures. Neophytes preparing to move from childhood to adulthood are without roles or status as though, in relation to the society from which they have come or the society into which they are to be incorporated later, they are anonymous, dead, nonpersons, deprived of all social roles other than just being initiates. Their state is "frequently . . . likened to being in the womb, to invisibility, to darkness . . . to the wilderness."[6] These initiates "have no status, property, insignia, secular clothing, rank, kinship positions, nothing to demarcate them structurally from their fellows."[7] The aim of this ritual stripping of former statuses is to dispose them to develop deep interrelations with one another and an openness to a new mythology and values that form the foundation of the culture of adulthood: "The neophyte in liminality must be a *tabula rasa*, a blank slate, on which is inscribed the knowledge and wisdom of the group, in those respects that pertain to the new status."[8] This is a frightening stage, a chaos stage, because the past securities have been destroyed.

---

[5] See Victor Turner, *The Ritual Process: Structure and Anti-Structure* (New York: Aldine, 1969), 95.

[6] Ibid.

[7] Victor Turner, *The Forest of Symbols: Aspects of Ndembu Ritual* (Ithaca, NY: Cornell University Press, 1967), 99.

[8] Turner, *The Ritual Process*, 103.

Mary Douglas concludes that social transition is perceived as dangerous simply because the status of neophytes remains temporarily undefined.[9] Rollo May comments on liminality: "*The loneliness of mythlessness is the deepest and least assuageable of all.* Unrelated to the past, unconnected with the future, we hang as it were in mid-air."[10] At the beginning of the *Divine Comedy*, the poet Dante Alighieri (1265–1321) dramatically describes the fear-evoking nature of liminal chaos (see Axiom 1, Chapter 1), particularly the feeling of utter loneliness and loss of direction. His words apply as much to the experience of cultures as to individuals caught in the turmoil and uncertainties of dramatic change:

> Midway upon the journey of life
> I found myself within a forest dark,
> For the straightforward pathway had been lost.
> Ah me! how hard a thing it is to say
> What was this forest savage, rough, and stern,
> Which in the very thought renews the fear.
> So bitter is it, death is little more.[11]

Communitas

In the state of liminality, neophytes experience a uniquely intense companionship that Turner terms *communitas,* that is, a bond of communion among members of a society.[12] This experience is usually an intense one; it belongs in the intuitive or emotional field, as

---

[9] See Mary Douglas, *Purity and Danger: An Analysis of Concepts of Pollution and Taboo* (Harmondsworth: Penguin, 1966), 116.

[10] Rollo May, *The Cry for Myth* (New York: Delta Publishing, 1991), 99.

[11] Dante Alighieri, *Divine Comedy*, trans. Henry W. Longfellow (New York: Charles Bigelow, 1909), 15.

[12] Victor Turner defines *communitas* as "a relational quality of full unmediated communication, even communion, between definite and determinate identities which arises spontaneously in all kinds of groups, situations and circumstances. It is a liminal phenomenon which combines qualities of lowliness, sacredness, homogeneity, and comradeship." Cited in Victor Turner and Edith Turner, *Image and Pilgrimage in Christian Culture* (Oxford: Basil Blackwell, 1978), 250.

opposed to the rational one.[13] It is either normative or spontaneous.[14] Normative communitas is integral to initiation rites; that is, circumstances are deliberately structured by ritual leaders to evoke deep bonding or oneness in initiates, but this does not necessarily happen. Initiates cannot experience communitas if they are unwilling to struggle through chaos for the conversion of their inner selves, that is, to move from an "I" to the "I-Thou" ethos as defined by the philosopher Martin Buber. This relationship takes place when there is mutuality, openness, presence, and directness.[15] The "I" relates to the "Thou" not as something to be studied, measured, or manipulated, but as an irreplaceable presence that responds to the "I" in its individuality. In communitas the ego fades away to become "We"; there is the blurring or merging of self and others, the creation of oneness and integrative harmony.

Spontaneous communitas is an unplanned experience of bonding, such as the sense of radical openness that people can feel when confronted with a shared experience like a natural disaster, or a sudden cultural disintegration as occurred during COVID-19. Anthropologist Edith Turner writes that spontaneous communitas has endless variations.

> Spontaneous communitas may arise in disasters: the Dunkirk spirit in World War II. Or it may happen during the rise of oppressed people. . . . Communitas dwells with the powers of the weak. The Universal Declaration of Human Rights shows that ethic today; the idea of democracy is founded on the value of the simple human being as undifferentiated, beyond the bailiwick of social-structural rules and status-made distinctions. . . . When communitas appears, one is conscious that it overrides psychological and sociological constructs.[16]

---

[13] See Tim Olaveson, "Collective Effervescence and Communitas: Processual Models of Ritual and Society in Emile Durkheim and Victor Turner," *Dialectical Anthropology,* no. 26 (2001): 89–124.

[14] See Victor Turner, *Dramas, Fields, and Metaphors: Symbolic Action in Human Society* (Ithaca, NY: Cornell University Press, 1996), 252.

[15] See Martin Buber, *Between Man and Man* (New York: Routledge, 2002), xii.

[16] Edith Turner, *Communitas: The Anthropology of Collective Joy* (New York: Palgrave Macmillan, 2012), 2, 3.

Liminality/Communitas: Subversive Power

Turner speaks of *root paradigms* in a culture's mythologies. A root paradigm consists of symbols and values in a group's creation myth that are considered crucial to the particular culture and its ongoing existence.[17] In initiation rituals the common root paradigm is death/rebirth. In traditional cultures the initiation of boys into adulthood insists there must be death to the childish, mother-centered ways and resurrection for service to others in the wider society of the adult world. The boys are to be "converted by the mystical efficacy of ritual into purified members of a male moral community, able to begin to take their part in the jural, political, and ritual affairs"[18] of the wider society. In these cultures the symbolic objects of the creation mythology that are used to foster the interiorization of this death/rebirth transformation in initiates are often highly dramatic and fear evoking. In traditional cultures, for example, the sacred symbols are tribal ancestors or heroes, gods and monsters.[19] In the rite of passage of the two disciples on the road to Emmaus Jesus speaks of "Moses and all the prophets" (Lk 24:27); in the initiation of Jesus into his public ministry the symbols are the desert and the devil (see Chapter 3).

The symbols provide physical, psychological, moral, and spiritual shocks to evoke in initiates critical reflection on foundational symbols and myths. Put another way, the leaders of the initiation process—the ritual guides—deliberately foster chaos in the liminal stage through various interventions, but this engineered disorder is carefully monitored lest it become excessive and damage the learning experience. The guides also recognize that conversion to mythology can remain superficial in their initiates, so they are vigilant and use manufactured or spontaneous events throughout the lengthy liminal phase to teach and test the depth of their learning. Turner writes, "Liminality is the mother of invention."[20] He also notes that liminality "may be partly described as a stage of reflection,"[21] or, to put it another way, that "liminality . . . breaks, as it were, the cake of custom and enfranchises

---

[17] See Victor Turner, *Ritual Process,* 67–68.

[18] Victor Turner, *The Forest of Symbols*, 265–66.

[19] See Victor Turner, *Ritual Process,* 103.

[20] Victor Turner, "Symbols and Social Experience in Religious Ritual," *Studia Missionalia,* no. 23 (1974): 10.

[21] Victor Turner, *The Forest of Symbols,* 105.

speculation"[22] about the mythology that should give revitalizing meaning to life. That is, in the liminality stage the experience of communitas has the power to subvert cultures for good or evil.

Reentry Stage

Entrance out of liminality is a dangerous stage. Mary Douglas describes why this is so: "It is consistent with the ideas about form and formlessness to treat initiands coming out of seclusion as though they were themselves charged with power, hot, dangerous, requiring insulation and a time for cooling down."[23] Tribal societies know from centuries of experience that neophytes need a "cooling off" period because (1) they become discouraged for not having adequately interiorized the mythology; (2) they are annoyed and cynical because their elders have failed to live according to the mythology; or (3) they want immediately to revolutionize the world.

Anthropologist Maurice Bloch, in his analysis of cultural rites of passage, further refines Douglas's conclusions. At the second stage, people make contact with the founding mythology of their culture, for example, clan, tribe, nation. This mythology has transcendental and revitalizing power. For Bloch, *transcendental* means that mythology has greater power than any individual; it is "godlike" in its ability to inspire people to act. So invigorating is this power that people transitioning into the reentry stage are tempted to violence and the scapegoating of others for their tribulations (see Axiom 7, Chapter 1). Bloch terms this "rebounding violence."[24] Dictatorial and populist leaders, well bolstered with conspiracy theories (see Axioms 4, 6, and 7, Chapter 1), take full advantage of this phenomenon. Hitler was able to obtain widespread support from Germans by evoking the mythology of anti-Semitism, and Serb Slobodan Milošević encouraged ethnic cleansing of Muslims in retaliation for Muslims having invaded and defeated Serbs in the fourteenth century. Likewise, Donald Trump encouraged the rebounding violence of the extremist supporters who assaulted the Capitol on

---

[22] Victor Turner, *The Ritual Process,* 106.

[23] Douglas, *Purity and Danger*, 117.

[24] See Maurice Bloch, *From Blessing to Violence* (Cambridge: Cambridge University Press, 1986); Gerald A. Arbuckle, *Violence, Society, and the Church: A Cultural Approach* (Collegeville, MN: Liturgical Press, 2004), 15.

January 6, 2021, inspiring them to act by making false statements about election fraud.

Communitas: Examples

Following are several historical examples of how accumulated collective grief can erupt into liminality and communitas, concluding at the reentry stage—except in the case of the United States—with autocratic populist leaders, rebounding violence, and further oppression. Economic and political crises lead to more collective grief and eventually to cultural trauma, which populist leaders can use to their advantage.

French Revolution

In the liminal years of the French Revolution[25] people recognized that radical change could still be possible (1789–99). For centuries the king had ruled by divine right; this was not seriously questioned. In the first stage of revolutionary trauma (1789–92) the revolution had the imprint of communitas, "a communion in hope and love, never to be wholly lost in the bitterest days of the Terror."[26] The National Constituent Assembly in 1791 created a constitutional monarchy, leaving the king with little power. The pent-up grief of centuries could not be silenced any longer. Widespread poverty, the fact that the majority still did not have political representation, and continuing suspicion that the king was seeking a return to full political control all intensified pressure for more radical political changes.

In 1792, in the second phase of the revolution, a new legislative body, the Convention, was formed; the monarchy was abolished. Then a renewed burst of communitas sparked the third phase of the revolution, the Reign of Terror (1793–95); the violence expanded and leader after leader fell victim to the Terror.[27] Liminality officially ended when the authorities sought to control the lawlessness; a new government was established with the support of the military (1795–99). For the exhausted

[25] See Edith Turner, *Communitas*, 96–105.

[26] Crane Brinton, *A Decade of Revolution 1789–1700* (New York: Harper and Row, 1934), 3.

[27] See Simon Sharma, *Citizens: A Chronicle of French Revolution* (New York: Random House, 1990).

population, societas was again restored with little having been achieved despite the enormity of the human costs. Stephen Clarke comments:

> [If] public discontent about the flaws in the constitutional monarchy of 1789–92 had been harnessed democratically instead of dictatorially, France might have been able to grow harmoniously, and relatively quickly, into a country that offered true *Liberté, Egalité* and *Fraternité*.[28]

But the accumulated collective grief of centuries of royal oppression in the liminality/communitas period (1789–95) was so explosively powerful that it could only have been channeled into democratic life by incredibly gifted leaders, and such leaders failed to emerge.

Nazi Germany

When the American stock market collapsed on October 29, 1929, it had disastrous consequences around the world. The impact on the German economy, however, was particularly catastrophic because following the First World War of 1914–18 the economy had been overly dependent on foreign capital, mainly loans from America and foreign trade. Runaway inflation and mass unemployment followed. Economic destitution, however, was only one reason for the rise of Nazism. The Great Depression came on top of the German defeat in the war and the severe and humiliating terms of the peace agreement. Germans deeply and collectively resented the massive demands for German reparations. They were in a state of grief overload. In this state of liminality the country was open to accepting populist leaders. Hitler promised to reverse the humiliation of the peace agreement of Versailles, and he inspired his followers with the mythology of a renewed Germany, no matter the costs: "Those who see in National Socialism nothing more than a political movement know scarcely anything of it. It is more than a religion: it is the will to create mankind anew."[29] This is communitas. There was to be a transformed

---

[28] Stephen Clarke, *The French Revolution and What Went Wrong* (London: Arrow Books, 2019), 518.

[29] Adolf Hitler, cited in Jonathan Glover, *Humanity: A Moral History of the Twentieth Century* (London: Jonathan Cape, 1999), 315.

people, even if this meant the destruction of traditional moral values. The fact that by 1939 the German economy was flourishing, together with the admiration of many outsiders, assured Hitler's followers that his vision was the correct one. The enthusiasm of their communitas blinded them to his abominable cruelties.

Russian Revolution

The Russian Revolution started during the First World War. The communitas of the revolution began when people rioted against the government's corruption, the rising death toll in the war, and the scarcity of food supplies. With Emperor Nicholas II's abdication there developed an initial liminal period of dual power in the Provisional Government: one center of power was held by representatives of the aristocracy, financial elites, urban middle class, and socialist groups; the other, more influential power was held by Bolsheviks under the populist leadership of Vladimir Lenin. Political chaos intensified. Finally, with the October Revolution in 1917, a Bolshevik-led revolution assumed armed control and transferred all authority to the Soviets, thus ending the liminal period. For some seven decades the lid was firmly kept on Soviet society by a ruthless, violent authoritarian elite. Once it became clear that under Mikhail Gorbachev an alternative system was possible, there was no stopping the onrush of the people's communitas. The breakup of the Soviet Union into nation states could not be halted. An attempted coup to stop the breakup failed; the people no longer feared the coup's leaders, who belonged to a former age.[30]

United States: New Deal

When Herbert Hoover became president in March 1929, he was confident that the economy of the United States would continue to flourish. But in October of that year the liminal stage began when the stock market collapsed, followed by the massive unemployment, poverty, and starvation of the Great Depression. No class was exempt from the trauma. Unemployment rates jumped from 4 percent to 25 percent.

---

[30] See William Taubman, *Gorbachev: His Life and Times* (London: Simon and Schuster, 2017), 574–619.

Shantytowns (called Hoovervilles) grew up outside major cities. Hoover thought that minimal intervention from government would revitalize the capitalist system, and that the market on its own would do the rest. But he was wrong.

When Franklin Roosevelt was elected president in 1933, he faced a colossal challenge: how to foster "effective federal programs that would not agitate public fears of a swing toward collectivism and away from individualism by a president reaching for too much power."[31] He responded to this challenge with what became known as the New Deal.[32] This consisted of a series of programs, public work projects, and financial reforms between 1933 and 1939. The New Deal, a rite of passage to a refounding of America, had three aims: relief for the unemployed and poor, recovery of the economy to normal levels, and reform of the financial system to block the development of future depressions. Through Roosevelt's efforts millions were able to obtain work or at least to obtain help to survive; for his followers this was a communitas experience, encouraged by the growing success of the New Deal and his regular radio fireside chats (1933–44).

Roosevelt as ritual leader skillfully overcame the political opposition in the reentry period of recovery. In his annual address to Congress in 1935 he sharply critiqued neoliberalism, with its excessive emphasis on market freedoms, as the cause of the 1930s cultural trauma—the Great Depression. In his State of the Union Address to Congress in 1935 he described the country's situation: "We find our population suffering from old inequalities, little changed by past sporadic remedies. In spite of our efforts and in spite of our talk we have not weeded out the overprivileged and we have not effectively lifted up the underprivileged." "Americans," he said, "must foreswear that conception of the acquisition of wealth which, through excessive profits, creates undue private power."[33] He believed the role of the

[31] Robert Dallek, *Franklin Roosevelt: A Political Life* (London: Allen Lane, 2017), 8.

[32] While some aspects of the New Deal followed Keynesian economic principles, Roosevelt still "regarded the economist as an indecipherable mystic." "John Maynard Keynes: Alive in the Long Run," *The Economist* (May 9, 2020), 67.

[33] Franklin Delano Roosevelt, "State of the Union Address 1935"; see David Harvey, *A Brief History of Neoliberalism* (Oxford: Oxford University Press, 2005), 183.

state was to ensure that poverty and hunger are eradicated. Though the emphasis in the founding mythology of the United States is on individual freedom and rights, he managed to build his New Deal policies on the weaker side of the mythology—community rights. Like every sound ritual leader he draws on the founding mythology of the country to validate his mission: "We have undertaken a new order of things, yet we progress to it under the framework and in the spirit and intent of the American Constitution. We have proceeded a measurable distance on the road toward this new order."[34]

Roosevelt had detractors, but although they were vocal they failed to destroy what he had created. For example, the National Union for Social Justice was an extreme right-wing movement founded in 1934 by a demagogic Catholic priest, Father Charles Coughlin, a young pastor and skilled communicator. At first in his radio broadcasts he was a strong advocator of the New Deal, proclaiming "Roosevelt or ruin!" Then, backed by millions of supporters, he quickly and bitterly turned against Roosevelt, changing the slogan to "Roosevelt *and* ruin!" The conspiracy-minded Coughlin claimed both that Roosevelt was too friendly with bankers and that the New Deal was inspired by communism—but he was not successful in undermining Roosevelt's plans and policies.[35]

Cultural Trauma as a Rite of Passage[36]

The aim of this section is to formulate a working model of what can happen to people and their cultures when confronted with cultural trauma. Under the direction of ritual leaders like Roosevelt, they can

---

[34] Roosevelt, "State of the Union Address 1935."

[35] See Chester Gillis, *Roman Catholicism in America* (New York: Columbia University Press, 1999), 231–32; Gerald A. Arbuckle, *Fundamentalism at Home and Abroad: Analysis and Pastoral Responses* (Collegeville, MN: Liturgical Press, 2017), 90.

[36] This model updates the one previously published by the author in the following volumes: *The Francis Factor and the People of God: New Life for the Church* (Maryknoll, NY: Orbis Books, 2015), 126–98; *Fundamentalism: At Home and Abroad: Analysis and Pastoral Responses* (Collegeville, MN: Liturgical Press, 2017), 62–96; and *Abuse and Cover-Up: Refounding the Church in Trauma* (Maryknoll, NY: Orbis Books, 2019), 102–17.

utilize the trauma as a rite of passage into a new cultural consensus based on values of solidarity, justice, and compassion—or, they can reject that opportunity, as Hitler did.

Cultural Trauma Defined

- *Medically*, trauma is "an objective force that deprives a subject of some part of his normal sovereignty."[37] Arnon Bentovim describes the psychological impact of trauma on individuals: "An event that . . . ruptures the protective layer surrounding the mind with . . . long-lasting consequences for psychic well-being. Helplessness overwhelms, mastery is undermined, defences fail, there is a sense of failure of protection . . . [and] acute mental pain as the memory of the event intrudes and replays itself repeatedly."[38]
- *Sociologically*, social institutions can experience trauma when their identity and the identities of their members are grievously threatened.[39]
- *Anthropologically*, cultural trauma occurs (see Axiom 1, Chapter 1) when trauma extends beyond individuals and institutions to embrace directly an entire culture.[40]

Cultural trauma happens "when members of a collectivity feel they have been subjected to an appalling event that leaves indelible marks upon their group consciousness, marking their memories forever and changing their future identity in fundamental and irrevocable ways."[41]

---

[37] Jürgen Habermas, *Legitimation Crisis* (Boston: Beacon Press, 1975), 3. See also Cathy Caruth, ed., *Listening to Trauma: Conversations with Leaders in the Theory and Treatment of Catastrophic Experience* (Baltimore: Johns Hopkins University Press, 2014).

[38] Arnon Bentovim, *Trauma-Organized Systems: Physical and Sexual Abuse in Families* (London: Karnac, 1992), 24.

[39] See Caruth, *Listening to Trauma*, 1–3.

[40] See Ron Eyerman, "Cultural Trauma: Emotion and Narration," in *The Oxford Handbook of Cultural Sociology*, ed. Jeffrey Alexander et al. (Oxford: Oxford University Press, 2012), 564–82.

[41] Jeffrey C. Alexander, "Toward a Theory of Cultural Trauma," in *Cultural Trauma and Collective Identity*, ed. Jeffrey C. Alexander et al. (Berkeley and Los Angeles: University of California Press, 2004), 1.

The founding mythology that emotionally and normatively binds the culture together in collective identity ceases to operate. With their culture shattered, people lose their established sense of belonging; they feel stunned and rudderless. There is a mythological vacuum, as people are no longer able to find an adequate mythological answer to the strains of living. For example, in New Zealand in the nineteenth century millions of acres of land were forcefully confiscated by white settlers from the indigenous Maori people, who fell into widespread grieving expressed in depression, apathy, disillusionment, despair, and hopelessness.[42] Destroy the land—the foundation of their mythology—and the people's spirit dies. One Maori elder forced from his land lamented on behalf of thousands: "Send me a handful of earth that I may weep over it."[43] Ponder the cries of Israelite exiles in Babylon, tormented by their captors, bemoaning the destruction of sacred cultural symbols:

> By the rivers of Babylon—
>   there we sat down and there we wept
>   when we remembered Zion.
> On the willows there
>   we hung up our harps.
> For there our captors
>   asked us for songs,
> and our tormentors asked for mirth, saying,
> "Sing us one of the songs of Zion!"
>
> How could we sing the LORD's song
>   in a foreign land? (Ps 137:1–4)

Further Clarifications

1. Potential of chaos

Over time, cultures frequently undergo cyclic regression into chaos, the radical breakdown of order, as a disturbing and protracted preliminary to a new creation or cultural integration (see Axiom 8,

---

[42] See Arbuckle, *The Francis Factor and the People of God*, 141–43.

[43] Cited in Raymond Firth, *The Economics of the New Zealand Maori* (Wellington: R. E. Owen, 1959), 370.

Chapter 1).[44] For example, in the United States the Great Depression of the 1930s was followed by the New Deal. The development of the European Union following the chaos of World War II is another example of how chaos can evoke creative thinking and action. Likewise, in the midst of Brexit deliberations "some of the fundamental ideas that have underpinned Western governments...for decades are being questioned. . . . Some of them are promising; others downright dangerous."[45] This process of regression to chaos, as a preface to new life, is a rite of passage.

Some cultures successfully pass through the rite; others stumble; still others fail and disintegrate. Cultures, like individuals, can deny in a variety of ways the creative potential for change in the liminal period and escape into an unreal world. To prevent chaos from undermining their way of life, people often create new laws or rules, believing that authoritative action alone will prevent disintegration. Yet more than laws are required. There must be individual and corporate conversion and revitalization from within. Unless this occurs, the destructive assault of chaos is inevitable. Even when chaos develops, there are people who refuse to admit its existence. They build walls of denial. Yet a culture cannot remain in the escapist denial stage of chaos indefinitely. The more rigid the defense of an untenable position, the more catastrophic and traumatic the crash when it happens. Nations or institutional cultures in chaos and trauma are not an appealing sight; the atmosphere becomes dense with confusion, tensions, polarizations, scapegoating, and low morale. Eventually, the nation or institution either further disintegrates or is led to a new stage of adjustment to a changed world.[46]

2. Ritual leaders: Key role

A successful process of adjustment can be led by innovative ritual leaders or refounding people,[47] but this can only happen if there is a

---

[44] See Mircea Eliade, *Myth and Reality* (London: Allen and Unwin, 1964), 187–93, and *The Myth of the Eternal Return or Cosmos and History* (Princeton, NJ: Princeton University Press, 1965).

[45] "Beneath the Chaos of the Brexit Talks, Big Ideas Are Forming," *The Economist* (September 29, 2018), 18.

[46] See Anthony F. C. Wallace's model, "Revitalization Movements," *America Anthropologist* 58, no. 2 (1956): 264–81.

[47] The qualities of ritual leaders are described in Arbuckle, *The Francis Factor and the People of God*, 207–25.

sufficient number of people who have come to hope in the possibility of the new adjustment. Usually it takes a bitter, protracted experience of malaise or chaos before some people begin to yearn for individual and corporate revitalization under the leadership of inventive persons. Charismatic leaders sense this yearning, articulate it, and call people to face the future by drawing strength from their original creation mythology. Myth specialist Joseph Campbell described the ritual leader of rites of passage as a "hero" who "ventures forth from the world of common day into a region of . . . wonder: fabulous forces are encountered and a decisive victory is won. The hero comes back from this mysterious adventure with the power to bestow boons on his fellow man."[48] Ritual leaders are heroes who have visited a new land and have been converted to the mythology and values of the world they yearn to lead; their behavior will mirror this interior transformation. Ritual leaders such as Winston Churchill,[49] Charles de Gaulle,[50] and Lyndon Johnson[51] had interiorized a mythology of solidarity well before they assumed political power to lead.

3. Social capital and solidarity

Political scientist Robert Putman defines social capital, a collective asset, as "connections among individuals—social networks and the norms of reciprocity and trustworthiness that arise from them."[52] It is the affinity that people feel for others in their society, people they may never have met. However, "social capital, by creating strong in-group loyalty, may also create strong out-group antagonism."[53] Thus, it can

---

[48] Joseph Campbell, *The Hero with a Thousand Faces* (Princeton, NJ: Princeton University Press, 1949), 30.

[49] See Andrew Roberts, *Churchill: Walking with Destiny* (London: Allen Lane, 2018). Churchill drew heavily on the heroic founding mythology of Britain during his second time as prime minister.

[50] See Julian Jackson, *A Certain Idea of France: The Life of Charles de Gaulle* (London: Allen Lane, 2018), 770–77.

[51] President Lyndon Johnson, when he pushed for civil rights in the mid-1960s, kept referring to the inclusion of human rights for all in America's founding mythology. See Laura Tingle, "Follow the Leader," *Quarterly Essay,* no. 71 (2018): 29–30.

[52] Robert Putnam, *Bowling Alone: The Collapse and Revival of American Community* (New York: Simon and Schuster, 2000), 19.

[53] Ibid., 23.

be directed toward positive consequences such as mutual support for the welfare of the common good, or toward antisocial behavior such as sectarianism, ethnocentrism, or corruption.[54] Solidarity differs from social capital; it describes the moral values of justice and compassion as seen in people working together (see Chapter 1).

4. Populist leaders: Dangers[55]

Some innovative individuals can play on people's fears of the unknown and their desire for an instant experience of order and meaning in their lives. It is "easy to be seduced by superheroes who could come and 'rescue' us, but who possibly then plunge us into greater peril."[56] In chaotic times populism can flourish, with its inevitable dangers. The term *populism* is applied to a variety of political movements, including fundamentalism, but the common quality is their appeal to people as a whole—not the existing political power elites—who are experiencing communitas. The elites are described as illegally trampling upon the rights, values, and voice of the legitimate people.[57] Populist leaders, such as Vladimir Lenin, Adolf Hitler, Benito Mussolini, Juan Peron in Argentina in the 1940s, Huey Long in Alabama, Mao Tse-tung, Joseph McCarthy, and Donald Trump, using extremist language and behavior, assert that innocent citizens are "beset by remote, powerful and malign

---

[54] See ibid., 22.

[55] See Pope Francis, *Fratelli Tutti (On Fraternity and Social Friendship)* (October 3, 2020), nos. 155–62; Gerald A. Arbuckle, *Loneliness: Insights for Healing in a Fragmented World* (Maryknoll, NY: Orbis Books, 2018), 44–47; Jan-Werner Muller, *What Is Populism?* (Philadelphia: University of Pennsylvania Press, 2016).

[56] Margarita Mayo, "If Humble People Make the Best Leaders, Why Do We Fall for Charismatic Narcissists?" *Harvard Business Review* (April 7, 2017), 4.

[57] An early example in the United States was the Populist Party of the 1880s and 1890s, a grassroots, politically oriented alliance of agrarian reformers who were unhappy because of crop failures, falling prices, poor credit services, and assumed neglect by politicians in Washington, DC. See Chris Lehmann, *The Money Cult: Capitalism, Christianity, and the Unmaking of the American Dream* (Brooklyn, NY: First Melville House, 2016), 210–12.

enemies"[58] who must be named and marginalized or silenced (see Axioms 4, 6, and 7, Chapter 1). Immigrants are vulnerable targets. Such is the case with Donald Trump, Nigel Farage, Marine Le Pen, Geert Wilders, and Kristian Thulesen Dahl of the Danish People's Party.[59] Yascha Mounk writes of the dangers of populism:

> The major political problems of the day, populists claim, can easily be solved. All it takes is common sense. . . . If immigrants are flooding the country, you have to build a wall. . . . What has to happen is obvious, then. All it takes for the crisis to be solved—for the problems to go away, for the economy to boom . . . is for a faithful spokesman of the people to conquer power, to vanquish the traitors, and to implement common sense solutions.[60]

Populism is a reactionary movement that seeks to turn back the dominant developments of contemporary times and return to an unreal utopian past. Moisés Naím writes that populists suffer from "ideological necrophilia": a blind fixation with dead ideas.[61] Populists keep demanding social, economic, and political changes that have failed in the past and will collapse in the future as well. Naím argues that there are many reasons why bad ideas endure, but perhaps the most important is people's need to believe in populist leaders amid rapid change and subsequent cultural trauma.[62] Such leaders give people

---

[58] See Michael Mann, ed., *Macmillan Student Encyclopedia of Sociology* (London: Macmillan Press, 1983), 298; Margaret Canovan, "Populism," in *The Social Science Encyclopedia,* ed. Adam Kuper and Jessica Kuper (London: Routledge and Kegan Paul, 1985), 629–31.

[59] See John B. Judis, *The Populist Explosion: How the Great Recession Transformed American and European Politics* (New York: Columbia Global Reports, 2016), 154–55.

[60] Yascha Mounk, *The People vs. Democracy: Why Our Freedom Is in Danger and How To Save It* (Cambridge, MA: Harvard University Press, 2018), 41.

[61] See Moisés Naím, "What Is Ideological Necrophilia?" *Atlantic* (February 24, 2016).

[62] Ibid.

the assurance of immediate protection from the threatening world of chaos, an unreal and temporary sense of belonging and self-worth, and the promise of an exclusive peace in the future.[63] But, as Pope Francis warns in *Fratelli Tutti*, "Lack of concern for the vulnerable can hide behind a populism that exploits them demagogically for its own purposes, or a liberalism that serves the economic interests of the powerful" (FT, no. 155).

Pope Francis also cautions that populist leaders can "exploit politically a people's culture . . . for their own personal advantage. . . . This becomes all the more serious when, in cruder or more subtle forms, it leads to the usurpation of institutions and laws" (FT, no. 159). One way of doing this is to flout democratic norms and conventions, for example, by chiseling "away at a free press, an impartial justice system and other institutions that 'form' part of liberal democracy—all in the name of thwarting the enemies of the people."[64] At heart, populist leaders are narcissistic, interested only in themselves and power; the two vices of a narcissist are envy and jealousy.[65] Envy is the sadness a person feels because of what someone else has and the desire or wish that the other did not possess it; jealousy is the sadness when a person either fears losing or has already lost a meaningful status or relationship with another to a rival. Both vices are potentially destructive. Those who cannot possess what they envy or are in danger of losing what they possess to another may destroy the object. Such was the motivation behind populist Adolf Hitler's scorched-earth tactic; as World War II drew to a close, he chose to destroy whatever he could no longer possess. Destruction becomes a cleansing ritual whereby envious or jealous persons seek to reassert their feelings of power and superiority. Fueled by narcissistic desires, the envious and the jealous can become so consumed by anger or rage that nothing matters but their own world of concern.[66]

Now that we have explored some of the foundations of cultural trauma, we describe a multistage model that delineates what can

---

[63] See Arbuckle, *Fundamentalism at Home and Abroad,* 77–78.

[64] "How Democracies Die," *The Economist* (June 16, 2018), 8.

[65] See Neville Symington, *Emotion and Spirit* (London: Cassell, 1994), 115–17.

[66] See Arbuckle, *Violence, Society, and the Church,* 126–36.

happen to cultures when traumatic events occur, such as a pandemic, which destroy or seriously threaten the accepted order.

Cultural Trauma: Grief-overload Model

Shakespeare puts it well in *Macbeth*:

> Give sorrow words: the grief that does not speak
> Whispers the o'er-fraught heart, and bids it break.

The Cultural Trauma: Grief-overload Model (see Figure 2.1) is based on two pivotal variables that take into account the emotional aspects of culture change and disintegration: the grieving dynamic and leadership. Loss evokes grief (see Axiom 9, Chapter 1). If leaders do not allow mourning rituals to be expressed—for example, through reforms or peaceful protests that help the bereaved to deal with grief—the grief becomes increasingly cumulative and suffocating. An institution then moves inexorably into deepening cultural trauma, concluding with symptoms of chronic paralysis and/or regressive fundamentalist movements. On the other hand, if new and skilled leadership manages what is happening democratically, creative refounding leaders and movements will emerge from the impasse. Movement through the stages is not automatic; some people may remain fixed in one stage; others may retreat to an earlier stage; still others move forward. Tensions particularly develop when the leader pressures people to move unwillingly from Stage 4: Liminality/communitas: Grief Overload, to Stage 5: Reentry: Impasse Options.

Now to explain the stages of the model. In Stage 1: Cultural Consensus, the mythological status quo is generally accepted by people, but in Stage 2: Separation: Cultural Trauma, mythological consensus is severely strained, as seen for example, in the Great Depression, World War II, and the aftermath of the 9/11 terrorist attack in New York. Some people accept the directives of leaders who try to control the trauma, while others become increasingly uneasy and fear for their cultural and personal identity/security; the latter especially begin to grieve the loss of predictabilities. Some leaders deny the trauma and refuse to act.

Stage 1: Cultural Consensus

Stage 2: Separation: Cultural Trauma

- grieving losses
- initial coping efforts
- communitas begins

Stage 3: Liminality/Communitas: Grief Intensifies

- leadership trust weakens
- grief symptoms intensify

Stage 4: Liminality/Communitas: Grief Overload

- tipping points
- leadership trust disintegrates
- adaptive reactions*
    - emotionally paralyzed
    - aggressive
    - nostalgic
    - innovative

Stage 5: Reentry: Impasse Options

- restorationism
- chronic paralysis
- proactive
    - Escapist: fundamentalist/populist movements
    - Democratic Conversionist: refounding movements

*Robert Merton's model of adaptive reactions to anomie (chaos) is helpful here. See Robert K. Merton, "Social Structure and Anomie," *American Sociological Review* 3, no. 5 (1938): 672–82.

Figure 2.1 Cultural Trauma: Grief-overload Model

In Stage 3: Liminality/Communitas: Grief Intensifies, the collective grieving intensifies as people become increasingly aware of the awesome implications of the cultural trauma taking place. The trust of people in their leaders further weakens.[67] Leaders do not grasp what is happening when confronted with the ever-increasing collective aspirations (communitas) of people for change. The insights of Alexis de Tocqueville are relevant here. Reflecting on the power of revolutionary forces, he writes that dissatisfaction becomes increasingly evident whenever the conditions that give rise to it cease to be seen as inevitable and the possibility for correcting them arises.[68] In these circumstances the momentum of communitas cannot be slowed down, even though some of the changes being introduced in the outpouring of enthusiasm may not be socially and political the most prudent.

In Stage 4: Liminality/Communitas: Grief Overload, a seething mix of fear and chaos develops. Internal or external events become tipping points that push the institution from chaos into emotional grief overload. People become increasingly disillusioned when the authoritative commands fail to fulfill their hopes, and all the cultural and personal disintegration symptoms of chaos further intensify. Cultural order totally disintegrates. Individuals and their cultures crushingly grieve the loss of the familiar; they stumble painfully and blindly in an unsuccessful attempt to find reference points for a new identity or the restoration of the old. But people can differ in the way they cope with emotional overload. Some are paralyzed by it; others dream of restoring the past; still others become aggressive; and yet others interiorize a mythology of creative change. People's trust in their leaders disintegrates.

Marek Kohn defines trust as "an expectation, or a disposition to expect, that another party will act in one's interest."[69] In Russia, Mikhail Gorbachev offered dramatic beneficial legislative changes to produce

---

[67] For example, the Thatcher and Reagan governments in the 1980s at first refused to highlight the dangers of the AIDS epidemic because they were unwilling to "create sympathy or identification with the homosexual practices their ideologues so stigmatized." Alexander, "Toward a Theory of Cultural Trauma," 21.

[68] See Alexis de Tocqueville, *L'Ancien Regime* (Oxford: Oxford University Press, 1904), 182.

[69] Marek Kohn, *Trust: Self-Interest and the Common Good* (Oxford: Oxford University Press, 2008), 9.

personal freedoms and socioeconomic growth. But most Russians, lost in cultural trauma, distrusted him—and legislation alone, without a trusting population, could produce no results. His inability to effect change quickly became a significant tipping point for Russians to remove him and his successor, Boris Yeltsin, from power. When trust crumbles, fear takes its place; trust then is in danger of becoming perverted and replaced by the blind or unquestioning confidence characteristic of fundamentalist movements.[70] Hence, the rise of the autocrat Vladimir Putin.

Stage 5: Reentry: Impasse Options in contemporary cultures is particularly dangerous. The situation is ripe for rebounding violence and for populist leaders to take control. If initiates have interiorized the original founding mythology, they will think deeply about how to change the world around them. They are then open to participating in democratic conversionist or refounding movements. On the other hand, they may have failed to interiorize the mythology and want to revert nostalgically to the past or become seduced by the siren song of nationalist, populist, and extremist leaders who tempt them with fundamentalist simplistic solutions to the problems of life (see Chapter 6).[71] Populist politicians build support bases through mythologies of fear and contempt of other people in the same country or beyond. "The resulting oppositional identities," concludes Paul Collier, "are lethal for generosity, trust and co-operation."[72]

Scriptural Reflection: Old Testament Rites of Passage

> In the beginning when God created the heavens and the earth, the earth was a formless void and darkness covered the face of the deep, while a wind from God swept over the face of the waters. (Gen 1:1–2)

---

[70] See Vamik Volkan, *Blind Trust: Large Groups and Their Leaders in Times of Crisis and Terror* (Charlottesville, VA: Pitchstone, 2004), 14.

[71] For a fuller explanation of fundamentalist movements see Arbuckle, *Fundamentalism at Home and Abroad,* 73–93.

[72] Paul Collier, *The Future of Capitalism: Facing the New Anxieties* (London: Penguin Books, 2018), 59.

Experiences of liminality, chaos, cultural traumas, and rites of passage are frequently evident in the scriptures. There are lessons aplenty there to guide us through chaotic experiences of cultural traumas. Chaos can be a blessing from God. This is one of the principal messages of the scriptures. In the Old Testament the Exodus of the Israelites from slavery in Egypt into the promised land is an example of a rite of passage from cultural trauma. Lamentation prayer is the appropriate prayer in times of trauma.

Liminality and Chaos in the Scriptures

The term *chaos* and its many alternative expressions is a dominant theme in both the Old Testament and the New Testament. Walter Brueggemann writes that "the Bible is much more preoccupied with the threat of chaos than it is with sin and guilt. . . . The storm produces a more elemental, inchoate anxiety, a sense of helplessness. . . . It is bottomless in size and beyond measure in force."[73] Chaos is first described at the beginning of the Book of Genesis. It means that the earth prior to God's creative act is formless, a void, and concealed deeply under dark waters (Gen 1:2). In the mind of the book's writer, chaos also describes the cultural trauma of the Israelites in the Babylonian exile: wanderers lost in denial, despair, malaise, desolation, and depression, who are hurting, benumbed, and burdened with guilt. To overcome this sad state, God decides once more to breathe new life into the chaos, and with that, chaos begins to give way to meaning and hope.

Walter Brueggemann comments that "chaos is to be understood not simply as a situation of disorder but as an active agency that is engaged in challenging YHWH, undermining the possibility for life, and so seeking to negate the prospect for well-being in the world."[74]

---

[73] Walter Brueggemann, *Inscribing the Text* (Minneapolis: Fortress Press, 2004), 51; see Bernhard Anderson, *Creation Versus Chaos: The Reinterpretation of Mythical Symbolism in the Bible* (New York: Association Press, 1967), 132. Biblically, *chaos*—and its many synonyms, such as *the Pit, grave,* or *wilderness*—denotes a state of utter confusion and fear, totally lacking in organization or predictability; it is the antithesis of *cosmos.*

[74] Walter Brueggemann, *Reverberations of Faith: A Theological Handbook of Old Testament Themes* (Louisville, KY: Westminster John Knox Press, 2002), 28.

Creation in its entirety is pictured as being constantly in danger of falling back into destructive chaos; only God as Creator can ultimately control chaos and order. The primary motif or symbolic use of chaos is that through God's creative power and mercy radically new and vigorous life can spring up, but this cannot happen without human cooperation.

To be creative, therefore, the experience of chaos must be openly acknowledged and personally and corporately owned. We cannot learn from this ordeal if we deny it is happening to us. In other words, by acknowledging chaos we can encounter afresh—if we choose to do so—the mythical roots of our being. There we rediscover our powerlessness and vulnerability, and at the same time the saving, recreative, energizing power of God. The message given to the prophet Jeremiah depicts the same dynamic. The destruction of the three pivotal symbols of Jewish culture—the monarchy, the Temple, and Jerusalem—is foretold. It is a description of a land devastated by appalling destruction, a land degraded to a state of primordial chaos and bereft of people:[75]

> I looked on the earth, and lo, it was waste and
>   void; . . .
> I looked, and lo, the fruitful land was a desert
>   and all its cities were laid in ruins
>   before the Lord. (Jer 4:23, 26)

He entreats the Israelites to acknowledge the chaos and their dependence on God, so that they might enter into individual and group conversion. If the chaos's potential is realized, then the seemingly impossible will happen. There will be creativity beyond all human imagination. God speaks:

> "See, today I appoint you over nations and over
>   kingdoms,
> to pluck up and to pull down,
> to destroy and to overthrow,
> to build and to plant." (Jer 1:10)[76]

[75] See Robert P. Carroll, *From Chaos to Covenant: Prophecy in the Book of Jeremiah* (New York: Crossroad, 1981),

[76] See Walter Brueggemann, *Texts under Negotiations: The Bible and Postmodern Imagination* (Minneapolis: Fortress Press, 1993), 83–85, 89–91.

The Israelite prophets and the psalmists use the imagery of chaos in order to highlight the opposite, namely, the ongoing inventive and redemptive action of God. God's face is suddenly hidden, throwing the Israelites into a state of despair:

> By your favour, O Lord,
> you had established me as a strong mountain;
> you hid your face;
> I was dismayed. (Ps 30:7)

Like all people trapped in social and political disintegration, the Israelites in the Old Testament are tempted to escape nostalgically into the past, to hide within the comforting memories of God's past achievements. The prophet Isaiah warns:

> Do not remember the former things,
> or consider the things of old.
> I am about to do a new thing;
> now it springs forth, do you not perceive it?
> I will make a way in the wilderness
> and rivers in the desert. (Isa 43:18–19)

Then through God's compassionate action they discover new life in their experience of the chaos.

In the midst of the people's shattering grief and despair Jeremiah foretells signs of revitalization, of the refounding of the nation (Jer 1:10). A new covenant between God and the revitalized culture will succeed the previous one (Jer 31:31–40), and the gift of personal and intimate union with God will be a sign of the authenticity of God's people (Jer 31:34). Even in the exile's darkness significant pastoral creativity emerges. The people learn to pray in small supportive groups without the presence of the temple, and traditional religious practices are updated in light of the changed situation—for example, circumcision becomes less important as an initiation rite but instead develops as a new symbol of cultural identity.[77] In other parts of the Old Testament the word *chaos* is synonymous with a barren wasteland:

---

[77] See Carroll, *From Chaos to Covenant,* 31–58.

> He sustained him in the desert land,
> in a howling wilderness waste. (Deut 32:10)

It is emptiness, nothingness. But, as in the Genesis story, this emptiness and nothingness is itself potentially creative. Through God's creative power and mercy, and with human cooperation, new and vigorous life can spring up.

To summarize:

- The cosmos is pictured as continually moving between the poles of chaos and order. We are in constant need of God's mercy and creative love, for it is God who leads us "out of darkness into this wonderful light" (1 Pet 2:9). From chaos to order, from suffering to joy, from sinfulness to justice—the theme runs constantly through the scriptures.
- But there is always this precondition: if chaos is to be a catalyst for hope, we must acknowledge our chaos in all its depth and desolation. The more we acknowledge the exhaustion of our chaotic journey in life, the more we are open to the incredible mystery of God's energizing love (Rev 21:1, 5).

The Exodus: Trauma and Rite of Passage

This interaction of chaos and hope is vividly evident in the Exodus story. In this cultural trauma[78] there is a tripartite pattern of initiation to new identity for the Israelites: separation, liminality, reentry.[79] For the Israelites the Exodus is the archetypal experience of initiation.[80]

---

[78] Ron Eyerman describes slavery as an African American trauma that shaped the African American identity. It is not the direct experience of slavery but the memory of slavery, its restructuring in the minds of later generations of African Americans, that constitutes cultural slavery. See Ron Eyerman, *Cultural Trauma: Slavery and the Formation of African American Identity* (New York: Cambridge University Press, 2002). The Exodus trauma that formed the Israelite identity over generations would have followed the same dynamic of memory and reconfiguration.

[79] See Arbuckle, *From Chaos to Mission*, 119–20.

[80] See Michael D. Coogan, "The Exodus," in *The Oxford Companion to the Bible,* ed. Bruce M. Metzger and Michael D. Coogan (New York: Oxford University Press, 1993), 209–12.

It is through this rite of passage that they formally become the people of God, bonded by a common experience (communitas). There is a separation phase: the journeying out of Egypt under the leadership of Moses, which is a mixture of joy and grieving. Their time in Egypt had been collectively traumatic under a slavery regime, and more trauma would come in their years in the desert,[81] which is the liminality stage. This will be followed by the reentry phase: entrance into the promised land. But as they wander through the desert there are the anti-structure symbols of suffering, darkness, and death, and there are many trials as they wander

> in a land of drought and deep darkness,
>   in a land that no one passes through,
>   where no one lives. (Jer 2:6)

Yes, there is frequent grieving and mourning in the liminal desert over the comforts they have left behind in Egypt (Num 14:2). In the midst of the people's mourning, Moses repeats the vision of the newness that lies ahead: "For the Lord your God is bringing you into a good land, a land with flowing streams . . . a land of wheat and barley" (Deut 8:7–8). God allows the Israelites to be tempted, and when they fall they think they can survive without him (Ex 32:1). They begin to rely on other gods, and their own strength fades as they descend into bickering and fighting among themselves, weariness, and total loss of direction, but God is waiting for them to admit to their self-made chaos. Now is the chance to teach them a lesson:

> For thus says the Lord,
> who created the heavens
>   (he is God!),

---

[81] See David M. Carr, *Holy Resilience: The Bible's Traumatic Origins* (New Haven, CT: Yale University Press, 2014), 110–20. Carr defines trauma as "an overwhelming, haunting experience of disaster so explosive in its impact that it cannot be directly encountered and influences an individual/group's behavior and memory in indirect ways. . . . [Biblical traumas] did not just produce pain and suffering for individuals. They shattered the identities of whole groups, requiring them to come to new understandings of themselves, understandings now inscribed and fixed in the Jewish and Christian scriptures." Ibid., 7, 9.

who formed the earth and made it
(he established it;
he did not create a chaos,
he formed it to be inhabited!):
I am the LORD, and there is no other.
I did not speak in secret,
in a land of darkness;
I did not say to the offspring of Jacob,
"Seek me in chaos." (Isa 45:18–19)

God invites them to acknowledge and embrace the chaos of their failings, but not to linger too long over what they have done. They must face the future in hope and wait to experience God's action of newness in their lives.[82] When they do so, they experience a communitas with God and one another beyond all human comprehension: "The LORD went in front of them in a pillar of cloud by day, to lead them along the way, and in the pillar of fire by night, to give them light" (Ex 13:21). They learn that

as a father has compassion for his children,
so the LORD has compassion for those who fear
him. (Ps 103:13)

When in the depths of chaos, generation after generation will recall and be energized by the hope-filled communitas experience:

Some sat in darkness and in gloom,
prisoners in misery and in irons,
for they had rebelled against the words of God. . . .
Then they cried to the LORD in their trouble,
and he saved them in their distress. . . .
Let those who are wise give heed to these things,
and consider the steadfast love of the LORD.
(Ps 107:10–11, 13–14, 43)

The reentry stage of the rite of passage is depicted in the Book of Joshua, which traced the history of the Israelites from the death of

---

[82] See Walter Brueggemann, *Interpretation and Obedience: From Faithful Reading to Faithful Living* (Minneapolis: Fortress Press, 1991), 317–18.

Moses to that of his successor, Joshua; the book recounts their entry into the promised land and its partition among the twelve tribes. Their proclaimed loyalty to God, marking the end of their liminality experience in the desert, is quickly tested in the reentry stage. They fail the test by disobeying God. They must learn anew that there is but one God and that whenever they cease to offer God total loyalty they must expect chaos: "Therefore the Israelites are unable to stand before their enemies; they turn their back to their enemies, because they have become a thing devoted for destruction themselves. I will be with you no more, unless you destroy the devoted things from among you" (Josh 7:12). So, from bitter experience, they relearn the fundamental lesson of their liminality time: "If you forsake the Lord and serve foreign gods, then he will turn and do you harm" (Josh 24:20).

Lamentation Prayer in Cultural Traumas[83]

Since lamentation prayers characterize biblical rites of passage in personal and cultural traumas, we need to turn to these prayers as we grapple with the chaos evoked by COVID-19 and its aftermath. Lamentation has two inextricably intertwined aspects: mourning and praise of God. In vivid opposition to the frequent presence of personal and corporate distress and grief, at times in the Old Testament there are eruptions of surprising, even dramatic, newness and hope when the people mourn before God. This happens, as we have seen, to the Israelites in the Exodus. And consider also that most poignant poetic expression of grief, David's lament over Jonathan: "I am distressed for you, my brother Jonathan; greatly beloved were you to me" (2 Sam 1:26). Then David in the depth of his mourning consults God, and God calls David to a startlingly new leadership role: "After this David inquired of the Lord: 'Shall I go up into any of the cities of Judah?' The Lord said to him, 'Go up . . . to Hebron.' So David went up there. . . . Then the people of Judah came, and there they anointed David king over the house of Judah" (2 Sam 2:1, 2, 4).

The lament psalms (sometimes called complaint psalms), which make up about one-third of all the psalms, teach us how to mourn

---

[83] See Gerald A. Arbuckle, "The People of God: Healing through Mourning," *Health Progress: Journal of the Catholic Health Association of the United States* (March–April, 2020): 47–50.

by complaining in the midst of the dark nights of our overwhelming sadness:

> You have put me into the depths of the Pit,
> in the regions dark and deep. (Ps 88:6)

These psalms are rituals of mourning through which griefs in the midst of chaos are abandoned, allowing the bereaved to look to the future again in hope. If the bereaved truly complain to God from the very depths and emptiness of their souls, trusting in God's willingness to listen, hope will come alive once more:

> He put a new song in my mouth,
> a song of praise to our God. (Ps 40:3)

This is the message of the lamentation psalms.[84]

Elisabeth Kübler-Ross developed a well-known framework for a ritual of mourning, namely, the stages of denial-isolation, anger, bargaining, depression, and finally acceptance.[85] Her ritual process contains two key functions found in all rituals: it articulates/legitimizes how people move through grief, and it also prescribes how they should act in expressing their emotions in grief situations. In the second stage of Kübler-Ross's model the angry bereaved may lash out at loyal friends, even blaming them for the misery they are experiencing. These friends, however, because they belong to a culture that encourages denial of loss, rarely know how to cope with such anger; they often may become annoyed and frustrated at what they see as ingratitude on the part of the bereaved.

However, the pattern in the lament psalms is significantly different. Here, anger is recognized as a powerful human expression that must not be suppressed. Because the people are united in one covenant with God, they have every right to let their partner know what they feel about their sufferings and how God is involved in helping to cause them. They know God can "handle it." The Israelites want to make their problems God's problems. Then, it is hoped, God will be

---

[84] See Arbuckle, *Grieving for Change,* 61–85.

[85] See Elisabeth Kübler-Ross, *On Death and Dying* (New York: Macmillan, 1969).

Kübler-Ross	Lament Psalm
Denial and isolation	Address to God
Anger directed at friends	Anger directed at God
Bargaining	Trust in God/Hope
Depression	Petition
Acceptance	Assurance
	Vow to praise God

obligated to do something about them.[86] Ponder the public lament of the Israelites as they agonizingly view the destruction of the pivotal symbol of God's presence, the Temple. Desolation reigns supreme. God receives all the blame, but once their sadness has been so dramatically proclaimed and put aside, the Israelites discover space within their hearts for a hopeful trust in God:

> O God, why do you cast us off forever?
> Why does your anger smoke against the sheep
> of your pasture? . . .
> Rise up, O God, plead your cause;
> remember how the impious scoff at you all the
> day long. (Ps 74:1, 22)

Unlike Kübler-Ross's model, in which there is denial and a feeling of isolation, a lament psalm starkly proclaims from the beginning that the psalmist or the community is afflicted. There is no camouflaging the loss. So miserable is the sufferer that there is nothing left but to trust God. The declaration of trust sparks off a hope-filled petition to God at the stage when, in Kübler-Ross's framework, there is bargaining that leads to depression. In the lamentation psalm, no matter how horrible the situation may be, there is still the hope that God will intervene, just as God has done in the past. Listen to the psalmist ponder

[86] See Walter Brueggemann, *The Message of the Psalms* (Minneapolis: Augsburg, 1984), 54; idem, "The Formfulness of Grief," *Interpretation: A Journal of Bible and Theology* 31, no. 3 (1977): 265–75; and idem, "Psalms and the Life of Faith: A Suggested Typology of Function," *Journal for the Study of the Old Testament* 17, no. 1 (1980): 3–32.

the desperate situation confronting the Israelites after the capture of Jerusalem by the Babylonians:

> Give ear, O Shepherd of Israel. . . .
> Stir up your might,
>   and come to save us!
>
> Restore us, O God,
> let your face shine, that we may be saved.
>   (Ps 80:1–3)

The psalmist retells the actions of God that have molded the Israelites into God's chosen people: the Exodus from Egypt and the entrance into the promised land (Ps 80:8–11). These interventions of God gave meaning to their lives then; the hope is that God will again intervene to restore meaning in the midst of their fearful misery and chaos (Ps 80:16–17). The lament proceeds from petition to trust and praise: "Give us life and we will call upon your name" (Ps 80:18).

The words of assurance in the lament psalms and the stage of acceptance in Kübler-Ross's model of mourning at first sight may appear to have an identical function. For her, "acceptance" seems to mean the same thing as a stoic resignation in the face of the inevitable. But this view is contrary to a fundamental assumption in the lament psalms. While loss or death is known to be inevitable, there is always the historically supported belief that God can transform every crisis into a stunning new beginning. The task of covenant members is never to give up hope. This is the mark of every true Israelite.

Walter Brueggemann does not denigrate the importance of Kübler-Ross's model of mourning (or other stage theories of mourning) as an aid to understanding how people can confront loss of any kind. Rather, his aim is to show that those with faith and hope similar to that of the Old Testament believers see things at a quite different level. They do not deny trauma or loss; on the contrary, they see chaos in its many forms as the occasion to rediscover the historical fact that God can intervene in human affairs:

> For I am about to create new heavens
>   and a new earth; . . .
> no more shall the sound of weeping be heard in it.
>   (Isa 65:17, 19)

While laments mirror the experience of God's absence, they are also praise of God; for example, in Psalm 22 we read:

> Why are you so far away from helping me, from
> the words of my groaning? (v. 1)

But later:

> I will praise you:
> You who fear the LORD, praise him! . . .
> For dominion belongs to the LORD,
> and he rules over the nations. (vv. 22, 23, 28).

Psalm 109 begins with praise:

> Do not be silent, O God of my praise. . . .
> For I am poor and needy. (vv. 1, 22).

Indeed, to live is to praise God; not to praise God is not to live. As Psalm 88 tells us:

> Do you work wonders for the dead?
> Do the shades rise up to praise you? *Selah*
> (v. 10).

In these pandemic times the lament psalms teach us how to complain prayerfully to God in the midst of the overwhelming sadness resulting from the enduring effects of COVID-19. Our loud, faith-based laments become rituals of mourning through which our griefs can be abandoned and we can again look to the future in hope. But mourning rituals need ritual leaders. In the Exodus story Moses acts as God's exemplary formal ritual leader. At Emmaus, Jesus himself is the ritual leader, challenging the two disciples to own up to the trauma of loss. He gives them space to express their anger and sadness that things have not turned out as they had hoped. Jesus does not judge or condemn their anger (Lk 24:17–24). Yet lamentations must also be carefully planned. For example, Moses was sensitive to the fact that the experience of intense grief in the Exodus, a precondition for forming a new people, could lead to further collective trauma if not guided prudently. Therefore, he sought the advice of Jethro, his father-in-law, who instructed him to group the people into small units for mourning under the direction of "men who fear God, are trustworthy, and hate dishonest gain" (Ex 18:21).[87]

Summary

- Cultural trauma is the dramatic collective breakdown of cultural order with distressing long-term consequences; not everyone will experience the trauma with the same intensity.
- When people and cultures are traumatized, their movement forward into new life through chaos can be a rite of passage with three identifiable stages: separation, liminality, and reentry. Ritual leadership is required at each stage.
- Liminality exemplifies the principle of communitas, an egalitarian and relatively unstructured social world, which is in a sense complementary to the more mundane, hierarchical social order. Liminality is the dangerous stage in a rite of passage: people grieving the loss of order may nostalgically dream of returning to the securities of the past; become paralyzed by the chaos they are experiencing; or, inspired by a vision of the future, creatively move forward.
- Experiences of liminality, chaos, cultural traumas, and rites of passage are frequently evident in the scriptures. There are lessons aplenty there to guide us through cultural traumas. Chaos can be a blessing from God. This is one of the principal messages of the scriptures.

Reflection Questions

1. Can you identify a liminal experience in your life? What did you feel? What did you learn from it?
2. Do you think that the pandemic crisis is an example of cultural trauma? If so, why?
3. Can you describe a rite of passage that you have experienced? Did you find it helpful?
4. Reread the section on lamentation prayer. Why is such prayer important during rites of passage, such as the present pandemic crisis and its aftermath?

---

[87] See Arbuckle, *The Francis Factor*, 201–3.

3

Successes and Failures of the Pandemic Rite of Passage

When dealing with . . . COVID-19, much of the focus is on the prevention and treatment of the disease. The immediate effects are of the utmost concern, but it is also important to consider the longer-term collective trauma of the pandemic.

—Kendra Cherry,
"Collective Trauma from COVID-19"

The marketplace, by itself, cannot resolve every problem, however much we are asked to believe this dogma of neoliberal faith.

—Pope Francis, *Fratelli Tutti*

Where are the individuals with the generosity of the Good Samaritan? . . . [We need] unconventional people to take on leadership roles. Those who are close to the poor, who can galvanise young people by being willing to try new approaches. We need to be challenged by people who are fired by the spirit.

—Cardinal Carlo Martini

This chapter explains that:

- A nation's operative mythologies, as evidenced by their health-care systems, influence the responses of political leaders and others to the pandemic.[1]
- Pandemic rites of passage succeed if their leaders base their actions on Good Samaritan values, especially the values of solidarity and compassion.
- Prophetic leadership necessitates conversion; the rites of passage of Jesus Christ into public ministry and as savior exemplify what is required.

The pandemic cultural trauma began in December 2019, in or around the Hunan Seafood Wholesale Market in Wuhan, China, a city of about eleven million people.[2] Country after country felt the impact within two months. On the day the lockdown was imposed in Sydney, I noticed a surprising change in the streets. Not only did people observe social distancing, but more remarkably, total strangers frequently greeted one another, sometimes with a nervous smile or hello. Our social statuses had ceased to be important. We all now shared a common danger that had abruptly bonded us in an unexpected communitas experience. Pope Francis states:

> The believer, contemplating his or her neighbor as a brother or sister, and not as a stranger, looks at him or her compassionately and empathetically, not contemptuously or with hostility.[3]

---

[1] Cultural mythologies profoundly influence economic decisions. See Robert Putman, *Making Democracy Work* (Princeton, NJ: Princeton University Press, 1993); Joel Mokyr, *A Culture of Growth: The Origins of the Modern Economy* (Princeton, NJ: Princeton University Press, 2017); J. Schulz et al., "The Church, Intensive Kinship and Global Psychological Variation," *Science* 366, no. 707 (2019): 1–12.

[2] See Mark Honigsbaum, *The Pandemic Century: A History of Global Contagion from the Spanish Flu to COVID-19* (London: Penguin Random House, 2020), 262. On December 30, 2019, Dr. Li Wenliang, an ophthalmologist at Wuhan Central Hospital in the Hubei province of China, alerted fellow physicians to the appearance of a worrying cluster of pneumonia cases.

[3] Pope Francis, General Audience, August 12, 2020.

The purpose of this chapter is fourfold: first, to show that the manner in which nations react to the pandemic is influenced by their political leaders and their national mythologies; second, to demonstrate that political leaders, as ritual guides, emphasizing the democratic value of solidarity, not individualism, are more likely to lead their countries successively through the tough tripartite rite of passage of the pandemic, namely, separation, liminality, and reentry (see Chapter 2); third, to describe how people freed from the normal cultural constraints in the liminal chaos stage may collectively claim their authority to protest social abuses such as poverty and institutional racism; and fourth, to show that prophetic leaders in the crisis relive Christ's initiation as Savior.

Governments' Options

When the pandemic struck, governments had a threefold choice: (1) to emphasize economic welfare, with a minimum of lockdown and self-isolating policies, as in the United States, Brazil, and Britain; (2) to protect lives through lockdown and self-isolating policies, as in the egalitarian welfare states of Australia and New Zealand; or (3) to adopt whatever policies were necessary to maintain autocratic centralized control, as in China and Russia. The first option prioritizes the rights of individuals; the second, the needs of their communities, including the well-being of the most vulnerable; and the third, the protection of the political elite. Neoliberal policies privilege and promote the capitalist market system, assessing states of affairs in terms of economic productivity and profit (see Chapter 1).[4]

Political analyst Francis Fukuyama claims that three factors are responsible for a successful response to the pandemic: a competent state system; a government trusted by its citizens; and leadership.[5] Of the countries discussed in this chapter, only the governments of New Zealand and Australia mostly fulfilled these conditions. In countries

---

[4] See Pippa Norris and Ronald Inglehart, *Cultural Backlash: Trump, Brexit, and Authoritarian Populism* (Cambridge: Cambridge University Press, 2019), 362–63; David Harvey *A Brief History of Neoliberalism* (Oxford: Oxford University Press, 2005), 195.

[5] See Francis Fukuyama, "The Pandemic and Political Order," *Foreign Affairs* 99, no. 4 (2020): 26–32.

such as the United States, Iran, Britain, Russia, India, and Brazil, which have the highest caseloads, presidents and prime ministers minimized the threat, vacillated, contradicted their experts on basic facts, published implausible numbers of deaths, propagated conspiracy theories, or seemed more interested in their own political fortunes than the well-being of their citizens—sometimes all simultaneously.[6] As was the case in previous pandemics,[7] COVID-19 spawned an array of conspiracy theories and scapegoats, such as the World Health Organization and migrants (see Axioms 6 and 7, Chapter 1).

Influence of National Mythologies

In order to discover a nation's mythologies that influence the decision-making of political leaders and their governments in the pandemic crisis, we must identify and examine the mythologies behind their healthcare systems. I particularly focus here on the mythologies of the health systems of New Zealand, Australia, Britain, and the United States.

Western Healthcare's Good Samaritan Foundations

The historical roots of Western healthcare systems are scriptural. The Christian tradition has always seen suffering as mysterious. Ultimately, Christians seeking to answer the question, Why suffering?, search for meaning in faith. Jesus Christ died for our sins, and Christians believe our pain must be related to the redemptive suffering of Christ who freely submitted to suffering and death. Suffering has significance when related to Christ's mission:

> Beloved, do not be surprised at the fiery ordeal that is taking place among you to test you, as though something strange were happening to you. But rejoice insofar as you are sharing Christ's sufferings, so that you may also be glad and shout for joy when his glory is revealed. (1 Pet 4:12–13)

---

[6] See "COVID-19 Is Here to Stay: People Will Have to Adapt," *The Economist* (July 4, 2020).

[7] See Honigsbaum, *The Pandemic Century*, 107, 110, 247–49.

In this tradition persons who are physically sick also experience inner affliction, for example, the inner pain of loneliness resulting from the breakdown of their predictable lifestyle and relationships (see Chapter 1).

Early Christians organized themselves to take care of the suffering, inspired by the example of Christ the Good Samaritan (1 Cor 12:26–27), emphasizing the unity of soul and body. The early Christian hospice was open to poor members of the community, and it developed by the fourth century into the hospital, where the sick poor were given assistance. Monastic orders and laity-led movements in the Low Countries and elsewhere in Europe continued the tradition for centuries, but in the nineteenth century more and more religious congregations were established with the primary task of caring for the poor sick, most often regardless of their church affiliation.[8] Particularly from the nineteenth century on, the state gradually assumed more responsibility for the building and staffing of hospitals.

At the heart of holistic healthcare, according to its founding mythology, is the principle of social justice or solidarity, namely, that people as a basic human right should have equal access to healthcare services.[9] Moreover, healthcare is a larger category than medical care; it embraces health education as well as socioeconomic and political structural change to provide people with opportunities—such as housing, education, and employment—to help develop their human potential and overcome discrimination. Thus, health can be broadly defined as "a complete state of physical, mental and social well-being, not merely the absence of disease and infirmity."[10] A society is in good health when it is struggling to liberate people from economic, social, political, and religious structures that diminish them as persons and cause medical ill health.[11]

---

[8] See Norman Vetter, *The Hospital: From Centre of Excellence to Community Support* (London: Chapman and Hall, 1995), 4–9.

[9] See Richard A. McCormick, *Health and Medicine in the Catholic Tradition* (New York: Crossroad, 1987), 75.

[10] Definition of the World Health Organization 1948, as cited in David Locker, "Prevention and Health Promotion," in *Sociology as Applied to Medicine,* ed. Graham Scambler (London: W. B. Saunders, 1997), 244.

[11] See Gerald A. Arbuckle, *Healthcare Ministry: Refounding the Mission* (Collegeville, MN: Liturgical Press, 2000), 152–93.

The Undermining of Healthcare Mythology

In the mythology of democracy there are two complementary poles: the rights of the individual and the rights of the community. The concept of fraternity is the resulting balance between these two mythological poles. For Americans, unlike Canadians, Australians, New Zealanders, and the British, fraternity means that the rights of the individual are primarily to be respected, even though the common good or community rights may suffer. Hence, any attempt by the American government to redress the imbalance in favor of the common good is met with strong, highly organized and emotional opposition. Medical healthcare reforms are branded, as we've seen in recent times, as "socialized medicine" and as "government interference in private affairs," characterizations that seriously limit efforts to provide much-needed healthcare for millions of people. Such is the power of mythology![12] As we will see, various other countries handle the tension between the opposing poles in healthcare mythology of universality (public healthcare services) and choice (private healthcare) in different ways. In Australia and Holland, a mixed system allows for a significant degree of both universality and choice, while Canada,[13] like Britain, has particularly emphasized universality.

Western democracies, with the exception of the United States, established egalitarian welfare states either before or following the Second World War.[14] The first was New Zealand, then Britain, then Australia, and eventually the European Union nations. Barbara Castle, when secretary of state for health in Britain in the 1970s, claimed that the National Health Service (NHS) "is the nearest thing to the embodiment of the Good Samaritan that we have in any aspect of our public

---

[12] For further background see Gerald A. Arbuckle, *Humanizing Healthcare Reforms* (Philadelphia: Jessica Kingsley, 2013), 90–94.

[13] See Esyllt W. Jones, *Radical Medicine: The International Origins of Socialized Health Care in Canada* (Winnipeg: ARP Books, 2020).

[14] The term *welfare state* can be confusing. The *egalitarian* welfare state, rather than just tampering with extreme medical, social, and economic inequalities, is highly interventionist; the *mediating* welfare state is less interventionist, but it also emphasizes compassion and social justice. In the *limited* welfare state some basic social services are provided, such as limited safety nets in times of individual crises. See Gary Taylor, *Ideology and Welfare* (London: Palgrave Macmillan, 2007), 156.

policy."[15] Good quality healthcare is a fundamental human right, embedded in human relationships and trust between health workers and patients. Aneurin Bevan, the founder of the British National Health Service in 1948, often emphasized this fundamental right:

> Society becomes more wholesome, more serene and spiritually healthier, if it knows that its citizens have at the back of their consciousness the knowledge that not only themselves, but all their fellows have access, when ill, to the best that medical skill can provide.[16]

In 1946, Bevan even more forcefully declared that "it is repugnant to a civilized community for hospitals to have to rely upon charity."[17] Michael Savage, New Zealand's prime minister from 1935 to 1940 and founder of the nation's welfare state, was of the same mind: "I want to see that people have security. . . . I want to see humanity secure against poverty, secure in illness in old age. . . . What is more valuable in our Christianity than to be our brother's keepers in reality."[18] Savage also called the Social Security Act of 1938 "applied Christianity."[19] There is no denying the explicit and implicit influence of Christian thinking on the original formation of the philosophy of the welfare state.

By the late 1970s and 1980s, however, egalitarian welfare governments were increasingly confronted with serious questions about the financial sustainability of their healthcare systems due to rising demands for choice, especially from wealthier middle classes and

---

[15] Barbara Castle, cited in Rudolf Klein, *The New Politics of the NHS*, 5th ed. (Abingdon: Radcliffe Publishing, 2006), 90.

[16] Aneurin Bevan, cited in Margaret Whitehead, "Is It Fair? Evaluating the Equity Implications of the NHS Reforms," in *Evaluating the NHS Reforms*, ed. Ray Robinson and Julian Le Grand (London: King's Fund Institute, 1993), 210.

[17] Aneurin Bevan, cited in A. O'Hagan, *London Review of Books* (March 3, 2011), 34. For background to Britain's welfare state see Martin Powell and Martin Hewitt, *Welfare State and Welfare Change* (Buckingham: Open University Press, 2002), 29–41.

[18] Michael Savage, cited in Department of Social Security, *The Growth and Development of Social Security in New Zealand* (Wellington: Government Printer, 1950), 17.

[19] Ibid.

aging populations. Governments sought some quick solutions. The answer? Society's readiness to provide support for the poor became the subject of passionate public debate and reexamination in the West. Neoliberalism, sometimes called market economy or economic rationalism,[20] won. Profit is to be the sole measure of value, and the economics profession is to serve as its priesthood.[21] What does not pay should be closed.

Recall that the assumptions behind neoliberalism are (1) sustained economic growth is the best way to distribute wealth; (2) free local and global markets, unrestrained by interference from governments, lead to the most efficient use of resources; (3) lower taxation and reduced government spending are to be promoted; (4) governments must privatize services; and (5) the primary task of governments is to support individual initiatives in commerce. Neoliberalism's mythology accepts the social Darwinist assumption, namely, that the poor are what they are through their own fault; welfare services make their poverty worse, so they must be reduced (see Axiom 7, Chapter 1).[22] The principles of the market economy and its management must be applied to healthcare and welfare services for the traumatized and sick and for otherwise disadvantaged individuals. Such an approach means that the primary focus is on profit.[23] People cease to be patients and become instead consumers or clients.[24] All this led to a rise in

---

[20] See Michael Pusey, *Economic Rationalism in Canberra: A Nation Building State Changes Its Mind* (Cambridge: Cambridge University Press, 1992), 59–75.

[21] See David C. Korten, *When Corporations Rule the World* (London: Earthscan, 1996), 69.

[22] "The former Speaker of the House [of Representatives] John Boehner (2011–2015) publicly equated joblessness with personal laziness." Nancy Isenberg, *White Trash: The 400–Year Untold History of Class in America* (New York: Penguin, 2016), 319.

[23] Alexander C. McFarlane and Bessel A. van der Kolk wrote in 1996: "Alarmingly, the need to ignore the reality of trauma in people's lives also pervades medical school departments of psychiatry, where the response to increasing levels of traumatization in society has generally been to ignore it." *Traumatic Stress: The Effects of Overwhelming Experience on Mind, Body, and Society,* ed. Bessel A. van der Kolk, Alexander C. McFarlane, and Lars Weisaeth (New York: Guilford Press, 1996), 30.

[24] See Allyson M. Pollock, *NHS plc: The Privatisation of Our Health Care* (London: Verso, 2005), 36–131.

for-profit hospitals in the United States and elsewhere, in which the primary aim of healthcare is a financial return to shareholders, not the quality of service to patients.[25]

Impact of Myth Substitution

During the years that Margaret Thatcher was prime minister in Britain (1979–90),[26] there was a deliberate effort at myth substitution (see Axiom 2, Chapter 1) in the National Health Service and in the country's economy as a whole.[27] Neoliberalism ideology, with its emphasis on maximizing corporate profits, was poised to supplant the Christian mythology of healthcare and welfare services. The neoliberal dogma was avidly promoted by devotees of the New Right in the United States such as William F. Buckley Jr., Barry Goldwater, and President Ronald Reagan,[28] its most effective communicator. The New Right claimed that the breakdown in morality and the increase in government aid for welfare services are avenues for undermining a nation's local and international strength. It is patriotic to support a laissez-faire market capitalism and a reduction in aid to the poor. Social historian Tony Judt comments on the impact of Thatcher's acceptance of neoliberal individualistic values:

---

[25] See Gerald A. Arbuckle, *Violence, Society, and the Church: A Cultural Approach* (Collegeville, MN: Liturgical Press, 2004), 169–71.

[26] See Charles Moore, *Margaret Thatcher*, vol. 3, *Herself Alone* (London: Allen Lane, 2019), 56–93; 824. For background see Martin Powell and Martin Hewitt, *Welfare State and Welfare Change* (Buckingham: Open University Press, 2002), 49–58; Michael J. Sandel, *The Tyranny of Merit: What's Become of the Common Good?* (London: Allen Lane, 2020), 62–66.

[27] Social historian Tony Judt writes: "In the course of little more than a decade, the dominant 'paradigm' of public conversation [in Britain] shifted from interventionary enthusiasms and the pursuit of the public goods to a view of the world best summed up in Margaret Thatcher's notorious *bon mot:* 'there is no such thing as society, there are only individuals and families' . . . and a consequential faith in the naturally benevolent workings of the global market for financial products." *Ill Fares the Land: A Treatise on Our Present Discontents* (London: Allen Lane, 2010), 96, 104; see also Christopher Pierson, *Beyond the Welfare State: The New Political Economy of Welfare* (Cambridge: Polity Press, 1998), 136–66.

[28] See Gene Sterling, *Economic Dignity* (New York: Penguin Press, 2020), 90–105.

> As an *economy* . . . Thatcherized Britain was a more efficient place. But as a *society* it suffered meltdown, with catastrophic long-term consequences. By disdaining and dismantling all collectively-held resources, by vociferously insisting upon an individual ethic that discounted any unquantifiable assets, Margaret Thatcher did serious harm to the fabric of British public life. Citizens were transmuted into shareholders, or "stakeholders," their relationship to one another and to the collectivity measured in assets and claims rather than in services and obligations.[29]

Sir Keith Joseph, widely regarded as the founder of neoliberal ideology in healthcare in Britain, called social justice a "will o' the wisp."[30] Equitable access for the vulnerable that was based on need, not income, became increasingly undermined. Welfare services were also drastically reduced. In brief, the New Right British government, despite its rhetoric to the contrary, broke with the postwar democratic consensus that healthcare had its mythological roots in the Good Samaritan mythological story. In New Zealand and Australia the same neoliberal reforms were adopted with astounding speed. After half a century of stressing community values, governments opted for competition and survival of the fittest as a superior organizing dynamic for society.

The consequences were disastrous—levels of poverty and social exclusion rose dramatically, with tragic results for the well-being of people on the margins.[31] "Values such as human dignity, distributive justice, and social cohesion [were] given second place to the pursuit of efficiency, self-reliance, a fiscal balance, and a more limited

---

[29] Tony Judt, *Postwar: A History of Europe since 1945* (London: Pimlico, 2017), 543. See Paul Collier and John Kay, *Greed Is Dead: Politics after Individualism* (London: Allen Lane, 2020), 51–87.

[30] Keith Joseph, cited in Francis David, Elizabeth Paulhus, and Andrew Bradstock, *Moral, But No Compass: Government, Church, and the Future of Welfare* (Chelmsford: Matthew James, 2008), 39.

[31] See Christine Cheyne, Mike O'Brien, and Michael Belgrave, *Social Policy in Aotearoa New Zealand*, 4th ed. (South Melbourne: Oxford University Press, 2008), 232–33. In Australia, health policymakers gradually shifted their concern from equity and social justice to cost containment and cost effectiveness.

state."[32] However, reacting in the late 1990s to the social failures of neoliberalism in New Zealand, Australia, and Britain, governments of those countries were forced to modify to a limited degree their laissez-faire policies. But the principles of market economics, while solidly intact in the United States, still remained to varying degrees in those countries, contrary to the founding mythology of the egalitarian welfare state.

We see the results today. The overwhelming evidence, prior to the pandemic, points to "the rise of the greater income and wealth inequality in the West," due in part to such innovations as technological automation, the shrinking of welfare safety nets, and neoliberal austerity policies.[33] The result? The "rising economic insecurity and social deprivation among the left-behinds has fueled populist resentment against Washington DC,"[34] as well as Britain and the West in general. This is the atmosphere that has encouraged authoritarian populist leaders, such as Donald Trump and promoters of Brexit, to feed on this resentment.[35] Prior to the pandemic crisis, Paul Collins, reflecting on the American scene, wrote: "In America, the emblematic heart of capitalism, half of the 1980s generation are absolutely worse off than the generation of their parents at the same age. For them, capitalism is not working. . . . Anxiety, anger and despair have shredded people's political allegiances, their trust in government and even their trust in each other."[36]

---

[32] Jonathan Boston and Paul Dalziel, *The Decent Society?* (Oxford: Oxford University Press, 1992), 88. The most complete and erudite condemnation of the neoliberal model is contained in the report "The Global Economic Crisis: Systematic Failures and Multilateral Remedies" (United Nations Conference on Trade and Development [UNCTAD], 2009). See commentary by Manfred B. Steger and Ravi K. Roy, *Neoliberalism: A Very Short Introduction* (Oxford: Oxford University Press, 2010), 131–37.

[33] See Norris and Inglehart, *Cultural Backlash*, 349.

[34] Ibid., 362.

[35] See Gerald A. Arbuckle, *Fundamentalism at Home and Abroad: Analysis and Pastoral Responses* (Collegeville, MN: Liturgical Press, 2017), 77–81.

[36] Paul Collins, *The Future of Capitalism* (London: Penguin Books, 2019), 4, 5. Collins is professor of economics and public policy at the Blavatnik School of Government, Oxford University. See also Mariana Mazzucato, *Mission Economy: A Moonshot Guide to Changing Capitalism* (London: Penguin Random House, 2021), 11–56, 204–12. Mazzucato, professor of the economics of innovation and public value at University College London, critiques contemporary capitalism and argues it must refound itself if it is

The countries examined in the following sections are divided according to their mythological orientation, namely, individualistic, community, or autocratic.[37] Recall that ritual "is a stylized, repetitive social activity which, through the use of symbolism, expresses and defines social relations," and that "ritual activity occurs in a social context where there is ambiguity or conflict about social relations, and it is performed to resolve or disguise them"[38] (see Axiom 7, Chapter 1). Ritual is action "wrapped in a web of symbolism,"[39] and thus it has a communicative role. Ritual leaders, either religious or secular, "devise new, or adapt old, rituals in order to uphold their definition of social relationships."[40] Political leaders must be skilled in the art of ritual communication. They must use existing rituals or create new ones in order to identify and reinforce their powers; to communicate effectively, their rituals of authority must elicit a positive emotional response. Remember that ritual is not just about

---

to survive. Pope Francis has personally endorsed this book. Also Jonathan Hopkin, *Anti-System Politics: The Crisis of Market Liberalism in Rich Democracies* (New York: Oxford University Press, 2020).

[37] See "Which Market Model Is Best," *The Economist* (September 12, 2020), 66. The article approaches the topic from a different angle by applying two economic models of capitalism designed by Peter A. Hall and David Soskice to the pandemic context. They distinguish between liberal market economies (LMES), for example, America, Britain, and Canada, and coordinated market economies (CMES), such as Germany, the Nordic nations, Austria, and Holland. The LMES are neoliberal, depending on market forces to direct their economies; the United States particularly stresses market forces to direct the economy with a very thin overlay of welfare spending. The Nordic countries are more egalitarian, emphasizing consensual social bargaining founded on strong but collaborative trade unions. France depends particularly on the state for both development and distribution. The CMES countries during the pandemic developed a reasoned strategy to control COVID-19 but, in the estimation of the authors, they will be less innovative in the virus's aftermath. The approach of LMES to controlling the virus, on the other hand, is less organized, even chaotic, but likely to be more creative economically in moving out of the pandemic. See "An Introduction to Varieties of Capitalism," in *Varieties of Capitalism: The Institutional Foundations of Comparative Advantage*, ed. Peter A. Hall and David Soskice, 1–68 (Oxford: Oxford University Press, 2001).

[38] Christel Lane, *The Rites of Rulers: Ritual in Industrial Society—The Soviet Case* (Cambridge: Cambridge University Press, 1981), 11.

[39] David Kertzer, *Ritual, Politics, and Power* (London: Yale University Press, 1988), 9.

[40] Lane, *The Rites of Rulers*, 14.

maintaining order in relationships, but more important, writes Victor Turner, it is a "patterned process in time."[41] This means that ritual is also "transformative,"[42] because society itself is a process, not something static. Society is being repeatedly recreated out of the struggles, the social dramas of life, in order to resolve the tensions between order and chaos. People can refuse to participate in ritual. When leaders refuse to take up their role as ritual directors, however, we can expect social disorder—the trauma of chaos.

I examine four of the political leaders in the following case studies as ritual leaders: Prime Minister Boris Johnson, Britain; President Donald Trump, United States; Prime Minister Jacinda Ardern, New Zealand; and Prime Minister Scott Morrison, Australia. They used their ritual power of office either to disguise what was happening during the pandemic *or* to lead appropriately. Of the four ritual political leaders, only Ardern and Morrison led their countries through the travails of the pandemic cultural trauma as a rite of passage (see Figure 2.1), consistently respecting a mythology of Good Samaritan solidarity. Once the pandemic threatened, they immediately assumed the role of ritual leadership by putting into place the appropriate restrictions and financial assistance to those in need. Mistakes were made but there was no attempt to hide them. Johnson delayed with tragic consequences; having taken action, however, he attempted to lead the country too soon into the reentry stage. Trump never assumed the role of ritual leader at any point. The last group of nations to be considered are those with an autocratic orientation. While the rest of the world is focused on the COVID-19 crisis, the governments of these countries are grabbing more power for themselves with less and less accountability for their actions to the public.

Case Studies: Individual-oriented Nations

Britain

Britain by the end of June had the highest overall death rate due to COVID-19 of any country in the developed world.[43] The reason? *The*

---

[41] Victor Turner, *The Forest of Symbols: Aspects of Ndembu Ritual* (Ithaca, NY: Cornell University Press, 1967), 95.

[42] Ibid., 45.

[43] As at January 3, 2021, 74,682 people had died of the virus, representing a mortality rate of 112.32 per 100,000 of the population. See the Johns Hopkins Coronavirus Resource Center.

Economist concluded: "[Britain] has the wrong sort of government for a pandemic—and, in Boris Johnson, the wrong sort of prime minister."[44] He had been elected as a populist leader with demagogic tendencies.[45] While the public mythology of healthcare and of the government in Britain is that of the Good Samaritan, the operative mythology (see Axiom 3, Chapter 1), as explained above, remains hauntingly neoliberal. The government was slow to take the pandemic seriously despite the fact that some countries in Europe—for example, Italy, Denmark, Spain, and France—had gone into full lockdown.[46] Moreover, when the country finally did impose restrictions—which were light at first—it was ill-prepared to undertake key precautions such as virus testing, identifying a contact-tracing app, and stopping visits to care homes for the elderly. The government made vague announcements, at times minimizing the risks of the virus and failing to report the seriousness of the rising death toll. Even when the second wave of the virus hit Britain, the government kept publishing a series of ever-changing orders that were broken with impunity by its own officials.[47]

Though many factors contributed to the deaths in care homes and in the country in general, it was Prime Minister Boris Johnson who initially failed to take the impact of the pandemic seriously. While continental Europe was already going into lockdown, he announced only light restrictions on movements. *The Economist* reported: "As a

---

[44] "Not Britain's Finest Hour," *The Economist* (June 20, 2020), 11; see also, "Could Do Better," *The Economist* (September 5, 2020), 44. Johnson's approval rating "sunk to minus 22%" in October 2020. "A Reputation for Incompetence Dogs the Government," *The Economist* (October 17, 2020), 48.

[45] See Geoffrey Wheatcroft, "The Opportunist Triumphant," *New York Review of Books* (February 13, 2020), 32–35. Wheatcroft comments: "In October [2019], Johnson called for Britain 'to be released from the subjection of a parliament that has outlived its usefulness'" (32).

[46] "Germany, Austria and Switzerland all imposed lockdowns before they had reached 60 deaths. By contrast, Britain already had 300 deaths by March 23rd, when its government ordered people to stay at home. This slow response allowed the virus to reach the entire country. . . . Sweden, which did not impose a lockdown at all, has suffered a similarly widespread epidemic." "How Speedy Lockdowns Save Lives," *The Economist* (July 4, 2020).

[47] See "Why Governments Get It Wrong," *The Economist* (September 29, 2020), 9.

result of the government's tardiness, Britons were slower to change their behavior than in France, Spain or Italy. When the country finally locked down, the virus had spread further than in those countries."[48] Little wonder that trust in the government to lead the nation successfully through the liminal stage acutely collapsed. Johnson was elected as a charismatic populist leader but failed to lead with consistency and with respect for the most vulnerable. This, together with the failure of past governments to invest in healthcare services due to the embrace of neoliberal values, made the country ill-prepared to act in response to COVID-19. One positive move to reembrace the mythology of an egalitarian welfare state, however, came when Johnson, contrary to neoliberal values, planned to stimulate the economy by large investments in works—a welcome, if small, change favoring the Keynesian policies of President Franklin Roosevelt.

Between March 2 and June 12, 2020, it is estimated that nearly twenty thousand residents in care homes in England and Wales died due to COVID-19. The *Tablet* comments: "How this appalling situation came about is a deeply political story. The care home system itself was collateral damage in the long-running ideological warfare over the relative merits of public and private provision of essential services. It was another victim of the policy of 'shrinking the state' that was aggressively pursued under the premiership of Margaret Thatcher."[49] An earlier editorial had complained about the rising rates of death in care homes: "This betrays an attitude of indifference to the elderly. . . . It looks as if the lives of the elderly have been sacrificed to protect the political reputations of government ministers. That is shameful and intolerable."[50]

United States

> The causes of America's great pandemic failure run deep, exacerbated by innumerable longstanding problems, from a weak public health infrastructure to institutional racism to systemic inequality in health care, housing and employment. If the pandemic forces the nation to meaningfully grapple with any of

[48] "Trust Me, I'm a Prime Minister," *The Economist* (June 20, 2020), 46.
[49] "Needless Deaths of Thousands of Elderly," *Tablet* (July 19, 2020), 2.
[50] Editorial, "Shameful Acts of Disregard," *Tablet* (May 2, 2020), 2.

> those issues, then perhaps all this suffering will not have been in vain.[51]

The reactions to COVID-19 in the United States will be considered under the following headings: Public Health Failures, Ritual Leadership Failure, and Ultimate Responsibility.[52]

1. Public health failures

American healthcare specialists are among the very best in the world, but treatment is inequitable, overspecialized, and neglects primary and preventative care. In 2017, a study of eleven countries by the Commonwealth Fund in New York ranked "the UK first followed by Australia and the Netherlands. In last place . . . is the United States, which fails in almost every category."[53] The consequence of this is poorer health when compared to other advanced countries and a healthcare system ill-prepared to manage COVID-19.[54] By late May 2020, America was the nation most affected by the virus. Almost 1.7 million had contracted the virus, with numbers increasing by twenty thousand daily. By August 2020, COVID-19 casualties soared to over 150,000. America's death toll due to COVID-19 and its caseload are both high, and not only in absolute terms. Per head, it has had twice as many cases as Europe, and about 50 percent more deaths.[55] The poor suffer far more than the rich.[56] Nursing homes were severely affected

[51] Opinion, "America Could Control the Pandemic by October: Let's Get to It," *New York Times,* August 8, 2020.

[52] As of January 3, 2021, 350,186 people had died of the virus, representing a mortality rate of 107.04 per 100,000 of the population. See Johns Hopkins COVID-19 Resource Center.

[53] Commonwealth Fund, cited in David Oshinsky, "Health Care: The Best and the Rest," *New York Review of Books* 68, no. 16 (2020): 28.

[54] For an overview of the American healthcare system see John W. Miller, "In Search of a Safety Net," *America* (June 8, 2020), 18–25; Ezekiel J. Emanuel, *Which Country Has the World's Best Health Care?* (New York: Public Affairs, 2020), 18–54, 385–405, 408; Oshinsky, "Health Care: The Best and the Rest," 27–29; Arbuckle, *Humanizing Healthcare Reforms,* 90–94.

[55] See *The Economist* (June 14, 2020), 26; in late August 2020, the death toll due to the virus reached 180,000.

[56] See Ed Yong, "How the Pandemic Defeated America," *Atlantic* (September 2020).

by the disease. By late June 2020, 282,000 residents and workers in twelve thousand facilities were infected; 43 percent of all deaths in the United States had occurred in nursing homes.[57] "Nursing homes have come to symbolize the deadly destruction of the coronavirus crisis. . . . Nursing homes nationwide are evicting old and disabled residents and sending them into homeless shelters, run-down motels, and other unsafe facilities."[58]

Noted US healthcare expert Henry Aaron bluntly describes the healthcare of the United States as an "administrative monstrosity, a truly bizarre mélange of thousands, with payment systems that differ for no socially beneficial reasons."[59] The United States has no universal healthcare; instead, people are expected to have some type of private health insurance plan. Failure to have such a plan has had disastrous consequences for millions of people during the pandemic crisis. Only in recent times has the government legislated to mandate that every citizen must have some form of health insurance from either an employer, an individual plan, or through a public program such as Medicaid or Medicare.[60]

What are the implications of this legislation? About half of all Americans depend on their employers for coverage, but this is of little or no help when people become unemployed. In the pandemic approximately sixty million people have no coverage, many finding themselves ineligible to receive help from Medicaid or Medicare; minorities and the poor are often inadequately served. While most Americans have some insurance, premiums before and during pandemic times are rising and the quality of the insurance policies declining. Around forty million

[57] "43% of US Coronavirus Deaths Are Linked to Nursing Homes," *New York Times,* June 20, 2020. By mid-November 2020 more than 1,450 inmates in US prisons had died from the virus, a rate more than twice that of the general public; there were also 98 deaths of staff members, a rate three times as high as that for the general public. Editorial, "Coronavirus Rages through Prisons," *Times Digest* (November 22, 2020), 8.

[58] "As Crisis Swirls, Nursing Homes 'Dump' Patients," *Times Digest* (June 21, 2020), 3.

[59] Henry J. Aaron, quoted in John Glasser, "Keep Formation In-House," *Health Progress: Journal of the Catholic Health Association of the United States* 92, no. 5 (2011), 27.

[60] US Medicare provides primary medical coverage for people aged sixty-five and over and for those with a disability, and Medicaid for those of limited income.

workers, almost two out of five, do not have access to paid sick leave. In summary, the US health insurance system is patchy and increasingly expensive, leaving millions with little or no coverage. African Americans in particular have been badly affected by the virus, in part because, being less likely to have adequate insurance than their fellow citizens, they tend to seek treatment later in the course of their disease, which typically leads to worse outcomes.[61]

In late July 2020, Alexis Marshall, writing in the *Atlantic,* concluded that

> the lack of containment by American authorities has resulted in not only lost lives, but also lost businesses, savings accounts, school years, dreams, public trust, friendships. The country cannot get back to normal with a highly transmissible, deadly virus spreading in our communities. There is no way to just "live with it." There will only be dying from it for the unlucky, and barely surviving it for the rest of us.[62]

Stimulus checks and expanded unemployment insurance have helped household finances, but the weekly US$600 benefits ceased in late July; a program of loans for small businesses in order to prevent bankruptcies ended in early August.[63] Not surprisingly, a poll conducted in late May 2020 suggested that an overwhelming majority of Americans feel the nation is "spiraling out of control. Two-thirds felt hopeless, lonely, depressed or nervous."[64]

2. Ritual leadership failure

President Trump failed to take up the role as national leader of the rite of passage in the pandemic, and so the country floundered from crisis to crisis. Instead of learning from the informed actions initiated in

---

[61] See "100,000 and Counting," *The Economist* (May 30, 2020), 13.

[62] Alexis C. Marshall, "A Second Coronavirus Death Surge Is Coming," *Atlantic* (July 15, 2020).

[63] See Jeanna Smialek and Jim Tankersley, "US Recovery Stalling amid Virus Resurgence," *Times Digest* (August 22, 2020), 5.

[64] Report of Emily Olson, Washington DC, cited by ABC News, Australia (June 12, 2020).

China, Taiwan, New Zealand, Australia, Singapore, and Vietnam, he refused to listen to healthcare experts or to coordinate a federal reaction. He frequently dismissed the pandemic either as a matter of no consequence or as well under control. The federal government, under his leadership, sought to limit testing, thus ensuring that the number of reported cases was understated. He presided over tens, even hundreds of thousands of avoidable American deaths, as well as the collapse of the entire economy, which has had lasting consequences globally. It has been estimated that if America had introduced social-distancing restrictions one week sooner, it could have lessened the nationwide infections by 62 percent and deaths by 95 percent.[65] When he did explicitly refer to the crisis, he often blamed immigrants, China, or "fake news," while repeatedly mocking expert advice. He frequently spoke of the need to adhere to neoliberal principles and to reopen the country to business as usual, all the time ignoring the rising death rates in the country.[66] Each denial was but another tipping point into national cultural trauma. He added to the overwhelming grief of millions of Americans by this appalling behavior. Never did he find time to mourn those who died or to express any empathy with the bereaved through traditional national rites such as flying flags at half mast or a moment of silence.[67]

Not surprisingly, therefore, by mid-2020 few countries had been as severely hit by the virus as the United States, which has only 4 percent of the world's population but 25 percent of its confirmed cases and deaths.[68] Because the nation has a strong system of state governments, some states decided to impose lockdown measures rather than wait for federal action. California, for example, responded immediately to identify cases. In Florida, county officers imposed lockdown restrictions when the governor, Ron DeSantis, took no action; he considered pro wrestling an "essential business" and permitted crowds to fill

[65] See "100,000 and Counting," 14.

[66] See Don Watson, "American Carnage: Donald Trump and the Collapse of the Union," *Monthly* (July 2020), 18.

[67] See Susan Glasser, "Fifty Thousand Americans Died from the Coronavirus, and a President Who Refuses to Mourn Them," *New Yorker* (April 23, 2020).

[68] See Yong, "How the Pandemic Defeated America."

beaches.[69] In New York, where deaths rose to over twenty thousand in May, Governor Andrew Cuomo strenuously promoted testing and lockdown restrictions.[70]

In summary, Donald Trump was elected president in 2016 despite his well-publicized "fear-mongering and narcissism and cheerleading for torture . . . racism, misogyny, and xenophobia."[71] Over the next four years his leadership style did not change.[72] The fact that his political party did not reject his leadership, and in fact praised and colluded with it, indicates that American democracy is subordinate to neoliberal capitalism, patriarchy, and an immoral racial order descended from slavery. During the trauma Trump continued to flatter his supporters "by articulating a dog-whistle version of racist and xenophobic rhetoric and by appeals to strongman executive rule, disregarding conventional constitutional checks and balances."[73] He repeatedly attacked the press, claiming it to be the "enemy of the people"; threatened to jail those who opposed him; called members of Congress "treasonous" for refusing to praise his speeches; encouraged foreign interference in the electoral process; lauded autocrats while belittling the nation's friends; and fabricated facts whenever it served his purposes.[74] Political theorist Hannah Arendt (1906–75) once provocatively asserted that lying is an integral quality of politics, a required skill for demagogues and statesmen in general.[75] At least

---

[69] See "America Begins Easing COVID-19 Restrictions," *The Economist* (April 22, 2020).

[70] See Michael Greenberg, "Emergency Responder," *New York Review of Books* 68, no. 8 (2020): 9–10.

[71] Mark Danner, "On the Election II," *New York Review of Books* (November 10, 2016), 19; Carol Anderson, *White Rage: The Unspoken Truth of Our Racial Divide* (New York: Bloomsbury, 2017), 161–80.

[72] See Arbuckle, *Loneliness: Insights for Healing in a Fragmented World* (Maryknoll, NY: Orbis Books, 2018), 74–82.

[73] Norris and Inglehart, *Cultural Backlash*, 338–39.

[74] See Pamela Karlan, "Our Most Vulnerable Election," *New York Review of Books,* (October 2020), 4–8; Lawrence Douglas, *Will He Go? Trump and the Looming Election Meltdown* (New York: Twelve, 2020).

[75] See Hannah Arendt, *Between Past and Future* (New York: Viking Press, 1954), 227. See comments by Leah Bradshaw, "Principles and Politics," in *Cruelty and Deception: The Controversy Over Dirty Hands in Politics*, ed. Paul Rynard and David P. Shugarman, 87–99 (Orchard Park, NY: Broadview Press, 2000).

in the case of President Trump, she was correct. His main concern throughout the trauma was to prevent being personally blamed for the virus and its implications; the more he could scapegoat the governors and others for the economic consequences, the better for him. His reactions and policies as the nation's ritual leader were, ultimately, self-serving and narcissistic.[76]

The already existing bitter division in the American body politic was intensified by President Trump's failure to assume the national role of ritual leader during his term. He governed as the leader of one political faction, not as the president of a whole nation. The result is that the scars of a polarized nation are now deeper and more enduring: "To his allies he is a saviour; to his opponents, a dangerously unhinged demagogue."[77] When Joe Biden was elected president in November 2020, Trump flouted democratic norms and conventions by denying without proof the validity of the election; it is claimed he later incited the January 6 rebounding mob violence against the Capitol.[78] At the same time, he refused to acknowledge the ongoing human tragedy of the pandemic in the nation; in a third wave of the virus the death toll continued to rise and the human costs to survivors and the nation as a whole are immeasurable. President Biden has pledged to heal the divided nation.[79] His first act as president-elect was to focus on leading the national rite of passage by planning a program to control the pandemic and move forward into the reentry stage, respecting the dignity of all. It will not be easy.

We can expect former president Trump, with the national support base of 48 percent of the popular vote, to remain a destructive

---

[76] Eliot Cohen from Johns Hopkins University writes that America has been from its beginning "a land of the future, a work in progress," but with a second Trump term the nation "might as well be understood as a monument to the past, not a failed state, but a failed vision, a vast power in decline whose time has come and gone." "The End of American Power," *Foreign Affairs* (October 27, 2020).

[77] "Part of the Problem as Well as the Solution," *Tablet* (November 11, 2020).

[78] Rebounding violence, as defined by Maurice Bloch, is described in Chapter 2.

[79] Biden is committed to rejoining both the Paris Accord on Climate Change and the World Health Organization.

force.[80] The vices of envy and jealousy that characterize a populist, narcissistic leader (see Chapter 2)[81] were evident both in Trump's first campaign for the presidency and throughout his four years as president. From the outset he promised to "Make America Great Again"; once in power he immediately demonized his predecessor and began to destroy as much of the previous administration's legislation as possible, such as Obamacare, international trade agreements, and immigration policies. "For Trump, the mark of a successful president is the degree to which he can expunge Obama's presidency."[82] Anyone who questioned his policies, including federal pandemic experts, became the target of vitriolic attacks.

3. Ultimate responsibility: Individualism[83]

Who bears most of the responsibility for the rapid spread of the virus in the United States and its disastrous consequences? Why is the world's richest country in such disarray? *Washington Post* columnist Eugene Robinson blames Donald Trump, noting that "a good president, or even a mediocre one, would have believed world-renowned experts . . . when they warned that the first few cases of COVID-19 had the potential to mushroom into a global crisis."[84] But President Trump, without an understanding of or sympathy for the language of

---

[80] Steven Levitsky and Daniel Ziblatt comment: "A refounding of America's major center-right party is a tall order. . . . To save our democracy, Americans need to restore the basic norms that once protected it." *How Democracies Die* (New York: Crown, 2018), 223–24, 231.

[81] See Arbuckle, *Loneliness*, 74–82. David Goodhart comments: "In the US and Latin America the term (i.e. populist) has generally been associated with the left and in Europe with the right. Actually there has been a left-wing anti-corporate elite strand to US populism and a right-wing strand that is also nativist and anti-immigrant. . . . Donald Trump combines aspects of both left and right populism." *The Road to Somewhere: The Populist Revolt and the Future of Politics* (London: Hurst, 2017), 54.

[82] Charles M. Blow, "Opinion: Trump's Obama Obsession," *New York Times,* June 29, 2017.

[83] See Arbuckle, *Loneliness*, 57–82; Collier and Kay, *Greed Is Dead*, 13–28.

[84] Eugene Robinson, "Opinion: We're No. 1! In a Pandemic, That's No Cause for Celebration," *Washington Post*, July 2, 2020.

the nation's founders,[85] tried to substitute the democratic myth with autocracy, flouting norms with impunity, thus subverting democracy.[86] For him, modern politics is like a type of tribal warfare. What a leader does is of less importance for him than whom he is for, and above all, whom he is against. Ed Yong of the *Atlantic* writes, "Trump is a comorbidity of the COVID-19 pandemic. He isn't responsible for America's fiasco, but he is central to it."[87] Journalist and Pulitzer Prize–winner George Packer, also writing in the *Atlantic,* is equally direct: "The crisis demanded a response that was swift, rational, and collective. . . . [But the] administration squandered two irretrievable months to prepare. From the president came willful blindness, scapegoating, boasts and lies. From his mouthpiece came conspiracy theories and miracle cures."[88]

Packer, however, while condemning Trump for his blatant ignoring of the crisis, goes even deeper into the cultural reasons for the catastrophe: "When the crisis came here, it found a country with serious underlying conditions, and it exploited them ruthlessly. Chronic ills—a corrupt political class, a sclerotic bureaucracy, a heartless economy, a divided and distracted public. . . . Russia, Taiwan, the United Nations sent humanitarian aid to the world's richest power—a beggar nation in utter chaos."[89] Others agree: "The fumbling of the virus was not a fluke. It has exposed the country's incoherent leadership, self-defeating political polarization, a lack of investment in public health, and persistent socioeconomic and racial inequities that have left millions of people vulnerable to disease and death."[90] And the ultimate reason? Packer writes: "We can learn from these dreadful days . . . that, in a democracy, being a citizen is essential work; that

---

[85] See Anne Applebaum, *Twilight of Democracy: The Failure of Politics and the Parting of Friends* (London: Allen Lane, 2000), 142–71.

[86] See Levitsky and Ziblatt, *How Democracies Die*, 61–65, 176–203, 205–6.

[87] Ed Yong, "How the Pandemic Defeated America."

[88] George Packer, "Dispatches: Underlying Conditions," *Atlantic* (June 2020), 9.

[89] Ibid., 9, 10. The aid referred to was test kits, masks, medical gowns, and ventilators.

[90] Joel Achenbach et al., "The Crisis that Shocked the World: America's Response to the Coronavirus," *Washington Post,* July 20, 2020.

the alternative to solidarity is death."[91] In other words, the individualism inherent in the founding mythology has gone to extremes.[92] Any solidarity that did exist has disintegrated, and Presdient Trump's failure to lead was but a sad consequence. Anthropologist Wade Davis concludes: "More than any other country, the United States in the post-war era lionized the individual at the expense of community and family. . . . What was gained in terms of mobility and personal freedom came at the expense of common purpose."[93]

The founding mythology of America is that an individual can achieve anything on his or her own—particularly wealth and material things.[94] And although individualism characterizes many cultures, there is something quite exceptional in American individualism: it is extreme. Other countries balance their individualism with their concern for the good of the community. That perceptive observer of the American scene, Alexis de Tocqueville, noted in the mid-nineteenth century—as something still emerging—the problems of growing individualism, loneliness, and alienation: "Selfishness blights the germ of all virtues; individualism, at first, only saps the virtues of public life; but in the long run it attacks and destroys all others and is at length absorbed in downright selfishness."[95]

One serious consequence of individualism is the breakdown of trust.[96] Prior to the Trump presidency the level of trust in the American

---

[91] Packer, "Dispatches," 12.

[92] Masha Gessen argues that Trump's actions to destroy the accepted norms of presidential power, including undermining any mechanisms of accountability, downgrading political discourse, embracing xenophobia, and praising foreign dictators while insulting democratic allies, are efforts to obtain autocratic power. See *Surviving Autocracy* (New York: Riverhead, 2020).

[93] Wade Davis, "The Unravelling of America," *Rolling Stone* (August 6, 2020).

[94] See Oliver Stone and Peter Kuznick, *The Untold History of the United States,* vol. 1 (New York: Simon and Schuster, 2014), 138–40.

[95] Alexis de Tocqueville, *Democracy in America by Alexis de Tocqueville*, vol. 2, ed. Phillips Bradley (New York: Alfred A. Knopf, 1953), 98.

[96] See Robert D. Putnam, *Bowling Alone: The Collapse and Revival of American Community* (New York: Simon and Schuster, 2000), 350–63; Robert D. Putnam and Shaylyn Romney Garrett, *The Upswing: How America Came Together a Century Ago and How We Can Do It Again* (New York: Simon and Schuster, 2020), 186–99.

government by its citizens had descended to an all-time low, but worse was yet to come. As John Coyne and Peter Jennings wrote in 2020:

> Just 17% of Americans say they can trust the government in Washington to do what's right "just about always" (3%) or "most of the time" (14%). Beneath this hugely destructive erosion of faith in democratic systems has been an erosion of foundational structures. . . . Into this void, post-truth populism, with its simplistic denial of reality, has been an attractive but temporary salve, but it can't be sustained because it does nothing to address the absence of a meaningful organizing principle for society. The COVID-19 crisis has been a demonstration of its limits.[97]

Individualism is no substitute for solidarity as the organizing principle for a society.

Narcissism is a symptom of exaggerated individualism. Narcissists are focused only on themselves as individuals; narcissism is self-admiration taken to an extreme. In consequence, narcissists "lack emotionally warm, caring, and loving relationships with other people . . . [and they] manipulate and cheat to get ahead, surround themselves with people who look up to them . . . exploiting people and viewing others as tools to make themselves look and feel good."[98] Commitments of all kinds are highly fragile, for every relationship, even marriage, is dispensable if it fails to serve the self-fulfillment aspirations of the narcissist.[99] The narcissism in American culture helps to explain why Trump and millions of admiring Americans have ignored the plight of those, particularly the poor, who have died from COVID-19.[100]

---

[97] John Coyne and Peter Jennings, "Introduction," in *After COVID-19: Australia and the World Rebuild*, vol. 1, ed. John Coyne and Peter Jennings (Sydney: Australian Strategic Policy Institute, 2020), 11.

[98] Jean M. Twenge and W. Keith Campbell, *The Narcissism Epidemic* (New York: Atria, 2013), 19.

[99] See Christopher Lasch, *The Culture of Narcissism* (New York: Warner, 1991); and Rollo May, *The Cry of Myth* (New York: W. W. Norton, 1991), 110–24.

[100] See Hadley Freeman, "Trump's Deep Narcissism Acted as a Distorted Mirror for Millions of Voters," *Guardian*, November 6, 2020.

In brief, the failures to address the pandemic crisis point to individualism as the ultimate cause of America's contemporary calamity. Trump is not the most distressing reality in America's cultural trauma. He is no longer president, but the culture of narcissistic individualism remains significantly present to gravely hamper collective action (see Chapters 4 and 5).[101] Social researcher Jean Twenge concludes: "No single event initiated the narcissism epidemic; instead, Americans' core ideals slowly became more focused on self-admiration and self-expression. At the same time, Americans' faith in the power of collective action or the government was lost."[102] All this is making it difficult for Trump's successor, President Biden, to develop national solidarity to combat the human costs of the pandemic. It will take far more than one presidential election to unite a profoundly divided nation.

Case Studies: Community-oriented Nations[103]

New Zealand[104]

As we will see below with Australia, the New Zealand government's top priority was the saving of lives in the liminal stage of the country's rite of passage—at great economic cost. After briefly flirting with neoliberal values in the 1980s and 1990s, the New Zealand government reverted to its traditional mythology of the egalitarian welfare state,

---

[101] See Watson, "American Carnage," 19.

[102] Twenge and Campbell, *The Narcissism Epidemic,* 67. Michael J. Sandel argues that a culture of individualism and neocapitalism made America morally ill-prepared for the pandemic: "The toxic mix of hubris and resentment that propelled Trump to power is not a likely source of solidarity we need now." Michael J. Sandel, *The Tyranny of Merit: What's Become of the Common Good?* (New York: Farrar, Straus and Giroux, 2020), 5.

[103] Canada also belongs to this category. As of December 4, 2020, 12,887 people had died of the virus, representing a mortality rate of 34.77 per 100,000 of the population. See Johns Hopkins COVID-19 Resource Center.

[104] As of January 3, 2021, only twenty-five people had died of the virus in New Zealand (out of a population of approximately 4.8 million), representing a low international mortality rate of 0.51 per 100,000 of the population. See Johns Hopkins COVID-19 Resource Center.

and Prime Minister Jacinda Ardern built her leadership on its values. Her aim in 2020 was to pursue an elimination approach rather than a policy of merely mitigating the virus.[105] She introduced one of the toughest national lockdowns in the world when the nation only had 102 cases of the virus and no deaths: "New Zealand, with a population of 4.8 million, had a total of 1476 cases and 19 deaths as at 30 April, while Ireland, with a population of 4.9 million, had 20,253 cases and 1190 deaths."[106] At the same time, the level of the people's trust in the government remained remarkably high, a sure sign of communitas and the strength of national social capital. In early April 2020, "just over a week after New Zealand moved into its full nationwide lockdown . . . 88% of respondents to a national survey stated that they could 'trust the government to make the right decisions on COVID-19,' compared to an average of 59% of people in G7 countries."[107]

What are the reasons for the success of the government's policies compared with most other countries, and for the high level of people's trust? I list four: (1) the clarity of purpose in announcing the goal of national lockdown and restrictions over individual freedom, namely, to lessen danger to lives and livelihoods and in consequence to position the country for a more rapid economic recovery; (2) the prime minister's policy of persistently reminding people that the nation is a "team of 5 million [citizens]"[108] based on a founding mythology of solidarity, implying that as a team the people can defeat the virus; (3) the government's willingness to listen to and be led by experts; and (4) the leadership style of Prime Minister Ardern. Communication was considered crucial: "How a country communicates the concept of elimination will be important for going forwards."[109] "Her leadership style is one of empathy in a crisis. . . . Her messages are clear,

---

[105] See Sophie Cousins, "New Zealand Eliminates COVID-19," *Lancet,* vol. 395 (May 9, 2020): 1474.

[106] Suze Wilson, "Pandemic Leadership: Lessons from New Zealand's Approach to COVID-19," *Hazetnet: The Magazine of the Canadian Risks and Hazard Networks* (May 26, 2020), 6.

[107] Ibid.

[108] "Elections in New Zealand: Jacindarella," *The Economist* (October 3, 2020), 21.

[109] Michael Baker, Otago University, cited in Sophie Cousins, "New Zealand Eliminates COVID-19," 1474.

consistent, and somehow simultaneously sobering and soothing."[110] And importantly, her behavior matched her words; she lived under the same constraints as her fellow citizens.

The reentry stage of the nation's rite of passage into a post-COVID-19 world will be long and tortuous because the economic and social costs as a consequence of Ardern's lockdown policies continue to be considerable. The economy's biggest sources of income—tourism and educational services for foreign students—have ceased, causing a significant rise in unemployment and an uncertain economic future.[111] There are no previous road maps to guide Ardern's policies forward, and the country cannot remain isolated from international contacts forever. Given Ardern's successful leadership emphasis on the mythology of solidarity in the rite's liminal stage, there is hope that she and the nation may discover positive ways to reconnect in the reentry stage with the international community. It is an uncertain journey.

Australia[112]

The Commonwealth of Australia consists of six states and ten federal territories. Its founding mythology owes much to its history as a penal colony and the harshness of most of its countryside. The internationally known song "Waltzing Matilda" recounts in a fictional way the very heart of this mythology. There are two central characters: a "swagman" (itinerant worker), representing society's underprivileged, and a "squatter," signifying the elite rich landowners. The swagman is discovered by the squatter stealing a sheep, and the squatter calls in the "troopers" (police) who rush to apprehend the thief. Then the swagman jumps into a "billabong" (small lake) and drowns, but the story does not end there. The swagman actually wins! His ghost lives on to haunt the rich and powerful, reminding them that the real hero in Australia is the disadvantaged underdog. Thus, in Australian public

---

[110] Uri Friedman, "New Zealand's Prime Minister May Be the Most Effective Leader on the Planet," *Atlantic* (April 16, 2020), 1–2.

[111] See "A Victorious Jacinda Ardern Must Deal with COVID's Economic Fallout," *The Economist* (October 24, 2020), 20.

[112] As of January 3, 2021, 909 people had died of the virus in Australia, representing a low international mortality rate of 3.64 per 100,000 of the population. See Johns Hopkins COVID-19 Resource Center.

mythology it is the community good that must be emphasized even though individual rights are consequently restricted; this egalitarian interpretation is summed up in the expression "Fair go, mate." The mate refers especially to those on the margins of society and economy: society's underdogs. Consequently, significant cynicism is directed toward people who show squatter-like qualities, that is, who dare to put on airs of superiority or artificiality.[113] Medicare, Australia's universal healthcare scheme since 1984, which ranks as one of the best in the world, was founded on this public myth and a reservoir of national social capital—concern for the community's underprivileged.

Over the last thirty years, however, the operative myth (see Axiom 3, Chapter 1) behind healthcare and social services became neoliberal capitalism. Former welfare recipients became a new working poor; economic liberalism contributed to an increase in unemployment, inequality, social dysfunction, and alienation.[114] Australian health policymakers gradually shifted their concern from equity and social justice to cost containment and, more recently, to cost effectiveness, while publicly proclaiming allegiance to the mythology of solidarity.[115] The decision especially affected people who are poor. Primary care such as health promotion and education is being deemphasized, and particular groups such as elderly people, Aboriginal peoples, and individuals who are mentally sick or have physical disabilities are being increasingly marginalized. They lack the political and economic power to be heard when they cry out about their plight.

The Australian federal government in power, under Prime Minister Scott Morrison, had long favored neoliberal policies and their individualistic values. However, the government, from the beginning of the liminal stage of the pandemic, openly discarded these policies in favor of solidarity, and the residual mythology of concern for the welfare of all resurfaced to guide governmental decision-making.[116]

---

[113] See Gerald A. Arbuckle, *Culture, Inculturation, and Theologians: A Postmodern Critique* (Collegeville, MN: Liturgical Press, 2010), 31–32.

[114] See Peter Saunders, *The Poverty Wars* (Sydney: University of New South Wales Press, 2005), 57.

[115] See Hal Swerissen and Stephen Duckett, "Health Policy and Financing," in *Health Policy in Australia*, ed. Heather Gardner (Melbourne: Oxford University Press, 1997), 33.

[116] See Katherine Murphy, "The End of Certainty: Scott Morrison and Pandemic Politics," *Quarterly Essay* 79 (Carlton VIC, Australia: Black Inc., 2020), 1–98.

Morrison's leadership style was similar to that of New Zealand's Ardern—collaborative, consistent, and empathetic—unlike that of Trump and Johnson. Medical experts were frequently and publicly consulted.

> Australia is showing great resilience in the face of COVID-19. Our public institutions are working together to deal . . . in new and effective ways. Federal and state leaders are working together through the National Cabinet process. Disparate stakeholders, such as trade unions and business groups, are being given real input into critical decisions. The public are changing their behavior and finding new ways of supporting each other within their communities.[117]

When the pandemic crisis struck, it quickly became clear, as virus cases began to rise exponentially, that the country's healthcare system was ill-prepared to react.[118] For example, the nation wrestled with the developing demand for protective equipment, and the structural weaknesses and staffing of care homes became startlingly obvious. Nevertheless, the government's policies of intervention and collaboration evoked widespread trust and the feeling of solidarity, communitas, among the Australian people. It soon became clear that things would never return to the previous status quo. The daily media reports of massive increase in overseas countries of virus victims, local growing queues of the unemployed seeking government assistance, and businesses threatened with bankruptcy, evoked increasing fear and trauma among citizens. Yet trust in government continued to remain high. With few exceptions citizens obeyed lockdown restrictions. In late June isolating restrictions began slowly to be lifted as the country moved into the reentry phase. In a survey in late June 2020, 80 percent approved the prime minister's handling of the crisis. His empathy, collaborative style, willingness to listen to healthcare experts, and the closure of national borders have been major contributors to the success of the federal government's policies.

---

[117] Jay Weatherill, "Rethinking Government: Lessons from the National Cabinet," in *What Happens Next? Reconstructing Australia after COVID-19*, ed. Emma Dawson and Janet McCalman (Melbourne: Melbourne University Press, 2020), 81.

[118] By the end of August 2020, Australia, with a population of 25 million, had 24,916 confirmed cases of COVID-19 and 517 deaths due to the virus (Johns Hopkins COVID-19 Resource Center).

Both New Zealand and Australia experienced second waves of COVID-19, and their governments immediately imposed successful regional lockdowns, but "even with these spikes, the performances of these countries, together with Japan and Hong Kong, show the United States, Latin America, parts of Europe and struggling India in a dismal light."[119]

Case Studies: Autocratic-oriented Nations

It was reported in late June 2020 that "political violence has risen in 43 countries and remained steady in 45 since the start of the pandemic."[120] Democracy is experiencing its worst crisis since the tragic explosion of nationalism in the 1930s, and the dangers are rapidly becoming evident. Globally, democracy and human rights are in retreat; the number of democracies has been decreasing.[121] Nationalisms and economic depressions are socially dangerous mixes; even "Western societies are currently regressing toward the authoritarian politics that is linked historically with economic insecurity."[122] Fragile democracies particularly are under threat in Africa and South America.

Autocracy—government by one person or a small group with unlimited power—is on the rise in parts of the world. Hard times often make people especially vulnerable to the simplistic solutions of populists and extremists. Thus, while the world's attention is on the pandemic, would-be autocrats are taking advantage to grab more power.[123] Dictatorial governments in the Philippines, China, Turkey, El Salvador, and Brazil have all assumed emergency powers; Bulgaria

---

[119] "A Second Wave of COVID-19," *The Economist* (August 1, 2020), 21.

[120] "Pandemics and War: Horsemen of the Apocalypse," *The Economist* (June 20, 2020), 50.

[121] See Yascha Mounk, *The People vs. Democracy: Why Our Freedom Is in Danger and How to Save It* (Cambridge, MA: Harvard University Press, 2020), 1–21; "COVID-19: No Vaccine for Cruelty," *The Economist* (October 17, 2020), 9, 50–52.

[122] Norris and Inglehart, *Cultural Backlash,* 464.

[123] Even Donald Trump claimed to have "absolute power" to decide when lockdowns should end, but he was quickly reminded that America's constitution forbade it. "COVID-19 and Autocracy," *The Economist* (April 25, 2020), 48.

has used the virus as an excuse to repress the Roma minority.[124] At the end of March 2020, Hungary's parliament issued a "coronavirus law," granting almost unrestricted powers to govern by decree, with no expiration time given. Under Andrzej Duda's populist leadership, Poland's democracy is shaky. In August 2020, peaceful protests in Belarus against elections rigged by President Alexander Lukashenko were being met by ruthless repression.[125] In the Balkans, where political trust is low, many people believe that their governments are lying about there even being a virus; in Bosnia, prominent people are promoting conspiracy theories in order to conceal the realities of the virus infections.[126]

China

When the virus first appeared in China, it was ignored because it endangered the good image that the government, led by President Xi Jinping, wished to project. But when it alarmingly spread wider, the government acted with severe authoritarian force. On January 23, 2020, the city of Wuhan was locked down. "The nation's extensive system of personal surveillance was called into service, using security cameras, facial recognition software, and GPS tracking to locate and isolate infected individuals and to identify and quarantine contacts."[127] China is taking advantage of the world distracted by COVID-19 to intensify its hold over Hong Kong and to persecute millions of Uighurs, a Muslim minority, living in an autonomous northwest region of China.[128] Hundreds of underground Catholics were prevented

[124] See Patrick Kingsley and Boryana Dzhambazova, "Lockdown Used as a Weapon to Repress Roma," *Times Digest* (July 7, 2020), 2.

[125] See "Belarus's Bogus Election," *The Economist* (August 15, 2020), 41. Earlier, Lukashenko had claimed that the best way to control COVID-19 was to drink vodka and drive a tractor.

[126] See "COVID-19 in the Balkans," *The Economist* (August 8, 2020), 39.

[127] Daniel P. Sulmasy, "The Virus and the Common Good," *Tablet* (April 18, 2020), 8.

[128] See Jen Kirby, "Concentration Camps and Forced Labor: China's Repression of the Uighurs," Vox Media (updated September 25, 2020). *The Economist* reports: "The persecution of the Uyghurs is a crime against humanity. . . . [It] is the most extensive violation in the world today of the principle that individuals have a right to liberty and dignity simply because they are people" (October 17, 2020), 9.

from celebrating the Feast of the Assumption on August 15 in the latest example of the government's suppressing of Christians under cover of COVID-19.[129] China is also bullying other countries—for example, through the use of trade bans—to expand its regional and global influence.[130]

The Chinese government has two political objectives: to preserve territorial integrity, and to maintain the rule of the Communist Party. The founding mythology of emperors of the past along with the ethnocentric belief of the unique importance of the Han Chinese people[131] underlie these objectives. This mythology has been reinforced by the cycle of stability and war in China over the millennia, where invasion, Mongol or Japanese, resulted in cultural trauma and poverty under a weakened emperor. Traditional mythology says that heaven is defined as Han territory; thus resolution of border issues, such as in Tibet, Xinjiang, South China Sea, Taiwan, and now Hong Kong, is critical for protecting and maintaining the identity of China. The communist party sees itself as the guardian of these borders; the president, successor of the emperors, resides at Zhongnanhai, alongside the Forbidden City, where the emperors once lived. The large portrait of Mao Tsetung, former ruler of the People's Republic of China (1949–76), rests above the front gate of the Forbidden City[132] to indicate that he and the party he founded are the new emperors. This is a prime example of myth substitution. The more President Xi Jinping steers authoritarian China toward one rule, the more the myth substitution is perfected.[133]

Brazil

The attitudes and actions of Brazil's populist president, Jair Bolsonaro, are causing a health and human disaster for millions. He scoffs

---

[129] UCA News, Hong Kong, "China Suppresses Catholics under Covid-19 Cover" (updated August 21, 2020).

[130] See "Why China Bullies," *The Economist* (June 20, 2020), 26.

[131] The Han Chinese form the largest ethnic group in China—92 percent of the population.

[132] The Forbidden City, the palatial heart of China, was built in 1420 during the early Ming dynasty.

[133] Information provided by Nicholas Curtis (personal conversation). See also Michael Wood, *The Story of China: The Story of a Civilization and Its People* (London: Simon and Schuster, 2020), 526–33.

at medical authorities, belittles social-distancing restrictions and widespread testing, and wrangles with state governors who decreed lockdowns that he fears will cause unnecessary economic damage. The results are a catastrophe: by the end of May, Brazil had 411,821 confirmed cases and 25,598 deaths.[134] The most vulnerable have suffered the most. It is estimated that in São Paulo, people who live in poorer areas and fall victim to the virus are up to ten times more likely to die than people in wealthy districts. Black residents in the city are 62 percent more likely to die of the virus than white residents.[135]

Russia

Vladimir Putin, who came to power in 1999, "most resembles Tsar Nicholas I with his policies of Autocracy, Orthodoxy, Nationality."[136] Putin seeks to reestablish Russia's power by returning to the corrupting autocratic mythology of the tsars. It is a mythology that assumes domination can be achieved in any circumstance, including anarchy, and that "collaboration on ever-shifting terms is possible with any partner, from organized crime to Christian clergy."[137] Today Putin is the controller of power and wealth that crushes dissent at home and projects force abroad.[138] His agents helped to elect Trump "with long-standing Russian links who would not only sow chaos, but systematically undermine America's alliances, erode American influence."[139] Russia briefly rose to number two globally in COVID-19 cases

---

[134] See "Losing the Battle," *The Economist* (May 30, 2020), 32–33.

[135] See Ishaan Tharoor, "Brazil Faces the Coronavirus Disaster Almost Everyone Saw Coming," *Washington Post,* June 15, 2020. As of February 2021, Brazil recorded over 230,000 deaths due to COVID-19. Johns Hopkins Coronavirus Resource Center.

[136] Simon Sebag Montefiore, *The Romanovs* (London: Weidenfeld and Nicolson, 2016), 656.

[137] "Power in Russia: Made Men," *The Economist* (April 25, 2020), 71. See also Catherine Belton, *Putin's People* (New York: Farrar, Straus and Giroux, 2019).

[138] See Belton, *Putin's People.*

[139] Anne Applebaum, "A KGB Man to the End," *Atlantic* (September 2020), 88.

in May 2020, "and manifested a conspicuous absence of decisive central leadership."[140] At first Putin tried to ignore the importance of COVID-19, then falsely claimed it was being skillfully handled: "The contagion did not elicit from Putin's regime a muscular response worthy of the best arguments for authoritarian discipline."[141]

Scriptural Reflection: Conversion to Gospel Values for Leadership

In the aftermath of COVID-19 the world faces an uncertain future. There are no proven road maps for recovery, and as Pope Francis notes in *Laudato Si'*, "We lack leadership capable of striking out on new paths and meeting needs of the present with concern for all and without prejudice towards coming generations" (no. 53). We need refounding leaders who are willing and able to return to the values of Jesus Christ and the Good Samaritan (see Chapter 1) and to apply them to contemporary needs. In *Evangelii Gaudium* Pope Francis defines the process of refounding the church in this way:

> Whenever we make the effort to return to the source and to recover the original freshness of the Gospel, new avenues arise, new paths of creativity open up, with different forms of expression, more eloquent signs and words with new meaning for today's world. Every form of authentic evangelization is always "new." (EG, no. 11)

Refounding is the process of returning to Christ's example and seeking with imagination and pastoral creativity to bridge the gap between this and the world in which we live (see Chapter 6). This is prophetic leadership. Pope Francis writes in *Fratelli Tutti,* "Everything . . . depends on our ability to see the need for a change of heart, attitudes and lifestyles" (no. 166). What ultimately does this mean? In two rites of passage Jesus teaches by his personal example what "a change of

---

[140] Alexander Baunov, "Where Is Russia's Strongman in the Coronavirus Crisis?" *Foreign Affairs* (May 27, 2020).

[141] Ibid.

heart" involves: (1) letting go of what holds us back from union with God; and (2) the yearning to do the will of God.[142]

Jesus Christ's Initiation into Public Ministry

Jesus entered his public ministry as the greatest of all prophets by rite of passage with its threefold pattern.[143] The Spirit is his initiation guide. In the separation stage there are two steps (Mt 3:23–4:1): the first is Jesus moving alone away from familiar Galilee to the Jordan to be baptized; the second is his passage into the desert, as we read that "Jesus was led up by the Spirit into the wilderness to be tempted by the devil" (Mt 4:1). Each step removes him further from societas, that is, from his familiar surroundings and kinsfolk, and into liminality. Significantly, Jesus travels into the desert,[144] the sacred Israelite paradigm of marginality, trials, and the realistic encounter with human vulnerability and the power of God—in brief, into chaos.

Jesus fasts, dramatically symbolizing the letting go of his former identity and disposing him to receive a new one. Now Jesus is confronted by the devil as the "cultural monster" whose temptations become the catalyst for significant learning and self-growth. In response to each temptation Jesus expresses his solidarity (communitas) with Moses and with all the prophets who followed him down to John the Baptist. Jesus comes through the tests: "Absolute loyalty to God, solidarity with the prophets, an ability to see through the devil's tricks and recognizing and driving away evil are all essential characteristics

---

[142] See Gerald A. Arbuckle, *From Chaos to Mission: Refounding Religious Life Formation* (London: Geoffrey Chapman, 1995), 121–23.

[143] See Mark McVann, "One of the Prophets: Matthew's Testing Narrative as a Rite of Passage," *Biblical Theological Bulletin* 23, no. 1 (1993): 14–20. See also Jerome H. Neyrey, "Ritual of Status Transformation in Luke-Acts: The Case of Jesus the Prophet," in *The Social World of Luke-Acts: Models for Interpretation*, ed. Jerome H. Neyrey, 333–60 (Peabody, MA: Hendrickson, 1991).

[144] John L. McKenzie comments: "The cultural influence of the desert on the Bible cannot be overestimated. . . . The desert is a perpetual reminder of the reality of danger, hardship, and death. . . . Israel first met Yahweh in the desert, and the story of the desert wandering remains the type of encounter of man with God." *Dictionary of the Bible* (London: Geoffrey Chapman, 1996), 195.

of the authentic prophet. Matthew's audience sees that Jesus has full and flawless possession of these faculties."[145]

The reentry stage in Matthew 4 consists of two scenes. The first is the appearance of the "angels who came and waited on him" (4:11), representing "the virtually unmediated presence of God," symbolizing "God's certification of Jesus' status as prophet, just as the Voice from heaven at the baptism declares that Jesus is God's Son."[146] In the second scene (4:12–25) Jesus enthusiastically assumes his role as the Son of God and prophet; he proclaims his mission, as foretold by the prophet Isaiah, summons his first disciples, preaches, and heals the sick. He not only has divine approbation as a prophet, but the people now publicly endorse it: "From that time, Jesus began to proclaim: 'Repent, for the kingdom of heaven has come near.' . . . Immediately they left their nets and followed him. . . . And great crowds followed him" (Mt 4:17, 20, 25). He is the fully anointed prophet.

Jesus Christ's Initiation as Savior

Our conversion to Jesus Christ deepens when we relive his rite of passage as savior of the world:

> And being found in human form,
> he humbled himself
> and became obedient to the point of death. . . .
> Therefore God also highly exalted him. (Phil 2:7–8)

All followers of Christ desiring to lead in these tumultuous times must be reliving this mystery of Christ's initiation. As St. Paul writes, "We are afflicted . . . always carrying in the body the death of Jesus, so that the life of Jesus may also be made visible in our bodies. . . . So death is at work in us, but life in you" (2 Cor 4:8, 10, 12).

The evangelist Matthew describes Christ's second rite of passage. There are several steps in the rite's separation stage (Mt 26:1–35), each one marking a further movement of Jesus away from the predictable order (societas) he had established as a preacher of the kingdom: (1) the anointing in anticipation of his burial (vv. 6–13); (2) the drama

---

[145] McVann, "One of the Prophets," 18.

[146] Ibid., 19.

of the last supper (vv. 17–19, 26–29), where he described by word and action how leaders are to lead in a collaborative way; and (3) the distressing actual and anticipated loss of friends—Judas and Peter (vv. 14–16, 20–25, 30–35). One senses in the narrative an ever-deepening sadness in Jesus as he begins the pilgrimage of withdrawing from a world of loving crowds and supportive friends and from an exciting ministry of preaching and healing.

In the liminality stage (Mt 26:36–56) there are many scenes, each one a further experience for Jesus of heightening marginality. It begins with the trial of the agony in the garden. There Jesus wrestles with the fear of facing death; there is a harrowing inner struggle, for he does not want to die: "I am deeply grieved, even to death" (Mt 26:38). The language used to describe his distressed state is extraordinarily forceful, calling to mind Psalm 116:3:

> The snares of death encompassed me,
> the pangs of Sheol laid hold on me;
> I suffered distress and anguish.[147]

There is the yearning to revive the bonding or communitas relationship with his three closest disciples, but in this he fails: "He said to Peter, 'So, could you not stay awake with me one hour? Stay awake and pray that you may not come into the time of trial.' . . . Again he went away for the second time and prayed, 'My Father, if this cannot pass unless I drink it, your will be done.' Again, he came and found them sleeping" (Mt 26:40–43). As Oliver Davies observes, from the time at which "Jesus accepted baptism from John, it was clear that he would take upon himself the burden of human sin as alienation from God."[148]

St. Mark pointedly comments on the inability of the disciples to comfort Jesus: "and they did not know what to say to him" (Mk 14:40). They cannot offer compassion, simply because they themselves have not as yet become fully converted to the saving message of Christ. They did not know what to say to Jesus because they have not yet admitted to their own inner need for compassion. And so

---

[147] See Oliver Davies, *A Theology of Compassion* (Grand Rapids, MI: Eerdmans, 2001), 205.

[148] Ibid.

they avoid offering Jesus the gift of fellowship (communitas) that would have consoled him in his loneliness; by sleeping, the disciples avoid in a very human way the challenge to respond. They abandon Jesus, a "vulnerable God," personally alive to the enormity of the gap between his mission from the Father and the frailty inherent in his human nature when he is faced with the agony he is shortly to undergo.[149]

Having subordinated his will to the Father, Jesus lets go of the bonding relationship with the disciples. In its place he discovers a new communitas experience with the Father (Mt 26:36–46). As is customary in initiation rituals, Jesus is presented with sacred cultural symbols, but they represent opposing views of what is considered traditionally authentic. Jesus must make a choice: the horrific powers of the Sanhedrin and the civil authority represented by Pontius Pilate, or the role of the suffering servant as portrayed in the messianic psalms and prophecies (Mt 26:57–68; 27:1–31): "He was despised and rejected by others; a man of suffering and acquainted with infirmity" (Isa 53:3). Fundamentally, the option in the chaos is God or the world. Jesus passes the test, expresses his total loyalty to the Father, and continues his pilgrimage of initiation as Savior.

The crucifixion and death of Jesus and his burial end this liminal stage, in which Jesus experiences marginality to an intense degree (Mt 27:32–56): mocked, shamefully stripped of his clothes, crucified between two rogues, with a few remaining friends "looking on from a distance" (27:55). Yet in the midst of this darkness a humanly impossible light begins to break through. Jesus recites the lamentation Psalm 22, the first time he addresses the Father without the intimate "Abba." Though the psalm is a cry of dereliction, it also expresses its opposite, that is, hope in the saving power of God. In the chaos of his dying, Jesus is already being initiated into the new life of hope that comes from a God in whom he has total trust (Ps 22:1, 24, 27). As in

---

[149] See Gerald A. Arbuckle, *Laughing with God: Humor, Culture, and Transformation* (Collegeville, MN: Liturgical Press, 2008), 80; see also comments by David J. Stanley, SJ: "By inserting the story of Jesus' prayer as a coupling between the eucharistic words and his account of the arrest, Mark has succeeded in showing the dark side of the cup Jesus is to drink." David J. Stanley, *Jesus in Gethsemane: The Early Church Reflects on the Suffering of Jesus* (New York: Paulist Press, 1979), 119–54.

his trials in the desert at the beginning of his ministry, Jesus triumphs over evil, proving himself fit for the greatest of all actions longed for by all the prophets of old (Jn 15:13).

In the reentry stage (Mt 27:62–66; 28:1–20) Jesus joins his disciples, but as the resurrected one—the one who has vanquished death and is about to join his Father. Because he has become the resurrected Savior through an initiation ritual, Jesus now has the Father's authority to pass on the mission of preaching to others: "All authority in heaven and on earth has been given to me. Go, therefore and make disciples of all nations" (Mt 28:18–19).

Summary

- The manner in which nations react to the pandemic is influenced by their political leaders and their national mythologies. Political leaders, as ritual guides, emphasizing the democratic value of solidarity, not individualism, are more likely to lead their countries successfully through the tough tripartite rite of passage of the pandemic.[150]
- People who are freed from the normal cultural constraints in the liminal stage collectively claim their authority to protest social abuses, for example, in the protests of the Black Lives Matter movement.
- When the pandemic struck, governments had three options: (1) to emphasize economic welfare, with a minimum of lockdown and self-isolating policies, assuming economic neoliberal policies are more important than the protection of lives, as in the United States, Brazil, and Britain; (2) to protect lives through lockdown and self-isolating policies, as in the egalitarian welfare states of Australia and New Zealand; or (3) to adopt whatever policies are necessary, including public healthcare services, to maintain autocratic centralized control, as in China and Russia. The first option prioritizes the rights of individuals; the second, the needs of their communities, including the well-being of the most vulnerable; and the third, the protection of the political elite.

[150] See Collier and Kay, *Greed Is Dead*, 91–156.

- In the United States the high infection and death rate is due to the failures of public health facilities, the poverty of federal political leadership, and the national mythology of individualism. Since New Zealand and Australia have national community-oriented mythologies that respect the value of solidarity, their political leaders successfully reacted to the pandemic by emphasizing the health and welfare of the citizens.
- The world desperately needs leaders who are willing and able to articulate and implement the values of the Good Samaritan parable. These prophetic leaders in the crisis relive Christ's rites of passage into public ministry and as Savior.

Reflection Questions

1. What points in this chapter particularly draw your attention? Why?
2. This statement is made in this chapter: "Democracy is experiencing its worst crisis since the tragic explosion of nationalism in the 1930s, and the dangers are rapidly becoming evident." Do you agree or disagree? Why?
3. In a General Audience on August 12, 2020, Pope Francis said: "The coronavirus is not the only disease to be fought, but rather, the pandemic has shed light on broader social ills." What are these broader social ills? Can you help to ameliorate them?

4

The Enduring Impact of Poverty

This pandemic arrived suddenly and caught us unprepared, sparking a powerful sense of bewilderment and helplessness. This has made us all the more aware of the presence of the poor in our midst and their need for help.

—Pope Francis, Homily, June 13, 2020

The measure of a society is the quality of life at the bottom of the pyramid, not the top. The willful indifference to the distribution of prosperity over the last half century is an important reason that the very survival of liberal democracy is now being tested by nationalist demagogues, as it was in the 1930s.

—Binyamin Appelbaum, *The Economist's Hour*

The ideas of economists and political philosophers, both when they are right and when they are wrong, are more powerful than is commonly understood. Indeed, the world is ruled by little else.

—John Maynard Keynes,
The General Theory of Employment, Interest, and Money

This chapter explains that:

- Poverty can be measured quantitatively and particularly qualitatively.
- Poverty is the deprivation of the societal structures and personal prospects to live according to God's design.
- The pandemic has increased the gap between the rich and the poor.
- The scriptures call for healing not only of COVID-19 but also of the "virus" of social injustices, inequality of opportunities, and marginalization.

Due to the lack of resources to prepare and protect against the coronavirus and/or the unwillingness of governments to act appropriately, people who are poor face a higher risk of contracting and subsequently spreading COVID-19. Moreover, not only has the pandemic reinforced existing poverty, it has thrust millions more into its grip. This chapter aims to highlight the impact of the pandemic on poverty levels and the necessity to define poverty not only statistically but especially in terms of its human costs.[1]

Economically poor countries face difficult choices in dealing with the pandemic. The loss of whatever little income people have can mean mass starvation for millions of people. Once a country experiences a rapid outbreak of the disease, its government can only respond with one of two disastrous choices for people who are poor. Permitting the pandemic to remain unchecked could mean a very large proportion of the population will become sick and many, particularly the poor, will die. But the indirect consequences resulting from the alternative—the containment actions of locking down public life—can also lead to widespread suffering from higher unemployment, lower production, and increasing rates of poverty, and higher mortality as a consequence of poverty.

Sadly, the fact is that people in poverty are rarely able to expect governments to support them. In sub-Saharan Africa, for example, an individual at the lowest income level has only a 4 percent chance

---

[1] This chapter is an updating and expansion of "Poverty as a Trigger of Loneliness," chapter 4 in Gerald A. Arbuckle, *Loneliness: Insights for Healing in a Fragmented World,* 89–115 (Maryknoll, NY: Orbis Books, 2017).

of obtaining governmental aid in normal times. The pandemic could cast 490 million people in seventy countries into extreme poverty with catastrophic consequences,[2] reversing almost a decade of advances.[3] Stateless people and refugees are especially vulnerable.[4] Hunger has devastating long-term physical and mental consequences for children. The pandemic is causing "the greatest education emergency of our lifetime, with 1.7 billion children—more than 90 percent of the global total—having been out of school. . . . In poor countries they may never go back."[5] Lockdowns threaten to stop normal vaccination services. For example, a breakdown in anti-tuberculosis vaccinations alone in Africa could lead to 1.4 million deaths in the next five years; a similar situation would result from disruptions of treatments for malaria and AIDS.[6]

Defining Poverty

Poverty as a concept is an observable global and local reality, but how to define it is widely contested by academics, policymakers,

[2] Maddison Moore reports: "Many food-insecure nations are facing multiple, unprecedented threats to their food access such as war, natural disasters, and locust plagues impeding access to food sources. Since late 2019, a Desert Locusts plague has been increasing pre-existing food insecurity for over 20 million people in East-Africa and 15 million in Yemen." "Food Insecurity, Health and Privilege and COVID-19," *Eureka Street* (September 1, 2020).

[3] See "The Pandemic Is Plunging Millions Back into Extreme Poverty," *The Economist* (September 26, 2020).

[4] See Laura van Waas and Ottoline Spearman, "The Life-or-Death Cost of Being Stateless in a Global Pandemic," Kaldor Centre for International Refugee Law, UNSW Sydney (July 9, 2020).

[5] Erik Berglof et al., "A COVID-19 Response for the World's Poor," *Project Syndicate* (June 3, 2020). It is estimated that young people "between the ages of five and nineteen constitute a bigger share of the population in poor countries than in rich ones (26% versus 17%) and therefore a more significant share of the future workforce. The hiatus in their schooling is also more likely to become permanent." "In Emerging Markets, Short-term Panic Gives Way to Long-term Worry," *The Economist* (August 1, 2020), 53.

[6] "After Lockdowns: The Cure and the Disease," *The Economist* (May 23, 2020), 8.

and politicians.[7] However, a definition is imperative because how a problem is articulated and then explained strongly affects what is actually done about it. Faulty measurements of poverty, and defective attitudes toward it, consistently result in harmful policies and practices that intensify the sufferings of people. Frequently poverty is measured only in quantifiable terms, such as low income, inadequate housing, sickness, or low levels of educational achievement. This gives an inadequate picture of the reality.

Qualitative analysis is also essential[8] because poverty includes immaterial realities, such as the loss of dignity, spiritual deprivation, being subjected to violence, lack of power, and an inability to protest injustices. Nobel Prize–winner economist Amartya Sen distinguishes *functionings, capabilities,* and *commodities.* What is important is not income or similar benchmarks but the kind of life that people are able to lead (functionings) and the choices and opportunities available to people in leading their lives (capabilities). Money, says Sen, is just a means to an end, and the goods and services (commodities) it procures are merely particular ways of achieving functionings.[9] Thus, poverty should be defined in terms of failures to attain minimally acceptable capabilities. In this chapter, therefore, we view poverty not only from a quantitative perspective but especially from a qualitative angle. As will be seen, qualitative poverty has many interconnected expressions, including but not limited to opportunity deprivation, stigma and discrimination, violence, loneliness, old age, and ecological crisis.

Poverty as Quantifiable

The International Monetary Fund's global economic outlook catalogues a high-speed economic train crash that will see unemployment, debt, and bankruptcies soar more precipitously than ever before as a consequence of the pandemic and its aftermath.[10] In the most

---

[7] See Pete Alcock, *Understanding Poverty*, 3rd ed. (Basingstoke: Palgrave, 2006), 4.

[8] Ibid., 98–101.

[9] See Amartya Sen, *Development as Freedom* (Oxford: Oxford University Press, 1999). See also Pope Francis, *Fratelli Tutti* (October 3, 2020), nos. 21, 162, 187.

[10] See *New York Times,* "I.M.F. Predicts Worst Downturn since the Great Depression" (April 14, 2020).

optimistic scenario the global economy will shrink thirty times more than it did during the global financial crisis of 2008. Absolute and relative poverty rates are rising dramatically especially in the developing world, and many poorer countries will find it extremely difficult to roll over the debts due this year on affordable terms, if at all. Consider the impact of the pandemic on the economy of Bangladesh. From the 1980s until the financial crisis of 2008, economic integration had globally intensified to a historically unparalleled level. The dismantling of international trade barriers encouraged Bangladesh to export its most tradable product—readymade garments—to richer countries. But since 2008, for a variety of reasons,[11] including the resurgence of nationalism in the United States and European countries, trade barriers began once more to rise.[12] Markets for readymade garments started to decline, and the pandemic has hastened this decline with increasing rapidity. At the same time, many thousands of migrant workers from Bangladesh laboring in the Middle East and North Africa have become unemployed, thus reducing the remittances normally sent back to their families for their survival.[13]

It is helpful here to delineate two types of poverty: absolute and relative. *Absolute poverty* is defined by a set income measure below which people experience complete destitution and cannot meet even minimum needs for food and shelter. The United Nations Development Programme has set this measure at US$1 per day for people living in third- and fourth-world countries. Below that income threshold people experience severe malnutrition and perilous levels of ill health.

---

[11] The pandemic has caused a massive rise in unemployment, but there is no certainty that jobs will be available when economies improve due to the growing use of automation. Economist Daniel Susskind writes: "Machines don't fall ill, they don't need to isolate to protect peers, they don't need to take time off work." Cited in Alana Semuels, "Millions of Americans Have Lost Jobs in the Pandemic," *Time* (August 6, 2020); see also Martin Sandbu, *The Economics of Belonging* (Princeton, NJ: Princeton University Press, 2020), 17–18, 56–62, 68–70.

[12] The term *slowbalization* was invented to describe the reduction of international trade, investments, loans, and supply chains; see Douglas A. Irwin, "The Pandemic Adds Momentum to the Deglobalization Trend," Peterson Institution for International Economics (April 23, 2020).

[13] See Tapash Candra Paul, "COVID-19 and Its Impact on Bangladesh Economy," *The Financial Express* (June 19, 2020).

Relative poverty, on the other hand, is more helpful in assessing material and income levels and their impact on people's lives. Relative poverty refers to "the lack of resources needed to obtain the kinds of diet, participate in the activities and have the living conditions and amenities that are widely approved and generally obtained by most people in a particular society."[14] Resources are so below others in society that sufferers are effectively excluded from ordinary, socially considered essential, living arrangements and activities.

In the United States five years before the pandemic it was estimated that 18.4 million people lived in *absolute* poverty according to the standard set by that country.[15] In the United States single people making less than US$11,770 a year and families of four making less than US$24,250 a year were judged to be below the poverty line. Poverty does not strike ethnic groups equally. A survey by the Census Bureau in late June 2020 concluded that since the pandemic had begun, the share of Americans who "sometimes" or "often" do not have enough to eat has grown by two percentage points, representing four million households. A shocking 20 percent of African American households with children at this point are in this position.[16]

In 2018, 25.4 percent of Native Americans were living below the poverty line; 20.8 percent of African Americans; 17.6 percent of Hispanics; 8.1 percent of white people, and 10.1 percent of Asian people.[17] In 2016 it was estimated that there were over a half million people in the United States classified as homeless.[18] Homeless people have no place to self-isolate in an epidemic other than the streets.

In 2015 there were an estimated 43 million Americans in *relative* poverty.[19] Four of ten adults would not have the resources available to cover an unplanned US$400 expense.[20] Since the start of the pandemic,

---

[14] John Pierson, *Tackling Social Exclusion* (London: Routledge, 2002), 9.

[15] See "Poverty Facts" at www.worldhunger.org.

[16] See "America's Huge Stimulus Is Having Surprising Effects on the Poor," *The Economist* (July 6, 2020).

[17] See "The Population of Poverty USA," povertyusa.org.

[18] See Statista Research Department, "Estimated Number of Homeless People in the U.S. 2007–2020," March 23, 2021.

[19] See Robert Joyce and James P. Ziliak, "Relative Poverty in Great Britain and the United States, 1979–2017," *Fiscal Studies* 40, no. 4: 485–518.

[20] See Patricia Cohen, "Broad Shutdown Pushes Americans to Economic Edge," *Times Digest* (April 17, 2020), 1.

however, both absolute and relative poverty have dramatically escalated following the abrupt uptick in unemployment, which is projected to rise as high as 20 percent, a rate not seen since the Great Depression.[21] By mid-April 2020, within a three week period 22 million people in the United States had registered for unemployment benefits.[22] Even middle-class Americans, once secure, fear what the future may bring.

Many Americans who were already on the margins before the pandemic have now been thrust over the edge. African Americans and Hispanics are becoming sick and dying at disproportionate rates. A forty-year-old Hispanic American is twelve times more likely to die from the pandemic than a white American of the same age.[23] Decades of racism have left many minority Americans with crowded housing, poor health, and little savings, making it more challenging to survive the pandemic. Before the pandemic hit America, the country was in the throes of a massive health crisis: "In 2015 life expectancy began falling for the first time since . . . 1993. The causes—mainly suicides, alcohol-related deaths, and drug overdoses—claim roughly 190,000 lives each year."[24] The cavernous divides in American society are widening in pandemic times; the impact of COVID-19 has not fallen evenly. In April 2020, in New York City, data showed that black and Hispanic residents were twice as likely to die of coronavirus as white city dwellers. As noted in Chapter 3, they were less likely to have health insurance and thus may have avoided seeking testing and treatment. Those living on low incomes have incidences of illness and poor health at much higher rates than people on high incomes. An "expensive and inefficient medical system" reinforces the degree of poverty of Americans; those "in the bottom fourth of the income

---

[21] See Jamelle Bouie, "The Racial Character of Inequality," *New York Times Digest* (April 19, 2020), 8; "Unequal Protection: American Inequality Meets COVID-19," *The Economist* (April 18, 2020).

[22] "Workers who are younger, poorer or lack a university education have disproportionately lost their source of income. For some, that has also meant losing their employer-sponsored health insurance in the middle of the epidemic." "Unequal Protection: American Inequality Meets COVID-19," *The Economist* (April 18, 2020).

[23] See "The Plague Year," *The Economist* (December 19, 2020), 15.

[24] Helen Epstein, "Left Behind," *New York Review of Books* 67, no. 5 (2020): 28. See Anne Case and Angus Deaton, *Deaths of Despair and the Future of Capitalism* (Princeton, NJ: Princeton University Press, 2019).

distribution die about 13 years younger on average than those in the top fourth."[25]

Poverty as Opportunity Deprivation

People can become so imprisoned by their low income that it is extremely difficult, if not impossible, for many to break through its crushing circumstances. We speak of a cycle of poverty, simply because the factors referred to are interconnected and self-perpetuating. The vicious cycle in which poverty breeds poverty occurs through time and transmits its effects from one generation to another. There is no beginning to the cycle and no conclusion. Being financially poor leads to poor diet, inadequate housing, limited access to health and educational facilities, unemployment and underemployment because of lack of qualifications, and reduced energy levels.

Since this crippling cycle of poverty prevents or obstructs people from participating as full members of society, poverty can be defined as "deprivation of opportunities" or simply "capability deprivation."[26] All have the right to work; to participate in society; and to grow intellectually, emotionally, and spiritually. All people have responsibility for one another's well-being; all should have opportunities to meet their responsibilities and to contribute to society.[27] But unjust structures in society can render these rights and responsibilities impossible for groups in society to achieve. People trapped in the circle of poverty have a restricted range of choices available to them. To be poor is "to be denied the chance to enjoy the consumption of goods, or the ability to achieve and maintain good health, or to participate in social activities or other aspects of community life."[28] Moreover, to be forced to live in segregated areas—common in American cities—which are beset with poverty and violence for generations, is to encounter continuous loss

---

[25] David Leonardt, "A Vulnerable Nation," *New York Times Digest* (April 19, 2020), 8.

[26] See Sen, *Development as Freedom,* 87–110.

[27] See Mary Jo Bane, "A Catholic Policy Analyst Looks at Poverty," in *Lifting Up the Poor: A Dialogue on Religion, Poverty, and Welfare Reform,* ed. Mary Jo Bane and Lawrence M. Mead (Washington, DC: Brookings Institution, 2003), 22–23.

[28] Peter Saunders, *The Ends and Means of Welfare* (Cambridge: Cambridge University Press, 2002), 143.

of opportunity. It destroys democratic solidarity by forming distinct domains of race and class—one for "them" and one for "us."[29]

Lack of equality of educational opportunity is a significant contributor to the rigidity of poverty. In the United States "virtually the entire increase in mortality has been among white adults without bachelor's degrees—some 70 percent of all whites."[30] The McKinsey Global Institute commented in 2020 that "Today the pandemic has put the educational divide in stark relief. Workers without bachelor's degrees are twice as likely to hold jobs we classify as vulnerable. They amount to 58 percent of the US workforce but 82 percent of all vulnerable jobs."[31] Educational needs in socioeconomically depressed areas require significant input of finance and specialized staff, but in fact, they get less than the demand needed in terms of buildings, facilities, equipment, and teachers, particularly those relating to special needs. Moreover, people with inadequate or no housing of their own find it extremely difficult, if not impossible, to obtain ordinary services such as a bank account or credit card, or to develop a regular relationship with local schools and medical services. In summary, therefore, as Pope Francis writes in *Fratelli Tutti,* "poverty must always be understood and gauged in the context of the actual opportunities available in each concrete historical period" (FT, no. 21).

Unemployment Due to COVID-19

There has been a massive rise in global unemployment rates since the pandemic. In response most governments in developed countries introduced systems of financial relief; many people may never find work again and will have to depend on government support for years to come. The human costs are far-reaching. Unemployment, especially when prolonged, has debilitating consequences for individual freedom, initiative, and skills. It results in losses of self-reliance, self-confidence, and psychological and physical well-being.[32] Recently

---

[29] See "African Americans: Slow Progress," *The Economist* (June 6, 2020), 28.

[30] Epstein, "Left Behind," 28.

[31] McKinsey Global Institute, "COVID-19 and Jobs: Monitoring the US Impact on People and Places" (April 29, 2020).

[32] See Sen, *Development as Freedom,* 13–34.

a United Nations report warned that the pandemic could weaken decades of gender equality advancement.[33] Another report published in July 2020 concluded: "While most people's lives and work have been negatively affected by the crisis . . . analysis shows that, overall, women's jobs and livelihoods are more vulnerable to the COVID-19 pandemic. The magnitude of the inequality is striking. Using data from the United States and India . . . we estimate that female job loss rates due to COVID-19 are . . . at 5.7 percent versus 3.1 percent respectively."[34] In Australia women are becoming unemployed faster than men, and "greater numbers of women—who make up the vast majority of casual and part-time workers—are also seeing their working hours drastically reduced."[35]

Mental Stress of Poverty

COVID-19 has focused attention on mental health—a previously neglected problem. The pandemic "presents nearly all the risk factors for PTSD.[36] COVID-19 has caused sudden death, life-changing events, large-scale social ruptures and chronic stressors like uncertainty and the added hassles of daily life." The most fortunate will have one or two of these results, but "more than at any other point in recent history, millions of people have been slammed by all of them."[37] In Britain an August 2020 survey shows that 29 percent fulfill the criteria for a general psychiatric disorder; in Spain, where almost one-sixth of all COVID-19 infections are of health workers, more than half are showing signs of PTSD.[38] In March 2020 more

---

[33] See Jess Hill, "The Gendered Pandemic," *Monthly* [Sydney] (July 2020), 12.

[34] Anu Madgavkar et al., "COVID-19 and Gender Equality: Countering the Regressive Effects," McKinsey and Company (July 15, 2020).

[35] Hill, "The Gendered Pandemic," 12.

[36] Post-traumatic stress disorder (PTSD) is a mental disorder caused by experiencing or witnessing a terrifying event, a condition that may last for months or years. Triggers can revive memories of the trauma, leading to intense emotional and physical reactions.

[37] "The Common Tragedy: Worldwide COVID-19 Is Causing a New Form of Collective Trauma," *The Economist* (August 29, 2020), 43.

[38] Ibid.

than one-third of Americans (36 percent) reported that the pandemic was seriously affecting their mental health; most (59 percent) felt that COVID-19 was having a serious impact on their daily lives, such as their finances.[39] In Australia it is expected that suicides could rise by 50 percent annually due to the pandemic's impact on mental health; people feel overwhelmed by sudden unemployment, loss of homes, and loneliness caused by required isolation.[40]

Frontline healthcare workers and chaplains face an added challenge—moral distress. Ethicist Andrew Jameton writes: "Moral distress arises when one knows the right thing to do, but institutional constraints make it nearly impossible to pursue the right course of action."[41] This has repercussions at three levels: moral, psychological and spiritual. "In the context of COVID-19 a severe moral stressor would be, for example, a healthcare worker having to, due to lack of resources, deny treatment to a patient they know will die without that treatment. This may give rise to reactions like anger and guilt, which if left unresolved may lead to moral injury."[42]

The Stigma and Discrimination of Poverty

Unless poverty is viewed from structural and cultural perspectives, people may be blamed for causing their own poverty and social

[39] See "New Poll: COVID-19 Impacting Mental Well-Being," *American Psychiatric Association* (March 25, 2020).

[40] See John Kehoe, "COVID-19 Lockdown Fuels Mental Health Crisis," *Financial Review* (August 5, 2020); "Will the Economic and Psychological Costs of COVID-19 Increase Suicides? The Signs Are Ominous," *The Economist* (October 5, 2020).

[41] Andrew Jameton, *Nursing Practice: The Ethical Issues* (Englewood Cliffs, NJ: Prentice-Hall, 1984), 6.

[42] Phoenix Australia–Centre for Posttraumatic Mental Health and the Canadian Centre of Excellence on PTSD, *Moral Stress amongst Healthcare Workers during COVID-19: A Guide to Moral Injury* (July 27, 2020), 4. See also N. Kenny et al., "A Catholic Perspective: Triage Principles and Moral Distress in Pandemic Scarcity," Canadian Federation of Catholic Physicians and Societies (July 9, 2020); Kate Jackson-Meyer, "Moral Distress in Health Care Professionals," *Health Progress: Journal of the Catholic Health Association of the United States* 101, no. 3 (2020): 23–29.

exclusion (see Axiom 7, Chapter 1). Statements like "the poor can themselves get out of poverty, if they truly want to" are dangerously simplistic and do nothing to clarify our understanding of the complexity of poverty and its ability to crush initiative and self-respect. In the United States people who are poor, especially if they are single mothers, African Americans, or Hispanics, are frequently blamed for being poor by members of the dominant culture. When cultures are under the pressure of change, such as the impact of the pandemic, this stigmatizing process intensifies. An investigation into the effects of systemic poverty in the United States reported in 2018:

> For one of the world's wealthiest countries to have 40 million people living in poverty and over five million living in "Third World" conditions is cruel and inhuman. . . . Shaming those who need assistance, and devising ever more obstacles to prevent people from getting needed benefits, is not a strategy to reduce or eliminate poverty. . . . Contempt for the poor has intensified under the Trump administration.[43]

The impact on victims from being blamed, stigmatized, and marginalized can be horrific and long-lasting. They feel shamed and think others consider them of no importance, having nothing to contribute to society, worthless, having no credibility. A sense of hopelessness can grip them as their self-worth and self-respect disintegrate. We need to ponder and become keenly aware of what happens to human dignity once hope becomes forgotten and the spirit of people is enslaved. The psalmist describes the inner anguish of people who have been stigmatized and socially marginalized:

> You have caused my companions to shun me;
> you have made me a thing of horror to them.
> I am shut in so that I cannot escape. (Ps 88:8)

Human dignity cannot be subjected to endless indignities and remain intact. In the United States a recent study by Carol Graham concludes:

---

[43] Philip Alston, Special Rapporteur on Extreme Poverty and Human Rights, "Contempt for the Poor in US Drives Cruel Policies," United Nations Office of High Commissioner (June 4, 2018).

> Empirical findings . . . confirm the increasingly consistent story of "two Americas" with the poor much less likely to be optimistic about their futures than the rich. . . . Lack of hope and faith in the future may seem intangible and far from the realm of policy, but is reflected in real-world outcomes. . . . The recent increase in mortality rates for middle-aged, uneducated whites is a stark marker of this ill-being and lack of hope.[44]

Economist Gene Sperling writes that "whites with low levels of education—a group that has suffered from deaths of despair at high rates— . . . report a lack of hope and optimism, and low satisfaction in life. . . . African American men have for generations, and still do have, lower life expectancy than white men. By 2014, midlife mortality was rising across all racial groups, again largely caused by deaths of despair." Sperling asserts that "shorter lives due to worse-quality health care, exposure to gun violence, and intergenerational poverty, or factors that stem from structural race-related inequities, are every bit as worthy of the label of deaths of despair."[45]

Poverty as Patriarchal Domination

Pope Francis writes:

> Doubly poor are those women who endure situations of exclusion, mistreatment and violence, since they are frequently less able to defend their rights. (FT, no. 23)

Institutional patriarchy is the social system in which men hold the primary power and predominate in roles of political leadership, moral authority, and social privilege. Varda Burstyn, in her study of male violence, speaks of the mythology of "coercive power" expressed in phrases such as "might equals right," "survival of the fittest," "rugged individualism," and "winners take all." Men are encouraged to accept

---

[44] Carol Graham, *Happiness for All? Unequal Hopes and Lives in Pursuit of the American Dream* (Princeton, NJ: Princeton University Press, 2017), 118, 147.

[45] Gene Sperling, *Economic Dignity* (New York: Penguin Press, 2020), 60–61.

"coercive entitlement," that is, since men are stronger than women, might is on their side and women must submit to this even if it means being subjected to violence.[46] It is common, for example, for men to be portrayed in movies and television as dominating women even in violent ways: "the woman who is beaten or raped may be seen as somehow deserving it."[47]

Sociologists Colin Samson and Carlos Gigoux, in their study of the impact of colonialism on indigenous peoples, conclude that dispossession from land had a foremost impact on gender relations:

> Even though the indigenous societies frequently did not permit male-only leadership, the subsequent land cession negotiations [with colonial powers] introduced and then embedded male authority in conformity with European patriarchal norms. . . . Colonial institutions of tribal governments in vastly reduced areas of land caused many men and women to seek consolation in alcohol and drugs. Their use caused rifts in families and marriages, precipitating domestic violence and child neglect, in which women almost always became victims.[48]

Poverty as Violence

Violence is rather slippery to define. It is not about damaging or destroying *things*; it is about abusing *people.* Violence can crush the spirit of people and make them submissive to violators for their purposes. It is not confined to killing or physical violence but also the creation of cultural conditions that materially or psychologically destroy or diminish people's dignity, rightful happiness, and capacity to fulfill basic material needs. During the COVID-19 pandemic many governments reported an increase in domestic and intimate-partner violence. Almost one in ten Australian women in a relationship experienced domestic violence during the coronavirus

---

[46] See Varda Burstyn, *The Rites of Men: Manhood, Politics, and the Culture of Sport* (Toronto: University of Toronto Press, 1999), 162.

[47] Daniel J. Sonkin and Michael Durphy, *Learning to Live without Violence* (Los Angeles: Volcano, 1982), 15.

[48] Colin Samson and Carlos Gigoux, *Indigenous Peoples and Colonialism: Global Perspectives* (Cambridge: Polity Press, 2017), 98, 100.

crisis, with two-thirds reporting the attacks started or became worse during the pandemic.[49] The World Health Organization reported that across European countries, interpersonal physical violence significantly increased due to the pandemic: "With job losses, rising alcohol-based harm and drug use, stress and fear, the legacy of this pandemic could haunt us for years."[50]

Governments confronted with the COVID-19 crisis had to choose either to protect lives through shutdown and self-isolating policies or to emphasize economic welfare. In those countries where governments favored the latter option (see Chapter 3),[51] people in poverty must solve their own problems. They live in fear of sudden and expensive illnesses and feel devalued as persons because they are classed as beggars dependent on the good will and charity of hospitals. They are victims of *structural* or *institutional* violence from political, economic, and social institutions that coerce them into remaining poor.[52] In addition they may be suffering the injustices of institutional racism (see Chapter 5). Where neoliberalist policies prevail, few question this violence. It is taken for granted.

Poverty as Loneliness

Loneliness is an unavoidable and distressing fact of human experience.[53] St. Teresa of Calcutta believed that loneliness, often accompanied by despair and hopelessness, is the most virulent affliction

---

[49] See Anthony Galloway, "Domestic Violence on the Rise during Pandemic," *Sydney Morning Herald,* July 13, 2020.

[50] Hans Kluge, WHO Europe, quoted in "Covid-19: EU States Report 60% Rise in Emergency Calls about Domestic Violence," *British Medical Journal* (May 11, 2020).

[51] See Robert Bellah et al., *Habits of the Heart: Individualism and Commitment in American Life* (San Francisco: Harper and Row, 1985), 275–96.

[52] See Gerald A. Arbuckle, *Healthcare Ministry: Refounding the Mission in Tumultuous Times* (Collegeville, MN: Liturgical Press, 2000), 65–66.

[53] See Arbuckle, *Loneliness*; Gerald A. Arbuckle, "Loneliness: A Global Epidemic," *Health Progress: Journal of the Catholic Health Association of the United States* 99, no. 4 (July–August 2018): 15–19; Bei Wu, "Social Isolation and Loneliness among Older Adults in the Context of COVID-19: A Global Challenge," *Global Health Research and Policy* 5, no. 27 (2020).

in the West.[54] Before the coronavirus pandemic, loneliness had been identified as the next global health epidemic of the twenty-first century. Loneliness is the feeling of being disconnected, excluded, and disengaged from others, an agonizing feeling of emptiness or desolation, a feeling that no one cares. It is a sense of distress people experience when their relations are not the way they would wish. When people struggle to describe loneliness, there is the common theme of a yearning to belong, a thirsting to be connected, a restlessness, a "panting"—to use St. Augustine's expression[55]—at last to belong, to make a satisfying relationship, to feel valued, to feel there is a pervading meaning in one's life if only it could be found. Yearning or thirsting for a relationship is frequently and poignantly expressed by the psalmist:

> As a deer yearns for flowing streams,
> so my soul yearns for you, O God. (Ps 42:1)

and

> My soul longs, indeed it faints
> for the courts of the LORD;
> my heart and my flesh sing for joy
> to the living God. (Ps 84:2)

Multidisciplinary investigation concludes that loneliness is "a serious risk factor for illness and early death, right alongside smoking, obesity and lack of exercise."[56] It has been estimated that living with air pollution increases one's possibility of dying early by 5 percent, being obese by 20 percent, misuse of alcohol by 30 percent, but

---

[54] See Mother Teresa of Calcutta, *A Simple Path* (New York: Random House, 1995), 83.

[55] St. Augustine, *Confessions*, Bk. 10, Ch. 27, v. 38.

[56] John T. Cacioppo and William Patrick, *Loneliness: Human Nature and the Need for Social Connection* (New York: W. W. Norton, 2008), 108. See also Noreena Hertz, *The Lonely Century: How to Restore Human Connection in a World That's Pulling Apart* (New York: Currency, 2021), 3–35. Hertz (of University College London) explains how COVID-19 has made it more difficult to make and maintain friendships at work, particularly for new employees, and notes that the consequent loneliness increases health risks.

the impact of loneliness by 45 percent.[57] Researchers conclude that "loneliness not only alters behavior, but shows up in measurements of stress hormones, immune function, and cardiovascular function. Over time, these changes in physiology are compounded in ways that may be hastening millions of people to an early grave."[58] Peter Shmigel comments on an Australian national survey of loneliness: "Loneliness wears down your resilience to crisis. . . . When you are lonely . . . your resilience drops . . . [the] risk of suicide increases."[59]

In early 2020, the COVID-19 pandemic intensified widespread isolation and loneliness beyond what had been imagined before the pandemic struck.[60] Because of the impact of the pandemic, this disease is fast becoming even more entrenched in all parts of the world; more and more people, young and old, are being gripped by loneliness, fear, and desperation.[61] Communities are further fragmenting. Once comforting personal and cultural identities are disintegrating as people lose their connectedness with each other and with their past. Loneliness exists where it did not before. Pope Francis writes: "We are more alone than ever in an increasingly massified world that promotes individual interests and weakens the communitarian dimension of life" (FT, no. 12). One of the unintended consequences of the safety guidelines of COVID-19 to self-isolate is a dramatic rise in loneliness among older adults. Family members and friends stop or curtail visiting in order to avoid exposing older people to the virus. During the pandemic the Vatican office for Laity, Family, and Life urged young people to keep in contact with the elderly trapped alone amid lockdown restrictions, urging "young people to seek out elderly people in their own neighborhoods and parishes and to 'send them a hug, according to the request of the Pope, by means of a phone call, a video call or by sending an image.'"[62]

---

[57] See Julianne Holt-Lunstad et al., "Loneliness and Social Isolation as Risk Factors for Mortality: A Meta-Analytic Review," *Perspectives on Psychological Science* 10, no. 2 (2015): 227–37.

[58] Cacioppo and Patrick, *Loneliness*, 108.

[59] Calla Wahlquist, "Lifeline Survey," *Guardian* (September 27, 2016).

[60] See Marcia G. Ory and Matthew Lee Smith, "Social Isolation: The COVID-19 Pandemic Health Risk," *The Conversation* (July 6, 2020).

[61] For an similar insight in 2013, cf. Pope Francis, *Evangelii Gaudium,* no. 52.

[62] Elise Ann Allen, "Vatican Launches Campaign for Lonely Elderly amid COVID-19," *Crux,* July 27, 2020.

Poverty as Old Age

Western Societies

> Let us admit that, for all the progress we have made, we are still "illiterate" when it comes to accompanying, caring for and supporting the most frail and vulnerable members of our developed societies. (FT, no. 64)

COVID-19 has spectacularly shown the urgent need to reform the care provided for the elderly in nursing homes. In the Western world almost half of all deaths from COVID-19 have occurred in nursing homes, even though less than 1 percent of people live in them. In the United Kingdom the disease has killed about 5 percent of all people living in care homes; in Canada 80 percent of all deaths from COVID-19 have happened in such homes.[63] In the United States more than 40 percent of the deaths from the disease have been residents or employees of nursing homes; many deaths could have been prevented because "well into the crisis, authorities kept these facilities strapped for masks, tests, and other desperately needed equipment . . . [and these homes] were already struggling with infection control before the pandemic hit."[64]

Certainly, the pandemic has revealed often grave weaknesses in the financing and staffing of care homes. Government funding is small—for example, in Canada, 1.3 percent of GDP, in Britain and the United States "a frugal monopsony payer (local authorities and Medicaid) typically reimburse less than the cost of residential care."[65] In addition to uncovering weak business models, the pandemic has stressed the conflict between ensuring that the elderly are kept safe and keeping them contented. Governments must urgently review methods of caring for the elderly, for example, by encouraging improved care in their own homes.

However, the pandemic is also challenging Western societies to review their attitudes toward aging in general. *Ageism* is the term that

---

[63] See "Care Homes: No Place Like Home," *The Economist* (July 25, 2020), 44–46.

[64] Olga Khazan, "The US Is Repeating Its Deadliest Pandemic Mistake," *Atlantic* (July 6, 2020).

[65] "Care Homes," 45.

describes the adverse stereotyping of and/or discrimination against people by reason of their age.[66] In the Western world the values of youthfulness are overemphasized, and the advertising world fosters negative stereotypes of senior citizens such as an inability to learn new skills, poor health, and overdependence on others.[67] The assumption is that they behave according to these images; as a result they commonly suffer work discrimination.[68] The stereotypes allow "the young generations to see older people as different from themselves, thus they subtly cease to identify with their elders as human beings."[69] The elderly may lose adult titles like Miss, Mrs., or Mr. and be treated like children, summoned by their Christian names "or given diminutive titles like 'dear' or 'love.'"[70] The reality is that most older people remain active, enjoying their independence, and often provide voluntary and compassionate assistance within families, such as childcare, or continue paid employment, if possible (many countries insist on compulsory retirement at sixty-five and/or employers discriminate against older people).[71]

At the same time, however, it is rarely appreciated that older people in Western societies, who tend to live longer than people in traditional cultures, experience multiple losses, for example, retirement from work and the social interaction that it involved; the loss of spouses and friends; increasing isolation as family members marry and geographically move elsewhere; loss of income; loss of

---

[66] See Gerald A. Arbuckle, *The Francis Factor and the People of God: New Life for the Church* (Maryknoll, NY: Orbis Books, 2013), 34–52.

[67] See Christina Victor, *The Social Context of Ageing* (London: Routledge, 2005).

[68] "60% of older people [aged 65 and over] in the UK agree that age discrimination exists in the daily lives of older people [and] 53% of adults agree that once you reach very old age, people tend to treat you as a child." "Later Life in the United Kingdom," Age UK factsheet (April 2017). In 1981 John Paul II wrote of the social exclusion of elderly people. *On the Role of the Christian Family* (*Familiaris Consortia*), no. 41.

[69] Robert Butler, *Why Survive? Being Old in America* (New York: Harper and Row, 1975), 35.

[70] Mike Featherstone and Mike Hepworth, "Images of Ageing: Cultural Representations of Later Life," in *The Cambridge Handbook of Age and Ageing*, ed. Malcolm L. Johnson (Cambridge: Cambridge University Press, 2005), 358.

[71] See Victor, *The Social Context of Ageing,* 400.

independence because of physical health problems that may prevent them from driving themselves to shops, cinema, and friends' houses; and the crippling consequences of chronic health problems such as heart disease and dementia.

The move to the restrictive qualities of a retirement or care home, if this is not managed with sensitivity by relatives and community officials, can also have devastating emotional consequences for elderly people. As one resident describes the experience: "[I received] the shock of loss because what happens is so quick. . . . There's the feeling of suddenly I'm in an institution. . . . So you lose your choices totally when you come into aged care."[72] So many fear this feeling of loss and loneliness that most want to stay in their own home as long as possible, keeping in touch with family members. When the pandemic struck and care homes went into lockdown, one of the most tragic losses for residents was their inability to hug their grandchildren. At times family members remained unsure if their loved ones were even alive, so rapid was the death rate in homes in Italy and elsewhere. Mourning was impossible. The wisdom enunciated by Walter Brueggemann could not be followed: "The public sharing of pain is one way to let reality sink in and let death go."[73] The inability to mourn publicly can cause paralyzing personal trauma, emotionally crippling the bereaved for decades or longer. The self-isolation required by authorities to control the pandemic forced the bereaved to hide their accumulated anguish.

Traditional Societies

COVID-19 also uncovered growing weaknesses in the care of older people in traditional societies. Village cultures commonly emphasize kinship, group harmony, cohesiveness, togetherness, solidarity, and stability.[74] Kinship refers not only to members of a nuclear family,

---

[72] Merle Mitchell, Commission Transcript, *Royal Commission into Quality and Safety: Interim Report,* vol. 1 (Canberra, ACT: Commonwealth of Australia, 2019), 103.

[73] Walter Brueggemann, *The Prophetic Imagination* (Philadelphia: Fortress Press, 1978), 111.

[74] See Gerald A. Arbuckle, *Violence, Society, and the Church: A Cultural Approach* (Collegeville, MN: Liturgical Press, 2004), 34; and idem, *The Francis Factor,* 44–52.

consisting of the two generations that is the norm in Western cultures, but also to members of an extended family. In Asia, as in most parts of Africa and the South Pacific, the ideology of the extended kinship family system, consisting of at least three generations, commonly reigns supreme.[75] One key rule in most traditional villages is that aging people are to be cared for by their extended family. But the economic implications of COVID-19 are making the system harder to maintain. Many young kinsfolk have lost low-level employment in the cities and are unable to send money back to help support their families and the elderly. Absolute poverty is the likely consequence.

In Japan, COVID-19 has drawn attention to structural weaknesses in the care of the aging. Traditionally older people were cared for by family members, but with the declining birth rate it has become increasingly difficult to find sons or daughters to support them. Anthropologist Harumi Befu comments that even when older people do live with their children, "they do not always enjoy the respected position that their parents formerly had and whatever task they perform around the house is usually menial and non-essential . . . which only helps to lower their status in the family."[76] For most older people living alone, the retirement allowance from their employer and the government grants are hardly enough to support them. The requirements of social distancing in the pandemic further intensified the vulnerability of aging people because neighbors were less likely to visit and offer assistance.

Poverty as Environmental Degradation

The global environmental crisis is characterized by the increasing consequences of climate change; degraded air and water quality; land contamination due to chemical or radioactive pollution; soil erosion;

---

[75] In some tribal cultures, especially in East Africa, central Brazil, and parts of Papua New Guinea, social groupings based on age cut across those based on kinship. Young people, most commonly young men, are grouped together into a named, corporate unit, and as they become older, they remain together in the same group. See Roger M. Keesing, *Cultural Anthropology: A Contemporary Perspective* (New York: Holt, Rinehart and Winston, 1981), 275–78.

[76] Harumi Befu, *Japan: An Anthropological Introduction* (New York: Harper and Row, 1971), 56.

and deforestation.[77] The poor and powerless are most affected but "there is widespread indifference to such suffering," writes Pope Francis in *Laudato Si'* (LS, no. 25). Indigenous communities are especially vulnerable to this crisis. "In various parts of the world, pressure is being put on them to abandon their homelands to make room for agricultural or mining projects which are undertaken without regard for the degradation of nature and culture" (LS, no. 146). Writing in *Querida Amazonia* (February 2020) about the plight of indigenous peoples in the Amazon, a region facing an ecological disaster, Pope Francis says that in the outskirts of the cities "they find no real freedom from their troubles, but rather the worst forms of enslavement, subjection and poverty" (QA, no. 10).

In addition to the destruction of their ecological environment, there is the undermining of indigenous peoples' personal and cultural identity. They are left bewildered, without roots. Pope Francis continues:

> The businesses, national or international, which harm the Amazon and fail to respect the right of the original peoples to the land and its boundaries, and to self-determination and prior consent, should be called for what they are: *injustice and crime*. . . . Nor can we exclude the possibility that members of the Church have been part of networks of corruption, at times to the point of agreeing to keep silent in exchange for economic assistance for ecclesial works. (QA, nos. 14, 25)

The Amazonian region is one of the epicenters of Brazil's COVID-19 pandemic. It has penetrated not only the large cities but many vulnerable communities in the countryside, including the villages of traditional peoples living in the rainforest, adding to their poverty and suffering.

Poverty as Paternalism

In January 1965, on my first day of research into the development of a credit union[78] in the then-British Colony of Fiji, I asked Joane, a

[77] See Robyn Eversole, "Overview: Patterns of Indigenous Disadvantage Worldwide," in *Indigenous Peoples and Poverty*, ed. Robyn Eversole et al. (London: Zed Books, 2005), 35.

[78] A credit union is a nongovernment controlled group of people, united by a common bond, who save money together and make loans to one another for provident and productive purposes at low interest.

Fijian, what his membership had brought him. I expected he would give me a list of material items he had bought by obtaining loans from his credit union. His reply surprised me:

> "I am a poor farmer. One day I decided to go to the agricultural department and ask for advice. I got as far as the door but I lacked confidence to enter. My knees trembled in fear because colonial people are educated and I am not. They tell us what to do, without listening to us. So I turned around and went home. Then I joined a credit union. I saved a little money for the first time. One day I said to myself: 'I am a man. I have saved money. I am the equal of the big colonial men.' I went to the official: 'I want your advice. You must listen to me first. Come! But listen!'"

This simple case study reveals universally powerful truths. Joane was rebelling against institutional paternalism, a social disease that commonly afflicts indigenous people and other receivers of aid. Institutional paternalism assumes that aid receivers must unquestionably listen to the development "experts" because they have "superior knowledge"; it destroys self-confidence and maintains a culture of dependency and inferiority.

There are two types of aid, though the line between them is not always clear: emergency aid and community development programs. Emergency aid concentrates on working *for* people. Development projects emphasize collaborating *with* people. Emergency efforts are short term, aiming to respond to a specific and urgent crisis, and generally have little direct impact on the structural causes of poverty. Community development programs such as the formation of credit unions, however, are longer term and are directed at the causes of poverty and injustice, attempting to change personal and social perceptions and promote self-reliance. As the proverb says: "Give a man a fish, and he'll eat for a day; teach a man to fish, and he'll eat for a lifetime."

Community development projects require skilled and accountable specialists willing and able to work *beside* local people. It is impossible for mutual trust to occur if the aid agent lacks an abiding respect for the dignity of people and the gift of listening. Serious intentional listening to marginalized peoples and cultures takes time, an openness to discover and remove within oneself prejudices of domineering power and cultural superiority, and a willingness to avoid hasty analyses and answers. Authentic listening conveys respect, and in subtle but powerful ways reinforces the idea that a person's full self is welcome here.

People, such as Joane and others, who struggle against poverty and marginalization have much to teach those of us who are privileged with human and material resources. Emergency and development aid must be a two-way process of learning. Through empathy, aid workers share to some degree in the sufferings of people on society's margins. Without some experience of solidarity with those who are marginalized, it is easy for aid agents to view such people as "them," the impersonal objects of aid. The founder of the Fijian Credit Union movement, Jesuit Father Marion Ganey, summarized his anti-paternalistic approach: "I was never able to do anything for the people . . . until I fully realized through my whole heart and soul that I was not doing the people a favor by coming, but that they were doing me a favor and a great one, by permitting me to come into their villages and into their lives. We are not the people's boss; we are their servant."[79] Patrick Dodson, an Aboriginal elder, comments on the need for aid agents to listen to Indigenous Australians:

> [We] must be prepared to enter into a genuine dialogue with the Indigenous community to determine the way forward in addressing the challenges that are before us. Unless the engagement and dialogue between us is premised on the concept of "the listening heart" then our relationship will remain out of balance and our endeavours will be doomed.[80]

Scriptural Reflection: Poverty in New Testament Writings

The ideology of neocapitalism negates solidarity, increases the gap between the rich and the poor, and promotes the belief that higher and

---

[79] See Gerald A. Arbuckle, "Economic and Social Development in the Fiji Islands through Credit Unions," in *Credit Unions in the South Pacific*, ed. Neil Runcie (London: University of London Press, 1969), 107–8.

[80] Patrick Dodson, "What Happened to Reconciliation?" in *Coercive Reconciliation: Stabilise, Normalise, Exit Aboriginal Australia*, ed. Jon Altman and Melinda Hinkson (Melbourne: Arena Press, 2007), 29.

higher consumption of material goods will lead to a happier society (see Chapter 1). This fundamentalist economic theory is so globally rampant that it has been called an "all-consuming epidemic."[81] It does not answer the social and economic sufferings caused by the pandemic trauma. Pope Francis writes in *Evangelii Gaudium*: "Today everything comes under the laws of competition and survival of the fittest, where the powerful feed upon the powerless. As a consequence, masses of people find themselves excluded and marginalized: without possibilities, without any means of escape. Human beings are themselves considered consumer goods to be used and then discarded" (EG, no. 53).

Corporate greed often spreads its economic power into developing countries ruthlessly to exploit workers in sweat shops. "In this context," the pope writes, "some people continue to defend trickle-down theories which assume that economic growth, encouraged by a free market, will inevitably succeed in bringing about greater justice in the world" (EG, no. 54). The theory is not confirmed by facts (see FT, no. 168). Profit-seeking without justice ignores the rights of the poor: "Almost without being aware of it, we end up being incapable of feeling compassion at the outcry of the poor, weeping for other people's pain, and feeling a need to help them, as though all of this were someone else's responsibility and not our own" (EG, no. 54).

What does the New Testament say about poverty and the unbridled pursuit of money so exalted by neoliberalism?[82] Jesus partly answers this question in the parable of the Good Samaritan (see Chapter 1; FT, nos. 56–83). We now consider further the scriptural foundations of Pope Francis's critiques of the unbridled pursuit of money, and, at the same time, the values that must guide collaborative social and economic responses to COVID-19. We first define poverty in the biblical sense, then provide a biblical illustration of solidarity, and finally offer some pastoral guidelines for helping people who are in poverty.

Defining Poverty

Biblically, poverty primarily means economic deprivation that renders people politically and socially powerless. It is biblically incorrect to equate poverty only with spiritual poverty. Scripture scholar John R.

---

[81] See John de Graff, David Wann, and Thomas H. Naylor, *Affluenza: The All-Consuming Epidemic* (San Francisco: Berrett-Koehler, 2005).

[82] See Arbuckle, *Loneliness*, 110–15, 142–48.

Donahue, SJ, writes: "Certain contemporary usages of 'spiritual poverty,' which allows it to be used of extremely wealthy people who are unhappy even amid prosperity, are not faithful to the biblical tradition."[83] The poverty of people who are economically marginalized causes not only social and political powerlessness but also an inner spiritual and psychological pain, such as shame and the loss of self-worth. God has a special concern and care for such people.[84] In St. Matthew's listing of the Beatitudes, Jesus speaks of two groups of people especially loved by God:

- First, there are those whose attitudes and lifestyles are contrary to the unjust culture that surrounds them. For them wealth, power, and selfishness have nothing to do with happiness. True contentment is to be found only in being just, compassionate and merciful. "Blessed are the poor in spirit," says Jesus, "for theirs is the kingdom of heaven" (Mt 5:3). If we are poor in spirit we surely become sensitive to the injustices around us and "to look at the world as it is, unvarnished and raw, means that we have to be able to look at ourselves in the same manner."[85]
- The second group of people are advocates who battle to protect the rights of the powerless and, suppressing self-love and ambition, show mercy. They struggle to develop peace in an unjust society and are prepared to suffer for the defense of justice: "for theirs is the kingdom of heaven" (Mt 5:3). They may be people with wealth and power who are detached from undue love of material goods and power. They offer themselves and their gifts for the service of God and their sisters and brothers. They seek to build solidarity with the economically poor and powerless and may even identify with them, sometimes in radical ways, just as Jesus does.[86]

---

[83] John R. Donahue, "The Bible and Catholic Social Teaching," in *Modern Catholic Social Teaching: Commentaries and Interpretations,* ed. Kenneth R. Himes (Washington, DC: Georgetown University Press, 2004), 22.

[84] See Norbert F. Lohfink, *Option for the Poor: The Basic Principle of Liberation Theology in Light of the* Series (North Richland Hills, TX: Bibal Press, 1995).

[85] Gerard Moore, *The Beatitudes and Justice* (Sydney: Australian Catholic Social Justice Council, 2004), 8.

[86] See Leonardo Boff and Clodovis Boff, *Introducing Liberation Theology* (Maryknoll, NY: Orbis Books, 1987), 48–49.

The gap between the rich and the poor at the time of St. Luke strikingly resembles our own contemporary pandemic world. It is a society in which working peoples' wages never allow them to be live far above the hunger line. One day without employment would cause hunger. In Luke's text Jesus speaks of the materially or sociologically poor: "Blessed are you who are poor" (Lk 6:20), and goes on with a warning, "But woe to you who are rich" (Lk 6:24).[87] The rich must use their resources to build a just community. These verses neither praise the lack of money nor condemn people having it; what the Beatitudes address, as in the Old Testament, is the chasm between the two that renders people powerless. The rich are challenged to forsake a substantial amount of their wealth and also to undertake disagreeable deeds, such as offering risky loans for the poor and canceling their debts (Lk 6:37).[88] Following his conversion, Zacchaeus, the chief tax collector of Jericho, is praised by Jesus for giving half his possessions to the poor. However, Zacchaeus still remains a wealthy man (Lk 19:1–10).[89]

Solidarity Illustrated

The parable of the Rich Farmer who is obsessed with profit has a twofold focus: human mortality, and the divine command to use money in solidarity for people who are marginalized (Lk 12:13–21). The wealthy farmer's properties have produced so much that his barns cannot store the plentiful harvest, so he plans to construct more storage buildings. At first sight the rich man seems to be acting responsibly in preparing for his future. But enough is never enough. He wants more for himself without considering the needs of others. He is more interested in his long-range security than in the immediate needs of people who are poor. He says to himself: "I will pull down my barns and build larger ones, and there will store all my grain and my goods, and I will say to my soul: 'Soul, you have ample goods laid up for many years; relax, eat, drink, be merry'" (Lk 12:18–19). God

---

[87] See Mary Elsbernd and Reimund Bieringer, *When Love Is Not Enough: A Theo-Ethic of Justice* (Collegeville, MN: Liturgical Press, 2002), 49.

[88] See David J. Bosch, *Transforming Mission: Paradigm Shifts in Theology of Mission* (Maryknoll, NY: Orbis Books, 1991), 103.

[89] See Robert Charles, *The Social Teaching of Vatican II* (Oxford: Platter Publications, 1982), 302.

then visits him: '"You fool! This very night your very life is being demanded of you. And the things you have prepared, whose will they be?' So it is with those who store up treasures for themselves but are not rich toward God" (Lk 12:20–21). The deep meaning of the story is that economic prosperity in itself does not give a lasting sense of personal satisfaction. If the farmer had been more concerned with the welfare of others, he would have distributed the excess harvest to people in need.[90]

The strongest statement by Jesus Christ supporting solidarity comes in his discourse on the Last Judgment (Mt 25:31–46), and it follows a lengthy series of parables and admonitions about living justly and compassionately to be ready for the coming of the Son of God. The statement is not a parable but an apocalyptic drama.[91] In the Sermon on the Mount, Jesus calls righteous those who have acknowledged him in the hungry, the thirsty, the strangers, the imprisoned, the naked, and the sick: "Truly I tell you, just as you did it to one of the least of these who are members of my family, you did it to me" (Mt 25:40). In Luke's Gospel, Jesus explained the imperative to love the neighbor by the parable of the Good Samaritan (Lk 10:25–37), but in Matthew, Jesus interprets this commandment in terms of his vision of the Last Judgment: "You shall love your neighbour as yourself" (Mt 22:39). No mention of grace, justification, or forgiveness of sins. What ultimately is important is whether one has acted with loving care for disadvantaged people.

The letters of John and Paul emphasize solidarity. John describes what Jesus Christ expects of a true follower: "How does God's love abide in anyone who has the world's goods and sees a brother or sister in need and yet refuses to help? Little children, let us love, not in word or speech, but in truth and action" (1 Jn 3:17–18). Paul spends time organizing a collection for people in poverty in Jerusalem and he reminds the Corinthians that their generosity is a sign of authentic love of God (2 Cor 8:8). He emphasizes the theme of community solidarity for justice when he uses the analogy of the human body: "For just as the body is one and has many members, and all the members of the body, though many, are one body, so it is with Christ. . . . Now

[90] See Charles W. Hedrick, *Many Things in Parables* (Louisville, KY: Westminster John Knox, 2004), 96–99.

[91] See M. Eugene Boring, "The Gospel of Matthew," *The New Interpreter's Bible,* vol. 8 (Nashville, TN: Abingdon, 1995), 454–59.

you are the body of Christ and individually members of it. . . . If one member suffers, all suffer together with it" (1 Cor 12:12, 27, 26). Each member of the body has a different task and duty (1 Cor 12:28). Just as a body has many diversified members—foot, eye, ear—so the church has many members with different functions.

This means that an official leader of a local church or a group will have more responsibility to work for justice than one who is not in leadership. But because of the unity and solidarity of the one body of Christ, whatever one person does in the name of justice, all share in that action: "Now there are varieties of gifts but the same Spirit; and there are varieties of services, but the same Lord. . . . To each is given the manifestation of the Spirit for the common good" (1 Cor 12:4, 5, 7). In Paul's letter to the Galatians he concludes with this mandate: "Bear one another's burdens, and in this way you will fulfill the law of Christ" (Gal 6:2). The final test of authenticity of followers of Christ is their concern for people in need, especially those on society's boundaries (see Rom 14:9; 1 Cor 8:11–13).

Guidelines for Helping People in Poverty

Conversion to solidarity as rite of passage

The parable of the Prodigal Son illustrates the moral stupidity of becoming a slave to money (Lk 15:11–32). At first sight the story seems to center on the conversion of one son, but in fact the description of his elder brother is equally enlightening because he refuses the chance to join his wayward younger sibling in a transforming rite of passage. The third figure in the story, the father, is the ritual leader of the rites of passage of his two sons.

The separation phase of the prodigal son's transformative rite of passage is brief (Lk 15:11–12): the foolhardy, narcissistic adolescent, acting within his rights according to the local tradition, demands that his father give him his share of the inheritance.[92] He leaves for a distant country where he wastes his wealth on "dissolute living"

[92] Kenneth E. Bailey notes: "The son has not broken the law. Rather, he has broken his father's heart. . . . To suddenly lose one third of their total wealth would mean a staggering loss to the entire family clan." *The Cross and the Prodigal: Luke 15 through the Eyes of Middle Eastern Peasants* (Downers Grove, IL: IVP Books, 2005), 42.

(Lk 15:13), seeing his father purely in economic terms, that is, as a financial resource. Then follows the liminal stage. Totally penniless and lonely, the son is forced to accept one of the most shaming employments for a Jew—working with pigs.[93] The pigpen is a potent symbol of the chaos in this adolescent's journey into mature adulthood.

In this liminal stage a process of conversion begins when he acknowledges that he alone is at fault. He recalls the love and compassion of his father, which in his self-centeredness he has long disregarded as unmanly. He must seek forgiveness and reconciliation, but he does not expect his father will receive him warmly. Hence, he will instead offer himself to his father as just another lowly hired laborer. But the father, seeing his son in the distance, runs to him and embraces him—a gesture of profound compassion and forgiveness: "He ran and put his arms around him and kissed him" (Lk 15:20). To this day one can feel the burst of communitas between the two men now bound together in compassionate solidarity. And it is sustained in festive celebrations (Lk 15:22–24).

The reentry stage of the initiation occurs when his father calls for a feast of celebration. The elder son's futile journey of initiation into maturity is in spectacular contrast to that of his brother. By tradition the elder son must act as the go-between in quarrels between younger brothers and his father, but he refuses to do so. But worse is ahead. Hearing of his sibling's return, he is overcome by jealousy and envy of his brother.[94] The elder son is jealous because he fears he will lose the farm and money he thinks are his due (Lk 15:29). He may also envy his brother, who now possesses what he lacks: a mature adult friendship with their father. Despite his protestations of maturity, the elder son has not grown up to be a responsible person concerned for the needs of others. Lacking compassion, he wants his brother punished for his earlier adolescent selfishness, so he tries to demean his brother and thus kill the joy of his father; the father refuses. The son rebuffs the chance for conversion, remaining instead consumed by envy and jealousy. No joyful communitas here.

Moreover, tradition dictates that the elder son should be the host of the party, but he refuses even to enter the house, thus publicly shaming the dignity of his father and his reconciliation with his brother.[95] But

---

[93] See ibid., 57.
[94] See Arbuckle, *Violence, Society, and the Church*, 126–36.
[95] See Bailey, *The Cross and the Prodigal*, 78–87.

the father does not give in. He again encourages him to begin the journey of conversion (Lk 11:31–32). As we are not informed if the elder son accepts the invitation the story ultimately ends on a melancholy note. The parable's deeper lesson is this: God's love is unconditional and God is persistently inviting us to be open to this love and to express it in action. We respond positively only if we acknowledge before God our own faults and pride. If we fulfill this precondition, we will effectively be initiated through God's compassion and love into union with Christ. The mythological heart of Christ's message is that in God's unqualified love, God is forever inviting us to abandon our attachments to worldly things.

Listening to people in poverty

Pope Francis forcefully concludes that the failure to listen to marginalized people is a form of violence: "Intolerance and lack of respect for indigenous popular cultures is a form of violence grounded in a cold and judgmental way of viewing them. No authentic, profound and enduring change is possible unless it starts from the different cultures, particularly those of the poor" (FT, no. 220). The detailed and emotionally moving account of the healing of the blind beggar Bartimaeus in Mark 10 by Jesus contains three relevant lessons about offering aid to people who are poor. First, Jesus by his attitude and action reassures Bartimaeus that he is a person of dignity. He inspires hope and empowers Bartimaeus to reject the cultural stigma that the poor must remain silent. Second, Jesus asks Bartimaeus what he would like: "What do you want me to do for you?" (Mk 10:51). And Jesus listens to his reply. Thinking about justice begins by *listening* to those who know about injustice. Third, the healing of poverty must be holistic—social, cultural, economic, and spiritual. Charity without justice is not holistic healing.

When Jesus heals Bartimaeus, he confronts multiple expressions of poverty. The authorities and wealthy citizens at the time of Bartimaeus would have been ignorant of these expressions of poverty, but the poor would have recognized them immediately. Bartimaeus would have been merely a statistic for the authorities of his time—just another annoying beggar, the sinful cause of his own misery. The grieving Bartimaeus is "sitting by the roadside" (Mk 10:46), a symbol of social rejection; because of a particular type of blindness he has been stigmatized by society, for he ritually endangers the clean. Excluded, he must silently sit by the roadside to avoid contact with people. For his family and former friends he no longer exists. He is utterly alone. Jesus is passing by, and Bartimaeus cries out for healing. The crowd does its best to silence him, "but he only shouted the louder" (Mk 10:48). He challenges the idea that poor people must remain silent, accepting their fate.

The crowd has followed Jesus and listened to his words on compassion and justice, but they remain blinded by their prejudice against people like Bartimaeus. Jesus will have none of this vicious stupidity. He calls Bartimaeus to his side and politely asks him what he wishes, to which Bartimaeus replies, "Rabunni, let me see again!" (Mk 10:51). The mourning cry of Bartimaeus is the cry of every poor person today mired in poverty: let me become again a full member of society, one who can freely contribute to society with a hope-filled sense of pride and responsibility. Jesus listens to Bartimaeus and by speaking directly to him—a nonperson in the eyes of society—Jesus breaks through the political, cultural, and structural barriers that are entrapping Bartimaeus and every other poor person. By defying these stigmatizing and discriminating walls, Jesus allows Bartimaeus to rediscover his ability to be and act like a human person with dignity. Filled with hope, not only is he medically healed but he returns to society, symbolized by his ability to walk once more on the road: he follows Jesus "on the way" (Mk 10:52). He is now a full member of society.

Avoiding exploitation of vulnerable people

The letter of James, written toward the end of the first Christian century, focuses on the evil of exploiting the rights of employees at harvest time. This letter is especially relevant in these times of the pandemic and its aftermath, because the poor, being powerless, are in danger of abuse by ruthless moneylenders and landowners. The language used to condemn the selfish rich is unforgiving and uncompromising. The letter also emphasizes the quality of powerlessness, which is integral to the biblical definition of people who are poor:

> Come now, you rich people, weep and wail for the miseries that are coming to you. Your riches have rotted, and your clothes are

> moth-eaten. . . . Listen! The wages of the laborers who mowed your fields, which you kept back by fraud, cry out, and the cries of the harvesters have reached the ears of the Lord of hosts. You have lived on the earth in luxury and in pleasure. . . . You have condemned and murdered the righteous one, who does not resist you. (Jas 5:1–2, 4–6)

Robust words! The message is clear. Injustice is murder; thus the oppressor is a murderer.[96] The letter was written when there were marked social differences existing in society. Some Christians were giving preferential treatment to the rich, and the writer heartily condemns this as contrary to the heart of the gospel: "You do well if you really fulfill the royal law according to the scripture, 'You shall love your neighbor as yourself.' But if you show partiality, you commit sin and are convicted by the law as transgressors" (Jas 2:8–9).

Care of aging people

In biblical times people depended on their kinship system for their own identity, housing, and food. A helpful custom, but the danger was that people could feel no obligation to care for others outside their kinship system. But such behavior goes against the fundamental commandment to love one another and show compassion to anyone in need (Lk 10:25–37). Converts risked being expelled from their kinship system when they went to the aid of a needy non-kinsman.[97] Jesus is referring to this when he says: "Do not think that I have come to bring peace to the earth; I have not come to bring peace, but a sword; . . . one's foes will be members of one's own household" (Mt 10:34, 36). Jesus hints at this tension also when he responds to the summons from "his mother and his brothers" to come to them (Mk 3:31). He replies that ultimate identity and support will not come from traditional extended family systems but from their faith communities: "Here are my

---

[96] See Gustavo Gutiérrez, *The God of Life* (Maryknoll, NY: Orbis Books, 1988), 129–30.

[97] See Jerome Neyrey, "Loss of Wealth, Loss of Family, Loss of Honor: The Cultural Context of the Original Makarisms in Q," in *The Social World of the New Testament: Insights and Models,* ed. Jerome H. Neyrey and Eric C. Stewart (Peabody, MA: Hendrickson, 2008), 100–101.

mother and my brothers! Whoever does the will of God is my brother and sister and mother" (Mk 3:35).

Consequently, converts, particularly elderly ones marginalized by their kinsfolk, needed care. Early Christians quickly responded: they "had all things in common; they would sell their possessions and goods and distribute the proceeds to all, as any had need" (Acts 2:44–45). The faith communities, where necessary, would assume the responsibilities of the kinship system, caring for "widows and orphans, the old, the unemployed, and the disabled."[98] St. Paul explicitly and in strong language reminds early Christians to take care of their relatives: "And whoever does not provide for relatives, and especially for family members, has denied the faith and is worse than an unbeliever" (1 Tim 5:8). By "family members" Paul is referring to the household, which included grandparents as well as younger relatives. Paul begins this section of his letter to Timothy by reminding Christians "not to speak harshly to an older man, but to speak to him as to a father . . . to older women as mothers" (1 Tim 5:1–2). But, according to Paul, following the teaching of Christ, concern for the aging must extend beyond one's relatives. To the Galatians, Paul writes: "So then, whenever we have an opportunity, let us work for the good of all, and especially for those of the family of faith" (Gal 6:10); baptism makes us into a family bonded together in faith. Paul in his letters frequently reminds Christians that the bonds between all Christians, including the relationship between the young and old—no matter whether they are biologically related or not—must be charity: "Love is patient; love is kind; . . . and now faith, hope, and love abide, these three; and the greatest of these is love" (1 Cor 13:4, 13); "Owe no one anything, except to love one another; for the one who loves another has fulfilled the law" (Rom 13:8).[99]

Summary

- The pandemic has intensified global poverty, reversing almost a decade of advances. Poverty is commonly measured only in *quantifiable* terms such as low-income, inadequate housing,

---

[98] Gary B. Ferngreen, *Medicine and Health Care in Early Christianity* (Baltimore, MD: Johns Hopkins University Press, 2009), 139.

[99] See Arbuckle, *The Francis Factor*, 28–30.

sickness, or levels of educational achievement. This gives an inadequate picture of the reality.

- *Qualitative* analysis is also essential; that is, poverty includes immaterial realities such as loss of dignity, mental stress, loneliness, spiritual deprivation, being subjected to violence, lack of voice and of power, economic exploitation, gender and racial inequalities, old age, environmental degradation, and paternalism. Poverty excludes people from participating in the social, economic, and political activity of society as a whole, forcing them into a world of powerlessness and loneliness. Poverty thus degrades their dignity.
- In responding to poverty, Benedict XVI's admonition in *Deus Caritas Est (God Is Love)* must be heeded: "We are dealing with human beings, and human beings need something more than technically proper care. They need humanity. They need heartfelt concern" (DC, no. 31).
- Biblically, poverty primarily means economic deprivation that renders people politically and socially powerless. It is incorrect to equate poverty only with spiritual poverty. The strongest statement by Jesus Christ supporting solidarity comes in his discourse on the Last Judgment (Mt 25:31–46), and it follows a lengthy series of parables and admonitions about living justly and compassionately in order to be ready for the coming of the Son of God. The statement is not a parable but an apocalyptic drama.[100]
- In the Sermon on the Mount, Jesus names as righteous those who have acknowledged him in the hungry, the thirsty, the stranger, the imprisoned, the naked, and the sick: "Truly I tell you, just as you did it to one of the least of these who are members of my family, you did it to me" (Mt 25:40). In Luke's Gospel, Jesus explains the imperative to love the neighbor by relaying the parable of the Good Samaritan (Lk 10:25–37), but in Matthew, Jesus interprets this commandment in terms of his vision of the Last Judgment: "You shall love your neighbor as yourself" (Mt 22:39). No mention of grace, justification, or forgiveness of sins. What is ultimately important is whether one has acted with loving care for disadvantaged people.

[100] See Boring, "The Gospel of Matthew," 454–59.

Reflection Questions

1. Have you ever felt excluded from a group? What did it feel like?
2. What groups in your country are now suffering poverty because of the pandemic? Who is defending them? Could you help in some way?
3. St. James warns against exploiting vulnerable people (Jas 5:1–2, 4–6). Who are the vulnerable people being exploited in your country? Is the ecological environment being exploited? If so, why is this contrary to gospel solidarity?

5

Racism and Institutional Racism Exposed

If something isn't done, and done in a hurry, to bring the colored peoples of the world out of their long years of poverty, their long years of hurt and neglect, the world is doomed.

—Martin Luther King Jr.

In brief, "unconscious racism" connotes how race can operate as a negative—yet not conscious, deliberate, or intentional—decision-making factor, due to the pervasive cultural stigma attached to dark skin color in Western culture.

—Bryan N. Massingale,
Racial Justice and the Catholic Church

When whiteness is normative (as is the case in the United States, historically, culturally, and institutionally), space is constructed to enforce white privilege, ensuring freedom and social mobility for whites while imposing unfair obstacles on people of color, especially African Americans.

—Marcus Mescher,
The Ethics of Encounter

This chapter explains that:

- The pandemic has highlighted the fact that racism continues.
- Prejudice reduces whole peoples to dangerous generalizations.
- There is a distinction between the terms *ethnic group* and *race*.
- Racism is the false belief that biologically superior and inferior groups exist and are called races.
- Institutional racism prioritizes white supremacy.
- Racism feeds on fear and contempt of others.
- Jesus Christ by words and actions vigorously condemned racist-like behavior.

The pandemic trauma starkly revealed the continuing evil of racism. Recall that liminality, a period when traditional cultural constraints temporally cease, as happened during the pandemic crisis, can be a time for reflection on the gaps between the founding story of a nation and contemporary reality (see Chapter 2). Evidence of this occurred dramatically in America following the killing of George Floyd by police in Minneapolis on May 25, 2020. Black Lives Matter (BLM) is a decentralized movement, founded in 2013, calling for nonviolent disobedience to protest against cases of police brutality and all racial violence.

The BLM movement, enlivened by Floyd's death, expanded spectacularly nationally, with reverberations internationally, to protest what had happened and the continuance of institutional racism (a term discussed later in this chapter). An estimated 15 to 26 million people participated in cities and towns around the nation; in June a Pew Research Center poll concluded that two-thirds of Americans of all ethnic groups strongly expressed support for the movement. Truly a rare national communitas experience of solidarity. The same poll found that Donald Trump's handling of race relations was considered significantly negative.[1]

Racism flourishes when there are economic and social inequalities. Since the pandemic has increased these inequalities, racism with its

[1] Pew Research Center reports: "Asked about Trump's handling of race relations more generally, about half (48%) say he has made race relations worse; 19% say he has made progress toward improving race relations; 19% say he has tried but failed to make progress and 12% say the president hasn't addressed the issue" (June 12, 2020).

pernicious effects will intensify. Sometimes, as is evident in American policing, racism is obvious, but more frequently it surfaces in humiliating comments, including racially inspired jokes, and in institutional biases. When people employ racially connected language, without obvious smears, linguists term it "racialization."[2] Because institutional racism is built into the way that institutions operate and need not be conscious or founded on individual prejudice, it is especially difficult to name and eradicate.

This chapter aims to explain the nature of racism, particularly institutional racism, its roots, and how it develops. To do so we must clarify key and often misunderstood terms, such as *prejudice, ethnocentrism, race, racism, institutional racism, race relations*, and *ethnicity.* I explore the reasons behind racism's persistence, as well some ethnic groups' reactions to racism. Finally, since Jesus Christ in his teachings and actions condemns racist-like attitudes and behavior, I show that the scriptures are a rich resource to guide our pastoral response to contemporary racism.

Clarifying Terms

Prejudice/Discrimination

Prejudice, at its irrational extreme, "is one of the most terrible manifestations of human nature. It is pervasive as well as cruel."[3] Prejudice has two dimensions: *meaning* and *feeling*. The *meaning* aspect is commonly referred to as a *stereotype*. Like the term *prejudice, stereotype* has been defined in various ways. For example, a stereotype reduces "whole peoples to some kind of generalisation."[4] Gordon Allport writes that "a stereotype is an exaggerated belief associated with a category."[5] It is a shorthand but faulty method of handling or grasping a complex world. By placing things and people into preformed categories, we try to control a world that threatens our sense of order or

---

[2] See "Snide and Prejudice," *The Economist* (June 13, 2020), 64.

[3] Cedric Cullingford, *Prejudice: From Individual Identity to Nationalism in Young People* (London: Kogan Page, 2000), 8.

[4] Ibid., 9.

[5] Gordon W. Allport, *The Nature of Prejudice* (Garden City, NY: Doubleday, 1958), 187.

meaning. For example, various immigrant ethnic groups in Australia have been stereotyped by white citizens as "taking over our country" or having "un-Australian values and customs."[6] The stereotype is a *pre*judgment. It is the judgment made without first checking the facts about things or people.

The second quality of prejudice is the *feeling* aspect. Prejudices are not just about stereotypes; they are stereotypes motivated by strong, and often powerful, feeling impulses. The feeling aspect is the "blinding power" in prejudice. It obstructs objectivity and the openness of dialogue; it forces the prejudiced person to see only what he or she wants to see, or even to see things that are not there at all. Jesus on one occasion spoke about how the people received John the Baptist and himself: "For John came neither eating nor drinking, and they say: 'He has a demon'; the Son of Man came eating and drinking, and they say, 'Look, a glutton and a drunkard, a friend of tax collectors and sinners!'" (Mt 11:18–19). No matter what Jesus does, his enemies only see evil in him.

Prejudice takes many forms; for example, it can be cultural, racial, sexual, religious, or related to social class. Prejudice and discrimination must be distinguished; the former refers to subjective feelings, the latter to overt behavior. For example, sexism is the *prejudice* that individuals are inferior in some way or other as human persons because they belong to a certain biological category. Sexist *discrimination* assumes that members of a particular gender are objects to be freely used for the pleasure and the preservation of the dominant position of the other gender.

People in every culture or nation can think their way of doing things is right and that other ways of acting are stupid, crude, uncivilized, unreasonable, evil, or superstitious.[7] This type of prejudice in favor of one's own group is technically called *ethnocentrism*. In its mild forms, ethnocentrism is normal, reasonable, and serves a useful purpose. Group identity (or ethnic identity) requires a feeling of pride in the group's achievements, the feeling that other ethnic groups have something to learn from our ethnic or cultural group. We call this patriotism. But unfortunately, such patriotism is apt to evaporate when

---

[6] See Robert van Krieken et al., *Sociology: Themes and Perspectives* (Frenchs Forest, NSW: Longman, 2000), 544.

[7] See Allport, *The Nature of Prejudice,* 24.

our group pride is transformed into prejudice. Then ethnocentrism ceases to be a positive value; we become excessively nationalistic.

Ethnic prejudice, therefore, can be defined as "an antipathy based upon a faulty and inflexible generalization. It may be felt or expressed, directed toward a group as a whole, or toward an individual because he is a member of that group."[8] Notice the reference to "antipathy" and "faulty and inflexible generalization," that is, words that refer to the two aspects of prejudice: the meaning and feeling dimensions. One evening, while visiting a Fijian village, I heard my hosts laugh every time they mentioned a person they called "the back-home man." On asking about him, I was told: "He is the New Zealander who has come to help us build a water supply for our village. That is good. But whenever he speaks, he begins like this: 'Back home in New Zealand we have the best road network in the world . . . the best education system . . . and so on!' He is not interested in our Fijian customs." Despite the genuine concern this New Zealander had to help the less fortunate, he was suffering from an overdose of ethnocentrism or ethnic prejudice; he assumed New Zealanders had nothing to learn from Fijians.

Race

Race is a confusing and emotional word. When it comes to awakening people's prejudices, hostilities, and fears, few words are the equal of *race.* It is also a vague and ambiguous word. The emotions and ambiguities evoked by the word are transferred to related expressions such as *racial discrimination, racial prejudice, racial segregation, racial group, race relations*, and *racism.*[9] And now we have the term *institutional racism.* Therefore, we need to be very clear about the historical origin of the word *race* and its different meanings.[10]

Race has two primary meanings: to connote the biological inferiority of designated groups of people; and as a synonym for *ethnic group.* Integral to the first meaning of *race* are power and subordination—one group of people claims to be biologically superior to another group

[8] Ibid., 10.

[9] See Michael Banton, *Racial Theories,* 2nd ed. (Cambridge: Cambridge University Press, 1998), 1–16.

[10] See Harriet Bradley, *Fractured Identities: Changing Patterns of Inequality* (Cambridge: Polity, 2016), 155–90.

and can act accordingly. Up to the Second World War it was commonly assumed by scientists and the public in general that humans were divided into races, normally distinguished by the color of skin and facial features, and that the causes of these differences are biological. Some races were consequently branded as innately superior, others inferior, such as African slaves in America. People could talk about "blacks" as if they were by nature not only different but less than human. There is no scientific foundation for this belief. Understood in this sense the term has no scientific validity whatsoever. No fixed or discrete racial categories exist in the world.[11]

When people are branded *nonhuman*, they can be discriminated against or even killed by the oppressing group with impunity, a reality tragically true for Jews in Germany under Hitler. The Nazis separated themselves from Slavs, Gypsies, and Jewish people, asserting that people in these groups were innately/biologically inferior as human beings. Apartheid in South Africa was also racist: "The basic principle of apartheid was the preservation of what is called white civilization. This is identified with white supremacy. . . . It is a purpose dwarfing every other purpose, an end justifying any means."[12]

In summary, race is not a scientific concept, but rather a social construct used by people in their everyday conversations to indicate different ethnic groups.[13] Often, however, people are unconscious of the historical racist connotations that the word can carry. By racism, we mean all three of the following:

- ethnocentric pride in one's ethnic group and preference for the distinctive qualities of that group;
- belief that these qualities are fundamentally biological in nature and are thus transmitted to succeeding generations; and

---

[11] See UNESCO, *The Race Concept: Results of an Inquiry* (Paris: UNESCO, 1951), 15–16.

[12] The South African Roman Catholic Bishops' Conference, cited in *The Church in Africa: Pastoral Letters of the African Hierarchies* (London: Sword of the Spirit, 1960), 11–12.

[13] In 1998 the American Anthropological Association stated that because of its historical origins the word *race* should immediately be replaced by a more correct term such as *ethnic group*. See Tony Bennett, Lawrence Grossberg, and Meaghan Morris, eds., *New Keywords: A Revised Vocabulary of Culture and Society* (Oxford: Blackwell, 2005), 292.

- strong negative feelings toward other groups who do not share these characteristics, coupled with the thrust to discriminate and exclude the outgroup from full participation in the life of the community.[14]

The essence of moral evil is the destruction of human persons made in the image of God. This includes not only killing but the creation of conditions that spiritually, materially, or psychologically destroy or diminish a people's dignity and their capacity to fulfil basic material needs. Evil are the "actions that have such consequences."[15] Prejudicial discrimination is evil. Racism is evil.[16]

Race is also used as another word for *ethnic group,* a term that refers to a group of people sharing an identity that arises from a collective sense of a distinctive history. Ethnicity derives from the existence of culturally distinctive, self-conscious groups (ethnic groups), each claiming a unique identity based on a shared tradition or common experiences and on social markers such as culture, language, religion, and physical characteristics. The social markers may indeed be quite simple, such as dress or style of house building; in other words, whatever a group of people feels particularly distinguishes it.[17] New ethnic groups are regularly forming, for example, African Americans, Latinx peoples in the United States, and a variety of blended ethnicities such as New Zealander Australian, Irish American, or Mexican American. Today most social scientists prefer not to use the term *race relations* and speak instead of *ethnic relations,* because the word *race* still carries biologically inferior connotations.

---

[14] See Keith R. McConnochie, *Realities of Race: An Analysis of the Concepts of Race and Racism and Their Relevance to Australian Society* (Sydney: Australia and New Zealand Book Company, 1973), 30.

[15] Ervin Staub, *The Roots of Evil: The Origins of Genocide and Other Group Violence* (Cambridge: Cambridge University Press, 1989), 25.

[16] See Bryan Massingale, "Conscience Formation and the Challenge of Unconscious Racial Bias," in *Conscience and Catholicism: Rights, Responsibilities, and Institutional Responses*, ed. David E. DeCosse and Kristin E. Heyer, 53–68 (Maryknoll, NY: Orbis Books, 2015); and idem, "The Systematic Erasure of the Black/Dark-Skinned Body in Catholic Ethics," in *Catholic Theological Ethics Past, Present, and Future: The Trento Conference,* ed. James F. Keenan, 116–24 (Maryknoll, NY: Orbis Books, 2011).

[17] See Gerald A. Arbuckle, *Violence, Society, and the Church: A Cultural Approach* (Collegeville, MN: Liturgical Press, 2004), 183–84.

We need to further distinguish between *ascribed* ethnic groups and *voluntary* ethnic groups. Jewish people were forced to become an ascribed ethnic group. In the 1960s, a little after African Americans began to demand respect for their history, there emerged among white Americans what is called voluntary, defensive, or backlash ethnicity. In recent times this backlash ethnicity has grown. The nation's increasing ethnic diversity, Barack Obama's election to the presidency, and the ever-expanding visibility of African Americans in colleges and corporations have fed fears that these achievements will eventually reduce the influence of white Americans politically, economically, and socially.[18] Donald Trump, backed by right-wing supporters,[19] has politically encouraged this fear with his xenophobic comments supporting white supremacists[20] and denigrating Mexicans, Muslims, and other would-be immigrant groups. Similar backlash ethnicity is found throughout Europe.[21]

Institutional Racism

In 1967, two black activists in the United States, Stokely Carmichael and Charles V. Hamilton, first used the term *institutional prejudice*—as opposed to *individual racism*—to highlight the fact that anti-black attitudes had become entrenched in key institutions of society, for example, education, justice, and government.[22] These institutions prevented African Americans from exercising their civil rights. *Institutional racism* is defined as

---

[18] See Carol Anderson, *White Rage: The Unspoken Truth of Our Racial Divide* (New York: Bloomsbury, 2017), 170.

[19] See Cas Mudde, *The Far Right Today* (Cambridge: Polity Press, 2019), 54.

[20] See Sarah Churchwell, *Behold America: The Entangled History of "America First" and "The American Dream"* (New York: Basic Books, 2018), 274.

[21] See Gerald A. Arbuckle, *Fundamentalism at Home and Abroad: Analysis and Pastoral Responses* (Collegeville, MN: Liturgical Press, 2017), 53, 106.

[22] A *Washington Post*-ABC News poll conducted in mid-July 2020 found that nearly 70 percent of Americans believed "black people and other minorities are not treated as equal to white people in the criminal justice system" and most still generally opposed "calls . . . to remove statues of Confederate generals or presidents who enslaved people." Charles M. Blow, "After Protests," *Times Digest* (August 10, 2020), 8.

> those situations where a racialized ethnic group is systematically disadvantaged by the ways in which social institutions, that may not be built around explicit racist ideas, nevertheless operate. People may not employ racist ideas—they may even disavow them—but they may, nevertheless, be involved in structures and processes that systematically disadvantage certain ethnic groups. This is racism. . . . Discriminating practices may result from institutional processes overseen by people who espouse tolerant and unbiased ideas. This is the central insight behind the concept of institutional racism.[23]

This definition has the advantage of highlighting the ease with which racial attitudes can originally shape institutions and then become normalized without people becoming aware that this has happened.[24] Racism can be structured into institutions without people being conscious that it is there or that they themselves are racially motivated.[25] But the evil racist consequences remain.

United States

> Racial attitudes were woven into every aspect of our nation's history.[26]

> People of color in the United States are systematically denied well-being in economic capital, bodily security, health, recreation, education, and ownership. Americans have come

[23] James Fulcher and John Scott, *Sociology* (Oxford: Oxford University Press, 2007), 202, 228.

[24] Tessa Blackstone illustrates how prejudices can become rigidly encased in institutions. She points to the difficulties faced by women in Britain who wanted to become engineers. She argues that the teaching profession fostered stereotypes stating what women could or could not do. The profession did not envisage women as engineers, and this institutional attitude transferred to girls graduating from school, who were then less likely to see themselves as engineers. "Why Are There So Few Women Scientists and Engineers?" *New Society* (February 21, 1980), 59.

[25] See Robert Livingston, "How to Promote Racial Equity in the Workplace," *Harvard Business Review* 98, no. 5 (2020): 64–72.

[26] Barack Obama, *A Promised Land* (New York: Viking, 2000), 405.

> to accept this structural reality as part of the order of things, normalizing dispossessions, placing it in the past, and ignoring its generational effects. But a world that is saturated and structured by White supremacy can only be described as a kingdom of evil.[27]

Rollo May notes that violence inherent in the founding experiences of nations can continue in different degrading forms. The racial violence in the founding mythology of the United States[28] continues mainly through institutional racism (see Axiom 3, Chapters 1 and 5), especially violence against minority groups such as African Americans, Mexicans, and Native Americans. The statues erected to honor Confederate generals and notable slave-owning citizens in the southern states symbolize the glorification of this racist violence. "We 'nice' Americans regularly identify with the pioneers who massacred Indians according to the will of God under a new name, manifest destiny. We make heroes out of gangsters."[29]

The Civil War may have shattered slave society, but the racial hierarchy that was pivotal to the survival of that society remained to

---

[27] Jeannine Hill Fletcher, *The Sin of White Supremacy: Christianity, Racism, and Religious Diversity in America* (Maryknoll, NY: Orbis Books, 2017), 94; for a historical overview of race relations in America see Robert D. Putnam and Shaylyn Romney Garrett, *The Upswing: How America Came Together a Century Ago and How We Can Do It Again* (New York: Simon and Schuster, 2020), 200–244.

[28] Robert G. Parkinson writes: "The refusal [by the nation's founders] to extend to African Americans and Indians the benefits of emerging concepts of liberal subjectivity in the form of citizenship had ghastly consequences, for it legitimated and excused the destruction of vast numbers of human beings." *The Common Cause: Creating Race and Nation in the American Revolution* (Chapel Hill: University of North Carolina Press, 2016), 665. See Ibram X. Kendi, *Stamped from the Beginning: The Definitive History of Racist Ideas in America* (New York: Bodley House, 2016); Sean Wilentz, *No Property in Man: Slavery and Antislavery at the Nation's Founding* (Cambridge, MA: Harvard University Press, 2018); Nicholas Guyatt comments in "How Proslavery Was the Constitution?" that "while individual slaveholders bore their share of responsibility, the Constitution allowed proslavery forces to use the power of the federal government to support appalling measures." *The New York Review of Books* 67, no. 9 (2019): 45.

[29] Rollo May, *The Cry for Myth* (New York: Delta, 1991), 100–101.

shape the outcome, especially in the absence of a prolonged program of radically restructuring the social and economic life of the South. The fact that slavery created "whiteness as personhood and blackness as property—as chattel,"[30] dies hard. The past is not the past. It is still present. Donald Trump's omnipresent campaign slogan "Make America Great Again" tapped into this racist mythology (see Chapter 3).[31]

Institutional racism became normalized in the United States after the Civil War, particularly in the Southern states, despite the ending of slave status for African Americans. There were people who were determined to give them status equal to that of other American citizens, but this had no support in the South and little appeal in the North. Eventually what became known as white supremacy and segregation for African Americans triumphed in the South. Immediately after the Civil War state after state in the South created laws, known as Black Codes, that equivalently re-enslaved them for years to come. Segregation and poverty, very often concentrated in racial ghettos, created a humanly destructive, traumatizing environment—educationally, socially, and economically. This institutionalized racial intimidation, sometimes subtle but often overtly violent, was geared to keep them second-class citizens.

> Segregation and poverty have created in the racial ghetto a destructive environment most totally unknown to most white Americans. What white Americans have never fully understood—but what the African American can never forget—is that white society is deeply implicated in the ghetto. White institutions created it, white institutions maintain it, and white society condones it.[32]

---

[30] Barbara Perry, *In the Name of Hate: Understanding Hate Crimes* (London: Routledge, 2001), 70.

[31] Carol Anderson comments: "Some 20 percent of Trump's supporters believed the Emancipation Proclamation had been bad public policy and that the enslaved should never have been freed." Anderson, *White Rage*, 170–71. Anderson is quoting a survey by Libby Nelson, "Nearly 20 Percent of Trump's Supporters Disapprove of Lincoln Freeing the Slaves," *Vox* (February 24, 2016).

[32] *Report of the National Advisory Commission on Civil Disorders* (New York: Bantam Books, 1968), 2; see Obama, *A Promised Land*, 398.

Today many Latinx and African American residents continue to be forced into inferior positions through poor education and social conditions, especially in the Southern states; they still live in suburbs with the worst schools, the worst jobs, and the worst healthcare services. In 1968 African American families earned about 60 percent as much as white families, and owned assets that were less than 10 percent of those of a typical white family; this is still the situation today.[33] In 2018 the average African American household income was approximately half that of the white population.[34] The fact that one in three African American boys born in 2001 will probably spend time in prison, compared with one in seventeen white boys, is the result of institutional racism.[35]

Not surprising, given this institutional racism, African Americans are not only more likely to be at higher risk for contracting COVID-19 but also have less access to testing. They have been three times more likely to become infected by COVID-19 as their neighbors. Black and Latinx people have been nearly twice as likely to die from the virus as white people. Also, African Americans are overrepresented in nine of the ten lowest-paid, high-contact essential services, which increased their possibility of catching the virus: they make up 30 percent of nursing assistants, 39 percent of orderlies, and 39 percent of psychiatric aides.[36] There is a similar pattern for Native Americans.[37]

New Zealand

Institutional racism is consciously or unknowingly created by the dominant group in society. In 1931, the editor of the *Journal of Polynesian Society*, Johannes Andersen, wrote: "It is significant that every Maori who has been able to overcome the inertia . . . who has been able to enter more or less fully into our complex civilisation, is a

---

[33] See "The New Ideology of Race," *The Economist* (July 11, 2020), 7.

[34] See "The Grim Racial Inequalities behind America's Protests," *The Economist* (June 3, 2020).

[35] See "The New Ideology of Race," 7.

[36] See Aria Florant et al., "COVID-19: Investing in Black Lives and Livelihoods," McKinsey and Company (April 14, 2020).

[37] See "How the Pandemic Threatens Native Americans—And Their Languages," *The Economist* (May 19, 2020).

Maori with a dash of Pakeha [white] blood."[38] This racist, biologically based stereotype of a minority people influenced educational decision-makers for years; Maori children were forbidden until the late 1930s to speak their own language at school. A Maori academic, Ranginui Walker, later highlighted ongoing institutional racism:

> The Pakeha [white New Zealander], who often controls the decision-making processes that affect the Maori [minority ethnic group], suffers from what I call ghetto-paranoia. It is a state of mind that is peculiar to the majority group and stems from fear, suspicion, ignorance and intolerance about the Maori minority.[39]

The New Zealand Race Relations Conciliator in 1972 argued that "there is no or little *racist intent* . . . either among the citizens, or within the system, or in the way of life" (emphasis added).[40] Though there may have been little racist intent on the part of politicians and educators, nonetheless powerful negative stereotypes continued to be reinforced by them and further entrenched in social, educational, and economic institutions. In 1964 the Department of Education circulated thousands of artistically designed booklets depicting sometimes smiling Maori elders and children living in atrocious conditions. The photographs reinforced the popular stereotype that all members of the minority group lived like this. Maori organizations objected strongly, but educators could not understand what the fuss was all about. In 1971 Prime Minister John Marshall noted that "Maoris do have a role to play in New Zealand society and I have been through factories and noticed they make particularly competent and happy machine operators."[41] Such negative stereotypes encouraged educators to have

---

[38] Cited in W. S. Dale, "The Maori Language," in *The Maori and Education in New Zealand and Its Dependencies*, 249–60 (Wellington: Ferguson and Osborne, 1931).

[39] Ranginui Walker, "Authority and the Individual: A Maori Viewpoint," *Salient* (July 26, 1973), 1.

[40] *Report of the Race Relations Conciliator* (Wellington: Government Printer, 1972), 14.

[41] John Marshall, cited in James Ritchie, *One Nation or Two? Maori and Pakeha in Contemporary New Zealand* (Auckland: New Zealand University Press, 1971), 15.

low-level expectations of Maori children with tragic consequences for them; rarely at this time were Maoris said to make good teachers, lawyers, or doctors.[42]

Much has improved since the 1970s, but much has yet to change.[43]

Britain

Most black, Asian, and minority ethnic groups in Britain are more likely to be assigned to overcrowded and unsatisfactory accommodation and more likely to be in low-paid and unskilled work without job security. Little has changed since 1986, when one social researcher wrote of the fate of black students in many schools:

> These days the racism of the wider society has drained many black children of motivation. They see the uphill task of doing well in the educational system as being rewarded with a lower-paid job—or no job at all . . . allotted by a society that does not wish them well or at best wishes them to gain the least valuable prizes, and to fill the lowest strata in the labour market.[44]

A disproportionate number of young black, Asian, and other minority ethnic individuals are in prisons; black people form 3 percent of the population in Wales and England but constitute 12 percent of prisoners. There is the problem of labeling—the assumption that nonwhite youth are given to crime makes it more likely that they will be stopped by police and questioned. In 1993 an official inquiry concluded that the Metropolitan Police was infected with institutional

---

[42] See Joan Metge, *The Maoris of New Zealand,* 2nd ed. (London: Routledge and Kegan Paul, 1976), 153–57, 292–95; Angela Ballara, *Proud to Be White? A Survey of Pakeha Prejudice in New Zealand* (Auckland: Heinemann, 1986), 147–50.

[43] See Health Quality and Safety Commission, *A Window on the Quality of Aotearoa New Zealand's Health Care 2019* (Wellington: New Zealand Government, 2019), 42–48.

[44] David Sutcliffe, "Introduction," in *The Language of Black Experience*, ed. David Sutcliffe and Ansel Wong (Oxford: Basil Blackwell, 1986), 8.

racism,[45] a social disease all too common in the country.[46] In the BLM protests in Britain, people held up placards naming black victims of police violence.

Australia

In Australia, indigenous peoples have experienced racism, including persistent institutional racism, for over two hundred years. Aboriginal Australians and Torres Straits Islanders are 3 percent of the population but 27 percent of prisoners. Their health is considerably worse than that of non-Aboriginal people, and their life expectancy at birth is about twenty-one years less for men and nineteen years less for women. An editorial in the *Sydney Morning Herald* comments:

> The failures by courts and the police are sending far too many Indigenous people to prison. The high incarceration rate of Indigenous people results in a very large number of deaths in custody. As a share of the population, they are 10 times more likely to die in jail. The scars of these wasted lives linger for generations.[47]

The fundamental reason for this situation is entrenched institutional racism.[48]

---

[45] See *The Stephen Lawrence Inquiry: Report of an Inquiry by Sir William Macpherson of Cluny* (February 1999), CM 4262–I.

[46] See Editorial, "Evil that Lives On," *Tablet* (June 13, 2020), 2; Anthony Heath and Lindsay Richards, "How Racist Is Britain Today? What the Evidence Tells Us," *Conversation* (July 1, 2020); Leroy Logan, *My Life as a Cop* (London: SPCK Press, 2020), 102–26.

[47] Editorial, "Systemic Injustice for Indigenous People Must Be Addressed," *Sydney Morning Herald*, August 24, 2020.

[48] See *Racist Violence: Report of the National Inquiry into Racist Violence in Australia* (Canberra: Australian Human Rights Commission, 1991), 158–80; Barbara R. Henry, Shane Houston, and Gavin M. Mooney, "Institutional Racism in Australia: Healthcare," *Medical Journal of Australia* 180, no. 10 (2004): 517–20.

Persistence of Racism

Academia abandoned racist thinking as unscientific following the defeat of the Axis powers in 1945. In addition there was widespread horror at the Nazi-inspired Jewish Holocaust, a consequence of racist theories. We must now grapple with the question: Why does racism still exist, despite the fact that it has no scientific foundation? A number of causes are listed, but in practice some will overlap and reinforce one another.

Normalization of Evil

Moral evil can be defined as any deviation of a person or institution from the commandments prescribed by God or by any legitimate human authority. Evil is the antithesis of good, that which is morally depraved, bad, wicked, cruel, or unjust. Evil in this sense is referred to by Pope Francis in his encyclical *Fratelli Tutti* sixteen times. It refers to evil actions by personal or institutions. Pope St. John Paul II speaks of "structures of sin," that is, the accumulation and concentration of many acts of evil by individuals over time (*Sollicitudo Rei Socialis,* no. 36). In today's world the word *evil* generally has come to connote that which causes "discomfort and/or pain, to be unpleasant, offensive and disagreeable, to be 'not good.' It is interchangeable with 'bad', 'unpleasant', 'harmful.'"[49]

Why is evil losing its grave moral quality? Why is racism rarely seen as morally corrupt and unjust?[50] The disappearance of evil as a moral concept "is one of the most extraordinary features of modern society."[51] Charles Taylor responds theologically: "Running through all these attacks [on the existence of evil] is the spectre of meaninglessness; that as a result of the denial of transcendence . . . we are left with a view of human life which is empty . . . and cannot answer the craving for goals we can dedicate ourselves to."[52]

---

[49] See Alan Macfarlane, "The Root of All Evil," in *The Anthropology of Evil,* ed. David Parkin (Oxford: Basil Blackwell, 1985), 57.

[50] See Bryan Massingale, *Racial Justice and the Catholic Church* (Maryknoll, NY: Orbis Books, 2018), 148–49.

[51] Ibid.

[52] Charles Taylor, *A Secular Age* (Cambridge, MA: Belknap Press, 2007), 717.

There is also an anthropological reason for evil losing its grave moral quality. Little Lisa, the saxophone-playing daughter of Homer in *The Simpsons* television show and the social conscience of the family, at one point becomes squeamish about watching television violence, but her delinquent brother Bart replies: "If you don't watch the violence, you'll never get desensitized to it."[53] What Lisa is complaining about is the "normalization of violence."[54] Recall that culture is about maintaining the predictable, the normal (see Axiom 1, Chapter 1). Racism is normal in society. So, why change it? Consider that it took centuries before the church—inspired by the great missionary Bartolomé de Las Casas, OP, in the sixteenth century—very hesitatingly began to question the morality of slavery.[55] And still the normalization of the evil of racism in our contemporary societies is all too rarely questioned.

Cultural Learning

Remember that culture is a silent language; we are rarely conscious of its powerful emotional and cognitive content (see Chapter 1). We are born into a racially biased culture in which the status quo is assumed to be normal. Rudyard Kipling grasped in a few lines the power of ethnocentric racism:

> All good people agree,
> And all good people say,
> All nice people like Us, are We
> And everyone else is They.[56]

---

[53] Quoted in Chris Turner, *Planet Simpsons* (London: Ebury Press, 2004), vi.

[54] "Among Americans who identify as Democrat or Republican, 1 in 3 now believe that violence could be justified to advance their parties' political goal—a substantial increase over the last three years." Larry Diamond, Lee Drutman, Tod Lindberg, Nathan P. Kalmoe and Lilliana Mason, "Opinion: Americans Increasingly Believe Violence Is Justified if the Other Side Wins," *Politico* (September 10, 2020).

[55] See Gustavo Gutiérrez, *Las Casas: In Search of the Poor Jesus Christ* (Maryknoll, NY: Orbis Books, 1993).

[56] Rudyard Kipling, *Debts and Credits* (London: Macmillan, 1926), 327–28.

We learn that idea of "All nice people like Us, are We" first and foremost through absorbing, often unconsciously, the prejudices of our own nation about people and things. The basic assumption of racist human inequality that pervaded the emergence of colonialism in the West, and which was subsequently "refined" by the Nazis, has remained in the popular imagination ever since; the belief in the inferiority of some groups of people, or races as they were named, has been transferred from one generation to the next, and continues to haunt "race relations." Theologian Bernard Brady wisely warns of the insidious presence of racism: it "often has a subtle effect on people. It is as if it leaves a hidden imprint. Like a genetic predisposition to a disease, racism may lie dormant in a person until provoked by particular environmental realities."[57]

Once cultural and racial prejudices against "different" people have been absorbed, it is difficult to eradicate them. For example, as an increasing number of people of color migrated to Britain in the 1980s and 1990s, black people began to be presented by news media as a problem. This is racial bias. Young black men were portrayed as crime prone and as disturbers of civil peace. In comedy shows, images were taken from colonial times that depicted black people as stereotypically stupid and ignorant.[58] Few people questioned the inaccuracy of this prejudicial branding of the migrants. Reflecting on the American scene, Bryan Massingale comments: "Because a racialized set of meanings and values permeates all of our society's cultural products, we learn our cultural 'racial code' almost by osmosis."[59] He is correct. On the power of racial biases to pervade cultures and to remain unquestioned, Massingale writes:

> This is how racism enters the picture, not in the sense of deliberate and intentional acts of meanness and cruelty. We are dealing with a more or less unconscious racial bias that is manifested in the pervasive cultural association of black with criminality, in the willingness to presume (or, at least, to give them the benefit of the doubt), and above all, in the inability

[57] Bernard V. Brady, *Essential Catholic Social Thought* (Maryknoll, NY: Orbis Books, 2008), 230.

[58] See Chris Barker, *Cultural Studies: Theory and Practice*, 4th ed. (London: Sage, 2012), 275.

[59] Massingale, *Racial Justice and the Catholic Church*, 27.

to empathize with the plight of a black teenager confronted by an armed adult.[60]

Fear, Contempt of Differences, and Scapegoating

Culture is about order, the comforting presence of the familiar, the normal; whatever threatens order evokes fear (see Axiom 6, Chapter 1). The greater the fear, the more likely we are to marginalize, even demonize, any group that causes the distress (see Axiom 7, Chapter 1).

Fundamentalist Anti-immigrant Movements[61]

Fundamentalism is "a proclamation of reclaimed authority over a [secular or religious] sacred tradition which is to be reinstated as an antidote for a society perceived to have strayed from its cultural moorings."[62] James Hunter calls fundamentalism a form of organized anger and says that all fundamentalist groups "share the deep and worrisome sense that history has gone awry,"[63] the consequence of modernity and postmodernity. Richard Antoun also emphasizes the emotional aspect of fundamentalism: it is "an orientation to the world, both cognitive and affective. The affective, or emotional, orientation indicates outrage and protest against (and also fear of) change."[64]

Populism was increasingly evident on both sides of the Atlantic even before COVID-19 (see Chapters 2 and 3).[65] In the United States,

---

[60] Massingale, "Conscience Formation and the Challenge of Unconscious Racial Bias," 60.

[61] Fundamentalism is more fully explained in Arbuckle, *Fundamentalism at Home and Abroad.*

[62] Anson Shupe, "Religious Fundamentalism," in *The Oxford Handbook of The Sociology of Religion*, ed. Peter B. Clarke, (Oxford: Oxford University Press, 2009), 481.

[63] James Hunter, "Fundamentalism in Its Global Contours," in *The Fundamentalist Phenomenon*, ed. Norman J. Cohen (Grand Rapids, MI: Eerdmans, 1990), 59.

[64] Richard T. Antoun, *Understanding Fundamentalism: Christian, Islamic, and Jewish Movements* (Walnut Creek, CA: AltaMira Press, 2001), 3.

[65] See Pippa Norris, *Radical Right: Voters and Parties in the Electoral Market* (New York: Cambridge University Press, 2005).

right-wing and white-supremacist groups,[66] encouraged by Donald Trump and others, claim that illegal immigration is a threat to social order.[67] At the same time, right-wing, anti-immigrant populism became active in Europe. Some examples: Marine Le Pen, leader of the National Rally in France, once compared Muslims praying in the French street to the Nazi Occupation; Geert Wilders, a Dutch politician and member of the Party for Freedom, believes that Muslim immigration should be halted; Siv Jensen, leader of the Progress Party in Norway, achieved large popular gains through her attacks on Muslim immigration; and an Estonian leader, Martin Helme, stated that "our immigration policy should have one simple rule: if you're black, go back. . . . I want Estonia to be a white country."[68] In Germany in early 2016 the Alternative for Germany Party (AFD) achieved double-digit results in elections in three German states; the party officials said it may be necessary to shoot at migrants trying to enter the country illegally and they have mooted the idea of banning mosques.[69] And in Britain, fear of immigrants provided strong backing for Brexit.

The supporters of these populist movements are angry people, harking back to simpler times. They are angry because unemployment in Europe is high and rising. Stagnant wages in America are enraging a large group of older working-class white men whose jobs are threatened by globalization and automation.[70] Moreover, they complain, there are immigrants and freeloaders who grab benefits, commit crimes, and spurn local customs. In addition, particularly in Europe, the refugee crisis and international jihadist networks are eroding confidence that state governments can continue to protect

---

[66] Geneva Sands of CNN comments: "White supremacists will remain the most 'persistent and lethal threat' in the United States through 2021, according to Department of Homeland Security draft documents" (September 8, 2020). See Cynthia Miller-Idriss, *Hate in the Homeland: The New Global Right* (Princeton, NJ: Princeton University Press, 2020), 6–9; for the origin of white supremacism, see David W. Blight, "An American Pogrom," *New York Review of Books* 67, no. 18 (2020): 25–27.

[67] See Miller-Idriss, *Hate in the Homeland,* 50–62.

[68] Martin Helme, cited in Cas Mudde, *The Far Right Today* (Cambridge: Polity Press, 2019), 27.

[69] See Jan-Werner Muller, "Beyond the New German Right," *New York Review* (April 14, 2016).

[70] See Martin Sandbu, *The Economics of Belonging* (Princeton, NJ: Princeton University Press, 2020), 28–29, 68–70.

their citizens.[71] These movements existed before COVID-19, but the pandemic has further inflamed anti-immigrant racism.

Racism through Humor

Humor is one of the most effective means of communication; it has a subversive quality because it relaxes people, thus disposing them to receive information. Humor is positive when it respects the dignity of people; it is negative, or unkindly, when it degrades or mocks people, as in commonly used ethnic jokes.[72] The goal of an ethnic joke is to "put down" members of other cultures. At the same time, one's own group is presented as normal and superior. Miller-Idriss comments on the contemporary use of humor by far-right youth to spread racist themes:

> [Where] the extreme far right might have previously embraced bold tattoos or posters of swastikas or racist phrases, today's far-right youth are more likely to display ambiguous messages, embedding racist or anti-immigrant sentiments in brightly colored iconography. . . . Part of this shift in communication styles is due to the wider use of humor, jokes, and irony in internet culture more broadly, especially through the creation and circulation of memes. . . . The widespread creation and circulation of racist . . . memes on social media . . . have effectively weaponized humor to help carry extremist ideas into the mainstream.[73]

Founding Mythologies

The consequences of history are long-lasting. Residual racist qualities of founding mythologies (see Axiom 3, Chapter 1) can be revived by populist leaders and others to discriminate against minority ethnic groups and reinforce institutional racism, as is evident today, for example, in the United States[74] and Australia. Donald Trump was elected president in late 2016 despite his well-publicized "fear-mongering

---

[71] See Arbuckle, *Fundamentalism at Home and Abroad*, 1–29.

[72] See Gerald A. Arbuckle, *Laughing with God: Humor, Culture, and Transformation* (Collegeville, MN: Liturgical Press, 2008), 1–18.

[73] Miller-Idriss, *Hate in the Homeland*, 65–66.

[74] Perry, *In the Name of Hate*, 70.

and narcissism and cheerleading for torture . . . racism, misogyny, and xenophobia"[75] (see Chapter 3). In his electioneering he described illegal immigrants as rapists and murderers and claimed that Mexicans and Chinese and others had "stolen our jobs." This is dangerous populist language that fosters racist fear and contempt.[76] Trump was drawing on a political tradition with deep roots, including the Know-Nothing Party in the nineteenth century and the America First Committee of the early 1940s (see Axiom 7, Chapter 1). The latter accused "decadent" Europeans and well-connected Jews of conspiring to draw America into a new world war. Trump confirmed his xenophobic penchants when he failed to condemn outright the white nationalists actively expressing their hate message in Charlottesville in August 2017 (as well as when, in the view of many, he incited mob violence against the Capitol in January 2021). White nationalists and fascist sympathizers were brought into mainstream politics for the first time in living memory. In brief, Trump revived the residual racist myth that African Americans and Indians were excluded from the public founding story. That myth remains to haunt the present;[77] at the very time when democracy and freedom were proclaimed, African Americans and Native Americans[78] were sentenced to an existence without rights.[79]

> "Good" blacks and Indians were all but invisible in patriot newspapers throughout the conflict (Revolution of Independence). Rather, they were lumped together, as Jefferson would in the Declaration, as "domestic insurrectionists" and "merciless savages." The totality of these printed stories created a

---

[75] Mark Danner, "On the Election II," *New York Review of Books* (November 10, 2016), 19; see Anderson, *White Rage,* 161–80.

[76] See Ruth Wodak, *The Politics of Fear: What Right-Wing Populist Discourses Mean* (London: Sage, 2015), 4–6.

[77] See Bryan Stevenson, "The Presumption of Guilt," *New York Review of Books* (July 13, 2017). E. J. Dionne writes: "We fought the Civil War over the question of who was included in the phrase 'all men are created equal.' And we still have not come to terms with that fact." "There's a Right Way to Judge America's Past," *Washington Post,* July 2, 2017.

[78] See Thomas F. Pettigrew et al., *Prejudice* (Cambridge, MA: Harvard University Press, 1982), 33–40.

[79] See Obama, *A Promised Land*, xv.

> convincing interpretation. . . . They were not eligible for any of the benefits of American independence.[80]

Racist rhetoric by populist leader Donald Trump also appealed to white working-class Americans who felt their cultural and religious securities were under threat from migrants and neglected by the politicians in Washington (see Chapter 3). They had begun to feel like strangers in their own land.[81] Responding to their nostalgia for the securities of the white dominance of the 1950s, Trump promised his followers throughout his presidency and in his campaign for reelection that America would be "great again." He astutely understood that the them-against-us fury has profoundly deep foundations in American history and can be used for political advantage.[82]

In Australia, in 1788, when British settlers first arrived on the Australian continent, they concluded that the country was *terra nullius*—a land without a people—that was theirs for the taking. If the Aboriginal Australians contested this assumption, they were killed or further pushed back into inhospitable parts of the country. Many died, if not from violent causes, then from new diseases to which they had no resistance. The Australian Constitution of 1901 did not—and still does not—make adequate provision for Australia's first peoples. In fact they were denied citizenship until 1967. The Constitution was intended to unite Australians, but the first peoples of the country were not included in this agreement; they continue to feel excluded today.[83]

Economic Exploitation

Historically, racial prejudice has been, and continues to be, used to legitimize economic and political gain through the oppression

---

[80] Robert G. Parkinson, *The Common Cause: Creating Race and Nation in the American Revolution* (Chapel Hill: University of North Carolina Press, 2016), 22.

[81] See Emma Green, "It Was Cultural Anxiety that Drove White, Working Class Voters to Trump," *Atlantic* (May 9, 2017); Arlie R. Hochschild, *Strangers in Their Own Land: Anger and Mourning on the American Right* (New York: Free Press, 2016).

[82] See Arbuckle, *Fundamentalism at Home and Abroad,* 79–81, 86–92.

[83] See "Racism in Australia Is Not Just a Thing of the Past," *The Economist* (June 20, 2020).

of minority groups by dominant cultures. Anthropologist Michel Foucault says that scientific knowledge is primarily a discourse of power, a way in which formidable bureaucracies, states, corporations, and other institutions wield power over others: "There are no power relations without the correlative construction of a field of knowledge, nor any knowledge that does not presuppose and constitute at the same time power relations."[84] When apartheid policies ruled in South Africa, the white elite felt threatened economically and culturally, but the assumption of superiority allowed them to dominate ruthlessly and economically the republic's nonwhite ethnic groups.[85] The elite, reinforced by their command of the media, police, and state bureaucracies, manufactured "scientific" knowledge to justify their suppression of nonwhites.

As Colin Samson and Carlos Gigoux observe, "Economic racism is the common practice of situating industries that emit hazardous wastes and cause general ecosystem degradation in close proximity to lands occupied by poor, minority and indigenous populations."[86] This gravely affects the health of these people. Moreover, in "the places where indigenous peoples have not already been displaced, their marginalization is often a reason to make lands available for commercially lucrative, yet toxic, industrial activities."[87] Such is the case in parts of Australia, Canada, India, China, and Brazil.

Personality Types

Deeply insecure individuals and cultures achieve for themselves a sense of self-esteem by downgrading the abilities of other people and cultures. Gordon Allport describes a personality type prone to racism: "The person with character-conditioned prejudice likes order, but especially *social* order. In his clear-cut institutional memberships, he finds the safety and the definiteness he needs. Lodges, schools,

---

[84] Michel Foucault, *The Foucault Reader* (New York: Pantheon, 1984), 175.

[85] See David Mason, "After Scarman: A Note on the Concept of Institutional Racism," *New Community* 10, no. 1 (1982): 338–45.

[86] Colin Samson and Carlos Gigoux, *Indigenous Peoples and Colonialism: Global Perspectives* (Cambridge: Polity Press, 2017), 125.

[87] Ibid.

churches, the nation, may serve as a defense against the disquiet in his personal life. To lean on them saves him from leaning on himself."[88]

Ethnic Groups: Reacting to Racism

The pandemic has had a grave impact on many minority and vulnerable ethnic groups and will continue to do so for years to come. "Human dignity," writes novelist Frederick J. Thwaites, "can't be subjected to endless indignities and remain intact."[89] For many oppressed peoples the pandemic is an experience of re-traumatizing, since they have been subjected, sometimes for generations, to exploitation and racism. James Ritchie describes the decades-long, distressing experiences of the indigenous Maori in New Zealand, experiences with which many an oppressed ethnic group can identify: "Maoris . . . have passed, as a people, through almost every kind of negative experience, save total extermination, that could possibly be."[90] The following are examples of what happens to the dignity of people when they are subjected to injustices such as overt and institutional racism.

Ghetto/Segregation

Ethnic or racist prejudices force people into ghettos, and this segregation imposes wide and impassable barriers to humanly respectful interaction with people of the dominant and oppressing culture.[91] Attempts to break these barriers may meet further, even violent, resistance from the dominant oppressing group, particularly from police.[92] We tend to assume that segregation is confined only to housing, but racial separation involves a whole range of life experiences. For ex-

---

[88] Allport, *The Nature of Prejudice*, 380.

[89] Frederick J. Thwaites, *Beyond the Rainbow* (London: Harcourt), 62.

[90] James Ritchie, "Understanding Maoris," paper presented to the Vocational Council and Employers' Association, March 24, 1976.

[91] See Douglas S. Massey and Nancy A. Denton, *American Apartheid: Segregation and the Making of the Underclass* (Cambridge, MA: Harvard University Press, 1993), 83–114, 148–85.

[92] See Elijah Anderson, *Code of the Street: Decency, Violence, and the Moral Life of the Inner City* (New York: W. W. Norton, 2000), 32, 34.

ample, many African American residents in inner cities can have little social communication with the world beyond their ghettoes.

Slave-like Conditions

Millions of Asians from India, Bangladesh, Pakistan, and the Philippines now live abroad, working mainly in other countries such as Saudi Arabia, Iraq, or Taiwan. Most are forced to migrate temporarily or permanently with the hope that what they earn can assist destitute families at home. Tragically, migrant workers are easily exploited, especially in Arab countries. Women migrants are in particular danger of exploitation; the most vulnerable who do not have social protection or ready access to health and essential services disproportionately bear more severe consequences of the pandemic crisis.[93] The plight of legal or illegal migrant farm and other workers from the Caribbean or Mexico in the United States has been well documented; they face "exploitation by growers and crew leaders who have almost total control over their lives."[94]

Cultural and Spiritual Abuse

In the United States not only were Native Americans denied political rights for years, but efforts were made to destroy their culture. This was done by forcibly removing children from their families and placing them in foster homes or institutions so that they could be "trained" as white people. Such was the fate of indigenous children also in Canada and Australia. From about 1905 through 1967 successive state and federal Australian governments had the policy of "breeding out the color" of "half-caste" Aboriginal children by segregating them, often by force, from "full blood" children. Eventually it was expected that these children would marry white people and thus "breed out" the color.[95] One survivor said: "Why me, why was

---

[93] See Jeremy Douglas et al., UNICEF, "End Stigma and Discrimination against Migrant Workers and Their Children during COVID-19 Pandemic" (June 5, 2020); International Labour Organization, *COVID-19: Impact on Migrant Workers and Country Response in Malaysia,* update (May 8, 2020).

[94] "Asian Migrant Workers: Voluntary Servitude," *The Economist* (September 10, 1988), 25–28.

[95] See Robert Manne, "The Stolen Generation," in *Reconciliation*, ed. Michelle Grattan (Melbourne: Bookman Press, 2000), 129–39.

I taken? It's like a hole in your heart that can never heal." Another: "Actually what you see in a lot of us is the shell, and I believe as an Aboriginal person that everything is inside me to heal me if I know how to use it, if I know how to maintain it, if I know how to bring it out and use it. But sometimes the past is just too hard to look at."[96]

Land for traditional peoples is sacred; their identities are intimately linked to the land of their ancestors. For example, for the Maori in New Zealand, the lands on which their ancestors had lived, had fought on, and were buried in are always objects of deep affection. As this proverb describes it: "Mine is the land, the land of my ancestor."[97] Pope Francis writes in *Laudato Si'* (*On the Care of Our Common Home*) of indigenous peoples: "For them, land is not a commodity but rather a gift from God and from their ancestors who rest there, a sacred space with which they need to interact if they are to maintain their identity and values" (LS, no. 146). Today governments and industrialists, motivated by racism, continue to destroy the culture of indigenous peoples. Over the past seventy or more years, indigenous peoples in regions of South America, Myanmar, the Philippines, and elsewhere have faced both the inexorable pressure to drive them from their lands and forests and deliberate efforts to destroy their spiritually based cultures. Some have fought back by organizing protest movements, even at times taking up arms, but with little success.[98] At Murujuga, West Australia, there is possibly the largest indigenous rock art site in the world, but "between 5 percent and 25 percent . . . has been removed or destroyed as a result of iron mining, industrial expansion and poor archaeological advice."[99] Aboriginal peoples have objected but they have rarely been listened to.

---

[96] "Bringing them Home: Report of the National Inquiry into the Separation of Aboriginal and Torres Strait Islander Children from Their Families" (Canberra, ACT: Commonwealth of Australia, 1997), 177.

[97] Quoted in Raymond Firth, *The Economics of the New Zealand Maori* (Wellington: R. E. Owen, 1959), 368.

[98] See Julian Burger, *Report from the Frontier: The State of the World's Indigenous Peoples* (London: Zed Books, 1987).

[99] Jose Antonio Gonzalez Zarandona, "Heritage as a Cultural Measure in a Postcolonial Setting," in *Making Culture Count: The Politics of Cultural Measurement*, ed. Lachlan MacDowall et al. (Basingstoke: Palgrave Macmillan, 2015), 180.

Resignation

It is particularly tragic when individuals internally and externally accept the stereotype of inferiority leveled at them by a dominant culture. They become indifferent to, or even oblivious of, their status and poverty. Having no will to resist, they fall into a state of apathy. In 1976, in a study of attitudes of senior Maori college students in New Zealand, I found that 73 percent accepted the dominant culture's view of their inferiority by agreeing to the statement that "Maoris have above-average gifts for manual and semi-skilled work." Teachers said that when these students of average or above-average ability found their studies hard, they would quickly lose confidence in themselves, saying, "What's the use! We Maoris don't have the skills anyway." African Americans, in the Southern states of the United States, had so interiorized the view of human inferiority that Martin Luther King Jr. found it extremely difficult to foster their support for his civil-rights campaign. Barack Obama speaks of "protective pessimism," a feeling of hopelessness about the possibility of moving forward that still grips many African Americans. For example, "Nothing in Black people's experience told them that it might be possible for one of their own to win a major party nomination, much less the presidency of the United States."[100]

Despair

Despair can be the fate of some who are exposed to endless racism. People give up trying to cope with the interminable pressures of prejudice, discrimination, poverty, deplorable housing, and unemployment. Noel Pearson, an Aboriginal leader in Australia, describes what happens:

> Racism . . . .attacks self-esteem and the soul in ways that those who are not subjected to it would have not an inkling of understanding about. Racism is a major handicap—it results in Aboriginal people not recognizing opportunities when they arise, in not being able to seize opportunities when they arise,

[100] Obama, *A Promised Land*, 116.

in not being able to hold on to opportunities when they have them.[101]

Aggression

There are two primary catalysts for physical or psychological aggression by individuals or groups: *frustration*, which results from interference with goal-directed behavior or the failure to achieve goals; and *attacks* on or *threats* to life, material well-being, or self-concept and self-esteem.[102] The targets of aggression can be members of the dominant oppressing society. The people who are verbally or physically attacked may not be directly responsible for oppression, but they symbolize the dominant society and its oppressive attitudes and structures. People who externally accept the image of inferiority while internally rejecting it are in danger of aggressive behavior. For the sake of peace they may see protesting against their oppression as useless, but violence is liable to erupt at any moment if attacks on self-esteem become unbearable.

Such was the case when riots occurred in Brixton, London, in 1981, the first large-scale racial confrontation between black British youth and white British police, or in the Watts African American ghetto of Los Angeles in 1965. Of the latter Milton Viorst writes: "Nobody wanted a riot, nobody plotted to start it. . . . But, as if they had been coiled for signal, ten thousand blacks took to the streets that week to loot and to burn."[103] This dynamic may well have motivated some of the rebounding violence (see Chapter 2), such as looting and burning, that occurred in several American cities in reaction to the death of George Floyd in June 2020. Martin Luther King Jr. reasoned: "At some point, glacial progress spills over into anger. I think America must see that riots do not develop out of thin air. . . . In a real sense

---

[101] Noel Pearson, quoted in Australian Institute of Family Studies, "Causal Factors of Family Violence and Child Abuse in Aboriginal Communities" (May 2002).

[102] See Ervin Staub, *The Roots of Evil: The Origins of Genocide and Other Group Violence* (Cambridge: Cambridge University Press, 1989), 35–50.

[103] Milton Viorst, *Fire in the Streets: America in the 1960s* (New York: Simon and Schuster, 1979), 311.

our nation's summers are caused by our nation's winters of delay. And as long as America postpones justice, we stand in the position of having these recurrences of violence and riots over and over again."[104]

Rape can also be a form of aggressive release from oppression.[105] Eldridge Cleaver, an early leader of the Black Panther Party, comments: "[The] particular women I had victimized had not been actively involved in oppressing me or black people. I was taking revenge on them for what the whole system was responsible for."[106] An especially tragic form of aggression occurs when the anger and frustration evoked by racism is redirected from the dominant culture to people the oppressed most love. I once interviewed a Maori person in New Zealand who had been imprisoned for assaulting his wife and child: "I was good at work as a building laborer. My white companions seemed to accept me, but so often they told funny stories about my people. I laughed outwardly but felt sad inside. One day after one of these 'jokes,' I became so angry that I went home and bashed my wife and child, saying all the time: 'I love you, I love you.' I hoped they would understand!"

Challenging Racism

Some individuals and ethnic groups, after suffering years of institutional racism, are able by their own efforts to break by peaceful means some of its entrapping powers. A Western Indian carpenter in Britain comments: "I decided to quit the disenchantment, the uncompassionate, yet impolite monstrosity of the white man's society. . . . I began to intermingle with my own people. . . . I felt wanted and desired by my own people. . . . I belonged."[107] Sociologist Ron Eyerman writes that the African American trauma of slavery has become a source of cultural identity for American blacks. It is not the experience of slavery as such but the memory of it, its reconfiguration in the minds

---

[104] Martin Luther King Jr., cited in "Measuring Racial Progress in America," *The Economist* (June 6, 2020), 28.

[105] See Roy F. Baumeister, *Evil: Inside Human Violence and Cruelty* (New York: W. H. Freeman, 1999), 138–39.

[106] Eldridge Cleaver, *Soul on Ice* (New York: Delta, 1968), 14.

[107] W. Collins, cited in Dilip Hiro, *Black British, White British* (London: Eyre and Spottiswoode, 1971), 80.

of later generations of blacks, that forms cultural trauma and its mythology. He argues that "African American" is a historically shaped identity that is embedded in the collective memory of slavery. "As former slaves began to die out the voice of direct experience began to disappear. . . . By the 1880s, as the dreams of full citizenship and cultural integration were quashed, the meaning of slavery emerged as the site of an identity conflict, articulated most clearly by the newly expanded and resourceful ranks of educated blacks."[108] Two opposing mythological narratives of the collective memory resulted: a liberal narrative promoted by the NAACP (National Association for the Advancement of Colored Peoples) and others, and a narrative by black nationalists. In the 1960s and 1970s nationalists preached political separatism because they became convinced the dominant political system could not be justly changed in their favor. Thus, Malcolm X of the Black Muslims could bitterly remark on the need for African Americans to go it alone: "It is not necessary to change the white man's mind. We have to change our mind."[109]

Scriptural Reflection: Jesus Christ Challenges Injustices

Pope Francis says, speaking of George Floyd:

> We cannot tolerate or turn a blind eye to racism and exclusion in any form and yet claim to defend the sacredness of every human life. At the same time . . . nothing is gained by violence and so much is lost.[110]

---

[108] Ron Eyerman, *Cultural Trauma: Slavery and the Formation of African American Identity* (New York: Cambridge University Press, 2002), 16; see also Ron Eyerman "Cultural Trauma: Slavery and the Formation of African American Identity," in *Cultural Trauma and Collective Identity,* ed. Jeffrey C. Alexander et al., 60–111 (Berkeley and Los Angeles: University of California Press, 2004).

[109] See Gerald A. Arbuckle, "Understanding Ethnicity, Multiculturalism, and Inculturation," *Human Development* 4, no. 1 (1993): 6.

[110] Pope Francis, "Message on George Floyd," quoted in *America Magazine* (June 3, 2020).

Racism feeds on social and economic inequalities. As Pope Francis writes in *Evangelii Gaudium,* "Until exclusion and inequality in society and between peoples is reversed, it will be impossible to eliminate violence" (EG, no. 59). Tragically, in the wake of the pandemic these inequalities are further increasing. At the time of Jesus Christ there were also huge gaps between the rich and the poor, much institutional bullying, and racist-like cultural customs that degraded people.[111] As we see in the following pages, Jesus by his methods of evangelizing and his teachings neither tolerated nor turned a blind eye to these realities. And neither can we. Vatican II states in *Gaudium et Spes* that "any kind of social or cultural discrimination in basic personal rights on the grounds of sex, race, social conditions, language or religion, must be curbed and eradicated as incompatible with God's design" (no. 29).[112] Jesus modeled this design. He was perceptively conscious of the prejudices and discriminations of his time, and he actively and publicly sought to identify them by words and actions.[113]

Challenging Oppressive Structures

Jesus challenges oppressive ritual regulations that forbid healing on the Sabbath (Lk 14:3), and he heals people who have been marginalized because of disease (Mk 10:46–52). Decrying the marginalizing behavior of the Pharisees, he deliberately associates with people they considered sinners: "Now all the tax collectors and sinners were coming near to listen to him. And the Pharisees and the scribes were grumbling and saying 'This fellow welcomes sinners and eats with them'" (Lk 15:1–2). Though frequently dissenting from the scribes and Pharisees theologically, Jesus remains open and friendly to them. For example, he dines with a Pharisee despite the fact that he does not receive a special welcome that is his cultural due. Jesus then respectfully reminds his host what authentic conversion entails; he points to the sincere repentance and love of the woman who tearfully washed his feet "and dried them with her hair" (Lk 7:44).

---

[111] See John Stambaugh, *The Social World of the First Christians* (London: SPCK, 1986).

[112] Austin Flannery, ed., *Documents of Vatican II* (Grand Rapids, MI: Eerdmans, 1975).

[113] See Arbuckle, *Fundamentalism at Home and Abroad*, 172–75.

Challenging Subjugation of Women

At the time of Jesus women were considered second-class Jews, banished from the worship and teaching of God, "with status scarcely above that of slaves."[114] Hence, his frequent actions toward them are indeed profoundly countercultural and prophetic. He speaks to a woman ritually considered to be unclean, causing amazement to his disciples: "They were astonished that he was speaking to a woman" (Jn 4:27). He also teaches women (Lk 10:38–42), giving them a status equal to that of men (Lk 13:10–17); overtly ministers to them (Lk 7:35–50); offers them the highest respect as persons without condescension (Mt 5:28); and includes them in his inner circle of close followers (Lk 8:1–3). In fact, women were the first witnesses of his resurrection (Lk 24:1–11; Jn 4:29; 20:18).[115]

Challenging Cultural Inferiority

The Jews regarded the Samaritans as culturally inferior, and the feeling was mutual (see Chapter 1). The Samaritans must consequently have been astonished when Jesus reaches out to them often with a concerned and friendly manner. By greeting people who were scorned and hated, he makes their enemies his own. The Samaritan is proposed as an example of compassion and justice (Lk 10:33–37); only one of the ten lepers, and he a Samaritan (Lk 17:16), returned to thank Jesus for healing him; and in Acts 1:8 we see that Samaritans are welcome aspirants for conversion.

One day Jesus wearily stops at Jacob's Well for water while the disciples are away buying food (Jn 4:1–42). He begins to converse with a demonized Samaritan woman of shaky morality and asks her for a drink of water. Being a Samaritan she is understandably astonished. How will she act? How will Jesus act? By custom, a Samaritan should refuse hospitality. All is well—Jesus creates a trusting and respectful atmosphere, letting her know he is aware of her immoral private life (Jn 4:16–17). With confidence established, Jesus seeks to explain to her two fundamental lessons: that knowledge of God is a

---

[114] Elizabeth Achtemeier, "Women," in *The Oxford Companion to the Bible*, ed. Bruce M. Metzger and Michael D. Coogan (New York: Oxford University Press, 1993), 807.

[115] See ibid.

gift of "living water" (Jn 4:11), and the revelation of his own identity (Jn 4:14). She is so thrilled by her conversation with Jesus that she hastens to share her new faith with fellow villagers (Jn 4:2–30, 39–42). When the disciples return, they discover what has been happening. They are startled, even annoyed and ashamed that Jesus has been conversing with a woman, and a Samaritan one at that. They reveal their cultural prejudices and then they press him to eat, but he answers in ways they find puzzling: "I have food that you do not know about. . . . My food is to do the will of him who sent me and to complete his work" (Jn 4:32, 34). And the conclusion to this episode is that "many Samaritans from the city believed in him because of the woman's testimony" (Jn 4:39).

Fostering Nonviolence[116]

Nonviolence as a pastoral response to injustices is not easy to define. Thomas Schubeck writes, "Generally speaking, nonviolence means refraining from all violent acts, including inflicting physical injury on persons, killing them or threatening to do so, as well as intentionally damaging the property of another."[117] Staughton and Alice Lynd advise the following guidelines for nonviolent protests: first, refusal to retaliate; second, acting out of conviction by demonstrative action; third, the vision of love as an agent of radical change; and fourth, deliberate lawbreaking for conscience's sake (that is, civil disobedience).[118] Martin Luther King Jr. insisted that love of one's neighbor is at the heart of nonviolence.[119]

John Paul II, when commenting on the success of the nonviolent movements in Eastern Europe in *Centesimus Annus,* speaks of the masses eschewing violence in favor of winning their oppressors over with love (no. 23). Compassion as a particular expression of love is at the heart of nonviolence (see Chapter 1); compassion is contrary to violence because, while violence inflicts hateful images on an opponent, compassion acknowledges that these malevolent powers can

---

[116] See Thomas L. Schubeck, *Love That Does Justice* (Maryknoll, NY: Orbis Books, 2007), 60–67.

[117] Ibid., 54.

[118] See Staughton Lynd and Alice Lynd, eds., *Nonviolence in America: A Documentary History* (Maryknoll, NY: Orbis Books, 1995), xii.

[119] Martin Luther King Jr., quoted in ibid., 217.

exist in oneself. We can judge someone while at the same time not condemn them because we are conscious of our own failings. Rollo May comments: "Compassion is felt toward another . . . because he doesn't fulfill his potentialities—in other words, he is human, like you or me, forever engaged in the struggle between fulfillment and nonfulfillment."[120]

The aim of nonviolent movements is to undermine the primary basis of the power of autocratic authorities, that is, the consent of the people they are unjustly controlling.[121] To collude with oppression is to reinforce the power of autocrats.[122] When people refuse to be subjugated—for example, through boycotts—they gradually eliminate the oppressor's capacity to control, Here is the wisdom of Thomas Merton: "Nonviolence is not for power but for truth. It is not pragmatic but prophetic. . . . Nonviolence . . . does not say, 'We shall overcome' so much as 'This is the day of the Lord, and whatever may happen to us He shall overcome.'"[123]

Jesus Christ by word and action denounces violence as the method to gain power over others or even to defend one's own rights. Jesus exceeds the hopes of the Israelite prophets and pronounces that the fullness of the reign of God ends all suffering, violence, and injustice. It is the arrival of a new community of love and justice: "He will wipe every tear from their eyes; Death will be no more, for the first things have passed away" (Rev 21:4). The mission given him by the Father is to proclaim in word and deed what must be done to achieve this vision (Lk 4:18). The universal standard in relating to others is: "So always treat others as you would like them to treat you" (Mt 7:12). Love must be the reason: "But I say this to you, love your enemies and pray for those who persecute you. . . . For if you love those who love you, what reward will you get?" (Mt 5:44, 46). Love for one's persecutors, rather than "an eye for an eye," is to be the motivating principle: "You have heard that it was said, 'An eye for an eye and a tooth for a tooth.' But I say this to you, Do not resist an evildoer"

---

[120] Rollo May, *Power and Innocence: A Search for the Sources of Violence* (New York: Norton, 1998), 251.

[121] See Arbuckle, *Violence, Society, and the Church*, 227–34.

[122] See Peter Ackerman and Jack Duvall, *A Force More Powerful: A Century of Nonviolent Conflict* (New York: Palgrave, 2000), 494–95.

[123] Thomas Merton, "Peace and Revolution," in *Peace and Nonviolence*, ed. Edward Guinan (New York: Paulist Press, 1973), 127.

(Mt 5:38–39). At no point does Jesus use violence to protect himself or his disciples.[124] Jesus blessed those who afflicted him. He prayed for his torturers. He died for his enemies, because he died for all of us.[125]

However, Jesus explains that not resisting is not the same as accepting powerlessness. The oppressor wants the oppressed to agree that they are powerless, of no value. To be in control of one's life, even under violence, is a central right of every person, for it is the root of one's self-esteem and the basis of the conviction that one has significance.[126] This is so important to Jesus that he gives several examples by way of explanation to illustrate graphically that non-violence is not synonymous with passivity (Mt 5:39–41). Rather, nonviolent action is claiming one's just right to self-respect. Roman soldiers could by law force people to carry their baggage a certain distance only; if a person offered to carry the load an extra mile, this placed the soldier in the publicly embarrassing position of violating Roman practice. The oppressed person is equivalently saying to the Roman soldier: "You are forcing me to carry your baggage. I have no alternative, but I object to the law!" Jesus says: "If anyone forces you to go one mile, go also the second mile" (Mt 5:41). Also, "If anyone wants to sue you and take your coat, give your cloak as well" (Mt 5:40). If the coat and cloak are given to the bully, this leaves the person publicly naked, but since nakedness violates Jewish law, this would surely shame the oppressor.[127]

Summary

- The pandemic has aroused concern for escalating the ongoing racism in countries. Racism is the deterministic belief-system that different "races" possess distinct characteristics, abilities, or qualities, especially so as to regard them as innately inferior or superior to one another. Anthropologists prefer the term *ethnic group* to *race* because the former is a cultural type,

---

[124] See Schubeck, *Love That Does Justice*, 56–66.

[125] See Jürgen Moltmann, *The Power of the Powerless* (London: SCM Press, 1983), 55–63.

[126] See May, *Power and Innocence*, 243.

[127] See Walter Wink, *Engaging the Powers: Discernment and Resistance in a World of Domination* (Minneapolis: Fortress Press, 1992), 175–84.

while the latter is often an imposed biological categorization. Racism flourishes when there are social, economic, and political inequalities.

- Institutional racism is the systematic allocation of power, resources, and work opportunities that benefits the majority ethnic group and disadvantages minority ethnic people. An example is the pattern of subjugation of blacks by whites at the social level resulting from the interaction of several social institutions such as systems of policing, the labor market, and education. There are many reasons why it continues, such as the dynamics of cultural learning, fear and contempt of difference, fundamentalist beliefs, founding mythologies of nations, economic exploitation, and personality types.
- Globally, institutional racism forces people to experience, for example, ghetto segregation, slave-like living conditions, cultural and spiritual abuse, resignation, despair, and aggression. Some individuals and ethnic groups, after suffering years of institutional racism, are able to break some of its entrapping powers by peaceful means.
- Jesus Christ, by his example and teaching, condemned injustices, including racist-like behavior. Never, however, did he use violence to defend himself or his followers: "But I say to you: Do not resist an evildoer. . . . Love your enemies and pray for those who persecute you" (Mt 5:39, 44).

Reflection Questions

1. "Each day," writes Pope Francis in *Fratelli Tutti*, "we have to decide whether to be Good Samaritans or indifferent bystanders" (no. 69). What ethnic groups in your city and in your parish are discriminated against in employment, education, and housing? How can you and others work together to help remove this discrimination?
2. "I am," writes English essayist Charles Lamb (1775–1834), "in plain words, a bundle of prejudices—made up of likings and disliking." What can you do to detect in yourself cultural and racist prejudices?
3. St. Paul writes: "As many of you as were baptized into Christ have clothed yourselves with Christ. There is no longer Jew

or Greek, there is no longer slave or free, there is no longer male and female; for all of you are one in Christ Jesus" (Gal 3:27–28). What do you feel as you read this text? What are the behavioral implications of the text for yourself and others?

6

The Call to Refocus on Christ and His Mission

> *Once we emerge from this pandemic, we will not be able to keep doing what we were doing, as we were doing it.*
>
> —Pope Francis, May 31, 2020

> *When the church isn't for the suffering and broken, then the church isn't for Christ. Because Jesus, with his pierced side, is always on the side of the broken.*
>
> —Ann Voskamp, *The Broken Way*

This chapter explains that:

- The pandemic trauma offers the chance to be pastorally creative.
- The refounding of the church involves fostering intentional faith communities.
- Challenging institutional racism demands prophetic courage.
- Catholic fundamentalists are rigidly selective of doctrines.
- Pastoral formation avoids the "splitting" dynamic in ministries.

We the people of God are stunned by two liminal traumatic experiences: the trauma of the church muddied by the sexual abuse and cover-up crises,[1] and now the trauma of the global pandemic. What are we to do? Pope Francis has sound advice to guide us. Therefore, this chapter has a threefold focus. The first is to summarize the relevant lessons of Pope Francis. Second, in response to these lessons I have selected four urgent pastoral strategies: (1) to foster faith-based intentional communities; (2) to challenge institutional injustices; (3) to understand Catholic fundamentalism; and (4) to avoid the business ethos dominating our ministries. Finally, in these distressing times we need to make difficult pastoral decisions. In a concluding scriptural reflection we look at the annunciation, where Mary teaches us the art of faith discernment.

Pope Francis: Pastoral Advice

The people of God in the midst of the pandemic chaos, says Pope Francis, can learn from the reactions of the disciples when caught in the fear-evoking experience of being at sea in a tumultuous storm.[2] The fragile faith of Peter, James, John, and the other disciples is exposed in the storm. Jesus uses the incident as a rite of passage (see Chapter 2), an initiation experience for the disciples to grasp the divinity of Christ and to grow in faith. Jesus is the ritual leader of the rite of initiation. The incident begins with Jesus climbing into the boat, followed by the disciples (Mt 8:23)—this is the rite's separation stage. They head out to sea (chaos is often biblically symbolized by the sea).

The chaos or liminality stage comes quickly and is graphically described: "The boat was being swamped by the waves" (Mt 8:24). Jesus, like Jonah in a similar setting, is in the stern, in the part of the boat that sinks first. He is asleep, despite the roaring of the wind and tossing of the boat. This is chaos. Jesus awakes to the desperate calls of the terrified disciples: "Lord, save us! We are perishing!" (Mt 8:25). They not only doubt the promises of Jesus to protect them,

---

[1] See Gerald A. Arbuckle, *Abuse and Cover-up: Refounding the Catholic Church in Trauma* (Maryknoll, NY: Orbis Books, 2019).

[2] See Pope Francis, Homily: "Facing the COVID-19 Storm," Vatican Dispatch (March 27, 2020).

but they reproach him for what they believe is his negligence. He criticizes their behavior, saying, "Why are you afraid, you of little faith?" (Mt 8:26). Jesus then calms the sea (Mt 8:26). In the process he encourages the faith of the disciples by revealing his divine powers over chaos.[3] The reentry stage of the initiation of the disciples into this deeper faith is marked by the astonishment that the disciples experience when the sea is suddenly calmed at the request of Jesus: "What sort of man is this, that even the winds and sea obey him?" (Mt 8:27). Pope Francis, following the example of Jesus, sees profound lessons for the people of God in this incident of the storm.

Lesson 1: Enter a rite of passage for deeper conversion

We are invited by our Savior to enter into a rite of passage, a liminal journey into a deeper faith. During the pandemic, Pope Francis notes:

> Like the disciples in the Gospel we were caught off guard by an unexpected, turbulent storm and we find ourselves afraid and lost. . . . The storm exposes our vulnerability and uncovers those false and superfluous certainties around which we have constructed our daily schedules, our projects, our habits and priorities. . . . It lays bare all the prepackaged ideas and forgetfulness of what nourishes our souls.[4]

Like the disciples, we realize that we cannot go on thinking of ourselves alone; only by working together in faith will it be possible to come through the crisis. In Jesus, Pope Francis reminds us, "we have an anchor; by his cross we have been saved. We have a rudder; by his cross we have been redeemed. We have hope."[5] "What we are living now is a place of *metanoia* (conversion)."[6]

---

[3] See Sjoerd L. Bonting, *Chaos Theology: A Revised Creation Theology* (Toronto: Novalis, 2012), 21.

[4] Pope Francis, quoted in Antonio Spadaro, "'A New Imagination of the Possible': Seven Images from Francis for Post-Covid 19," *La Civiltà Cattolica* (July 14, 2020).

[5] Ibid.

[6] Pope Francis, "Take Care of Yourselves for a Future That Will Come," *Tablet* (April 11, 2020), 6.

Lesson 2: Be pastorally creative

It is time to rearticulate the mission of Christ to the world in turmoil, "to reset the course of life toward You, Lord, and toward others,"[7] a mission of solidarity especially focused on people who are poor. We need to find radically new pastoral ways of implementing this mission: "It's a time for inventing, for creativity . . . a propitious time to find the courage for a new imagination of the possible, with the realism that only the Gospel can offer us."[8]

Earlier, Francis writes in *Evangelii Gaudium*: "Pastoral ministry in a missionary key seeks to abandon the complacent attitude that says: 'We have always done it this way.' I invite everyone to be bold and creative" (EG, no. 33). In this rite of passage, what pastoral methods and governance structures must be abandoned that no longer serve the mission of Christ to the world? "Some of these customs may be beautiful," Francis writes, "but they no longer serve as means of communicating the Gospel. We should not be afraid to re-examine them" (EG, no. 43). Let mourning begin.

Lesson 3: Be a listening church

Pope Francis frequently emphasizes the need for "a synodal church [that] is a listening church, aware that listening is more than hearing. It is a reciprocal listening in which each one has something to learn."[9] Listening at all levels of the church leads to solidarity and participation for mission.[10]

---

[7] Pope Francis, "Un plan para resucitar: una meditación," in *Vida Nueva* (April 18–24, 2020), quoted in Spadaro, "A New Imagination of the Possible."

[8] Ibid.

[9] Pope Francis, "Pope Calls for 'Synodal' Church," *National Catholic Reporter* (October 17, 2015); see also Pope Francis, *Fratelli Tutti* (*On Fraternity and Social Friendship*), nos. 48, 190, 198, 261.

[10] See Massimo Faggioli, *The Liminal Papacy: Moving Toward Global Catholicity* (Maryknoll, NY: Orbis Books, 2020); and idem, "From Collegiality to Synodality: Promise and Limits of Francis's 'Listening Primacy,'" *Irish Theological Quarterly* 85, no. 4 (2020): 352–69; see also International Theological Commission, *Synodality in the Life and Mission of the Church* (March 2, 2018).

Lesson 4: Be a refounding church

A listening church is a refounding church (see EG, no. 11). Refounding is the pastoral process of returning to the original founding of the church and being so inspired by this experience that we respond by creatively bridging in radically fresh ways the pastoral gaps between Christ's mission and the world in which we live.

Refounding focuses on the roots of problems, while renewal focuses on their symptoms. President Franklin Roosevelt's New Deal was the epitome of chaos converted into opportunity. In his State of the Union Address of 1935, in which he explains his reasons for inaugurating the New Deal, he distinguishes between refounding and renewal: "The attempt to make a distinction between recovery and reform is a narrowly conceived effort to substitute the appearance of reality for reality itself. When a man is convalescing from illness, wisdom dictates not only cure of the symptoms but also removal of their cause." Roosevelt believed that unemployment benefits merely reacted to the symptoms of poverty, that is, renewal. But the policies of the New Deal, based on the original founding experience of the nation, were to be directed at removing the deep causes of poverty, and thus at refounding.[11]

In the church both refounding and renewal require personal and group conversion to Christ. The difference between them is the degree of imaginative creativity that is required: the innovative action of refounding evokes dramatically novel pastoral responses while renewal focuses on improving existing pastoral methods.[12] But existing pastoral methods may have become irrelevant. To believe that a brilliant pastoral strategy will hold indefinitely into the future is a certain recipe for failure. It is no longer sufficient in this postmodern turbulent world to confine ourselves only to improving present pastoral processes (renewal). The chaos within the church and the world calls for the refounding of governance structures and pastoral services in the church. This is what Pope Francis means when he writes: "Pastoral ministry in a missionary key seeks to abandon the complacent attitude that says: 'We have always done it this way.' I invite everyone to be bold and creative" (EG, no. 33).

---

[11] See Martin Sandbu, *The Economics of Belonging* (Princeton, NJ: Princeton University Press, 2019), 1–13.

[12] See Arbuckle, *Abuse and Cover-up*, 130–34.

Examples of Refounding

The Council of Jerusalem under the leadership of apostles and elders is historically the most notable example of refounding (Acts 15:4–29). The gathering took place after unnamed Judeans raised questions in Antioch about the status of converted Gentiles and the need for their circumcision and observance of Mosaic Law. St. Peter goes to the root of the problem: Judean customs are smothering the gospel. He settles the question by recounting his experience with the centurion Cornelius; that is, converted Gentiles had already received the Holy Spirit without the need to adhere to the Law (Acts 10:1–48). If the council had not agreed, the church would have remained a Judean sect, closed in on itself and imposing customs that were irrelevant or contrary to the gospel (Gal 3:25–26).

The council's example challenges us today. In Australia the Catholic Church maintains 75 acute care hospitals and 550 residential and aged care facilities, founded most often by religious congregations with their different charisms. In recent times, with the rapid withdrawal of religious congregations from direct involvement in these institutions, the merging of once-competitive facilities, and the introduction of new lay governance structures,[13] the question arose: "Who now is the primary founder of these ministries? Is it the former religious congregations with their different founders, or is it Jesus Christ?" A pastoral discernment process concluded: "Central to the approach to care provided by Catholic health ministries is the Gospel of the Good Samaritan. The Good Samaritan is our model."[14] Improving the presentation of the charisms of different congregations would not address the need for a new founding narrative to support new governance structures of the ministries. That would have been pastoral renewal. Instead, a new foundational charism is necessary that gives identity to the new structures and the overall national unity of the ministries. Catholic healthcare ministries, therefore, are being refounded on the story of the Good Samaritan; at the same time, the secondary founding stories of the religious congregations, the former

---

[13] For example, the new ministerial Public Juridic Persons (PJPs). A PJP is a legal entity that permits ministries to act in the name of the Catholic Church. See Arbuckle, *Abuse and Cover-up*, 155–61.

[14] Patrick Garcia, CEO Catholic Health Australia, "Good Samaritan Is Our Model for Health Care," *CathNews* (February 11, 2020).

sponsors of the ministries, are being reenergized by rediscovering their original links to this fundamental story.[15]

The late Jesuit superior general, Father Adolfo Nicolas, SJ, well understood this need for the ongoing refounding of pastoral structures and methods. He warns of myth drift in Jesuit university ministries, of unwittingly accepting market mythology to the detriment of gospel values (see Axiom 2, Chapter 1): "It would be a tragedy if [Jesuit] universities simply replicated the rationality and self-understandings of our secular, materialistic world. Our reason for being in education is completely different."[16] He asks this question: "What kind of universities, with what emphases and what directions, would we run, if we were refounding the Society of Jesus in today's world?" His answer: "I think every generation has to re-create the faith, they have to re-create the journey, they have to re-create, that is, refound, the institutions. This is not only a good desire. If we lose the ability to re-create, we have lost the spirit."[17] To re-create is to go to the roots of contemporary pastoral problems and imaginatively respond with Christ's message. We cannot assume, Father Nicolas says, that the reasons for the original founding of these institutions remain valid today:

> Imagination grasps reality. . . . The starting point . . . will always be what is real . . . a world of suffering and need, a broken world . . . with many people in need of healing. . . . Imagination is a creative process that goes to the depth of reality and begins re-creating it.[18]

Earlier he wrote of religious life:

> [Refounding] is an invitation to transcend chaos in a double movement: backward to the original emptiness; forward to a

---

[15] See Gerald A. Arbuckle, *Catholic Identity or Identities? Refounding Ministries in Chaotic Times* (Collegeville, MN: Liturgical Press, 2013), 173–98.

[16] Adolfo Nicolas, quoted in Christopher Pramuk, "A New Kind of Humanity: The Legacy of Adolfo Nicolas," *America* (July 2020), 37. The quotation is an excerpt from a recorded interview by Antonio Spadaro with Adolfo Nicolas, posted on the *Jesuit Post* (July 20, 2013).

[17] Ibid., 38.

[18] Ibid., 36, 37.

> new [pastoral] creation. Both movements are essential for the enterprise of refounding. . . . Neither the denial of chaos nor the ability to hide it under the blanket of visible institutional success or simple unenlightened good will can bring religious life forward to new service or new fidelity to God's call in the coming age.[19]

In a previous book I detailed pastoral responses to the trauma of sexual abuses, such as including laypeople in the governing structures of the church.[20] In the next section here, inspired by the pastoral lessons of Pope Francis, I focus on four pastoral strategies, the need for which have become more evident in these pandemic times: (1) fostering intentional faith communities; (2) challenging institutional injustices; (3) responding to Catholic fundamentalism; and (4) forming mission-driven ministries.

Pastoral Strategy 1: Fostering Intentional Faith Communities

Pastoral Challenge

Even before COVID-19 there is no denying that the Catholic Church has been in a crisis of membership. Many people are withdrawing from membership for a variety of reasons,[21] including the earnest desire for spiritual sustenance. Pope Francis writes that the parish should be "a community of communities, a sanctuary where the thirsty come to drink in the midst of their journey." But he admits that "the call to review our parishes has not yet sufficed to bring them nearer to the people" (EG, no. 28). Many parishes are threatened with closure, often because of the lack of priests.

- "44 percent of British cradle Catholics, and 34 percent of American ones now no longer identify as Catholic."[22]

---

[19] Adolfo Nicolas, review of Gerald A. Arbuckle, *Out of Chaos: Refounding Religious Congregations* (New York: Paulist Press, 1988), in *Human Development* 10, no. 4 (1989): 46.

[20] See Arbuckle, *Abuse and Cover-up*, 64–211.

[21] See Stephen Bullivant, *Mass Exodus: Catholic Disaffiliation in Britain and America since Vatican II* (Oxford: Oxford University Press, 2019), 56–84.

[22] Ibid., 250.

- In the United States, it is the Catholic Church that has experienced the most significant net loss.[23]
- In Australia, "across all age groups, more than 20,000 Australians *every year* are ceasing to identify themselves as Catholics."[24] The parish has been the foundation of the Catholic Church in Australia, "but its survival in many parts of the country is no longer assured."[25] One in four parishes no longer has a full-time resident priest.[26]
- The most common reason given for former Catholics in the United States joining a Protestant denomination is that the church has failed "to deliver what people consider fundamental products of religion: spiritual sustenance and a good worship service."[27]

There is an urgent need to find ways to refound parishes so that they may become "communities of communities" (EG, no. 28). The people of God are yearning for spiritual sustenance, liturgies that touch the hearts, to connect in supportive ways with one another. Why is this not happening? Streaming mass during the months of lockdown has been a creative act, but it can never satisfy people's needs, including the millions of people who are poor and with no access to computers. What fundamental change is necessary?

Pastoral Response

For refounding the parish, what model of church should be our guide? The answer is the early church, which grew by forming

---

[23] See Pew Research Center, "Strong Catholic Identity at a Four-Decade Low in US" (March 13, 2013).

[24] See Robert Dixon and Stephen Reid, "The Contemporary Catholic Community: A View from the 2011 Census," *The Australasian Catholic Record* 90, no. 2 (2013): 145–46.

[25] Robert Dixon, Stephen Reid, and Marilyn Chee, *Mass Attendance in Australia: A Critical Moment* (Melbourne: Pastoral Research Office, 2013), 8.

[26] See Peter J. Wilkinson, *Catholic Parish Ministry in Australia: Facing Disaster?* (Canberra: 2011), 3, 19.

[27] Thomas Reese, "The Hidden Exodus: Catholics Becoming Protestants," *National Catholic Reporter* (April 18, 2011).

prophetic, intentional faith communities following the example of Jesus Christ and the apostles. The early chapters of Acts contain several significant summaries of the idealized life and mission of these communities in Jerusalem (Acts 2:42–47; 4:32–5:16; 6:1–7). Community members worship together, share goods, and witness to the values of the gospel. For Luke, the church will grow only through intentional faith communities.[28] Today, as then, writes Walter Brueggemann, "The central task of ministry is the formation of a community with an alternative, liberated imagination that has the courage and freedom to act in a different vision and a different perception of reality."[29] Such small, faith-based communities are needed not only in parishes, but also in ministries, such as schools and healthcare facilities.

But what does *community* mean?[30] This is not an easy word to define because community as a concept is one of the most elusive and vague in the social sciences.[31] Definitions tend to fall into one of three broad categories depending on their particular emphasis. First, *community* is synonymous with *place*; for example, a particular parish is called a community because it belongs in an identifiable geographical suburb. The second definition emphasizes a *type of relationship* that people experience; for example, when people have a feeling of belonging they say they are experiencing community. In this definition it is not at all necessary to be present in a physical place and be face-to-face with people, because the key point in this definition is the feeling of belonging. When letter writing and then the telephone were invented, community was liberated from the constraints of place; the ultimate place-liberated community today is the spatially unlimited

---

[28] See Robert W. Wall, "The Acts of the Apostles," *The New Interpreter's Bible,* vol. 10, 70–74 (Nashville, TN: Abingdon Press, 2002); John Stambaugh and David Balch, *The Social World of the First Christians* (London: SPCK, 1986), 54–60; Etienne Nodet and Justin Taylor, *The Origins of Christianity: An Exploration* (Collegeville, MN: Liturgical Press, 1998).

[29] Walter Brueggemann, *Hopeful Imagination: Prophetic Voices in Exile* (Minneapolis: Fortress Press, 1986), 99.

[30] See Gerald A. Arbuckle, *Intentional Faith Communities in Catholic Education* (Strathfield: St. Pauls Publications, 2016), 77–82, 140–49, 204–7.

[31] See Ann Casson, *Fragmented Catholicity and Social Cohesion: Faith Schools in a Plural Society* (Bern: Peter Lang, 2013), 108–27.

virtual communities of the Web.[32] The third definition highlights the *quality of relationships*; this definition emphasizes the actual commitment or the willingness in practice to do something together.

Community Models

Using the third definition, we can distinguish three models of communities situated on a continuum: two dysfunctional communities at one polar extreme, namely, the *enmeshed* and the *disengaged*; and at the other pole of the continuum the *intentional* type. This last is the most supportive of personal and group growth in maturity.[33]

- In *enmeshed communities* members look almost exclusively to one another for emotional, spiritual, and intellectual security. The group's regulations extend to members' inner lives, but there is an overdependence on the leader that hinders or prevents individuation and differentiation of members.[34] Enmeshed communities are closed in on themselves, a point well expressed by Pope Francis in *Fratelli Tutti*: "Closed groups and self-absorbed couples . . . tend to be expressions of selfishness and mere self-preservation" (FT, no. 89).
- In *disengaged communities* individual rights take precedence at all times over the common good; there is no accountability by members to the group, nor is it expected. Community exists solely to satisfy the self-centered needs of neoliberal governments and individuals (see Chapter 3).[35] An example of disengaged communities comes from Pope Francis: "Digital

---

[32] See James Fulcher and John Scott, *Sociology* (Oxford: Oxford University Press, 2007), 496–97. For incisive comments on how the web is challenging traditional assumptions about community, see Charles Heckscher, *Trust in a Complex World: Enriching Community* (Oxford: Oxford University, 2015), 1–17.

[33] See Lucy Malarkey and Dorothy Marron, "Evaluating Community Interaction," *Human Development* 3, no. 3 (1982): 117–24.

[34] See Parker J. Palmer, *The Courage to Teach: Exploring the Inner Landscape of a Teacher's Life* (San Francisco: John Wiley, 2007), 93, 94.

[35] See Martha C. Nussbaum, *Not for Profit: Why Democracy Needs the Humanities* (Princeton, NJ: Princeton University Press, 2010), 95–97.

relationships . . . do not really build community; instead, they tend to disguise and expand the very individualism that finds expression in xenophobia and in contempt for the vulnerable. Digital connectivity . . . is not capable of uniting humanity" (FT, no. 42).

- In an *intentional community* members deliberately and consciously strive to nurture a culture in which all are willing to coordinate and, if necessary, sacrifice their personal aspirations and actions for the common good. The word *intentional* means "deliberate" or "consciously chosen." Community is only alive when members are willingly and actually committing themselves to an agreed-upon action. That is, intentional communities "represent a kind of 'voting with the feet'—a call to action that is personal and communal, bringing together the needs of the individual with those of other individuals, reestablishing the bonds that connect human beings in a particular fashion."[36] For Pope Francis, community is never static: "Love . . . impels us toward universal communion. No one can mature or find fulfillment by withdrawing from others" (FT, no. 95).

Intentional Christian Communities

Pope Paul VI, in 1975, writes in *Evangelii Nuntiandi (Evangelization in the Modern World)* that

> the Christian community is never to be closed in upon itself. . . . The intimate life of this community . . . only acquires its full meaning when it becomes a witness. (EN, no. 15)

I define an intentional faith community as *a small group of people who willingly commit themselves to develop a gospel-centered intimacy to be expressed in shared faith, ongoing conversation, and shared action for mission.*[37] The quality of community life is gospel solidarity (see Chapter 1). Intentional faith communities acknowledge that members will be different from one another, but, in the words of

---

[36] See Susan L. Brown, ed., *Intentional Community: An Anthropological Perspective* (Albany: State University of New York Press, 2002), 1–13.

[37] See Bernard J. Lee and Michael A. Cowan, *Dangerous Memories: House Churches and Our American Story* (Kansas City: Sheed and Ward, 1986), 91.

Pope Francis, "We must walk united with our differences: there is no other way to become one. This is the way of Jesus."[38] In contrast to the enmeshed or disengaged types, an intentional community has the following qualities: members work together to clarify the mission of the community, which is the primary source of bonding and energy for the group; they actively commit themselves to live and work according to the mission; formal community structures are few and are regularly evaluated by the community in light of its vision and mission.[39]

A faith community, for example, will meet *some* of the social, emotional, and intellectual needs of its members; supportive friendships within and outside the group are encouraged. Because of the level of trust within the community, members feel at ease to challenge one another's behavior in light of a commonly accepted vision, mission, and strategies. In "I-Thou"[40] relationships there is space for both autonomy and mutuality; dialogue and open interaction are encouraged before any significant decisions are made about community affairs.[41] As a prophetic community, it emphasizes the call to repentance, love of one's neighbor, and the option for the poor. In other words, members strive to live the truths of the Good Samaritan (see Chapter 1).

Biblical Examples

God desired to build an intentional community with the Israelites.[42] The community would be noted for its justice, unity, collaboration, dialogue, and mutuality. Jesus deliberately first chooses twelve people as companions and collaborators in his mission of teaching and mercy

---

[38] Pope Francis, interview with Antonio Spadaro, "A Big Heart Open to God," *America* 209, no. 8 (2013): 28.

[39] See Charles F. Elbot and David Fulton, *Building an Intentional School Culture* (Thousand Oaks, CA: Corwin Press, 2008).

[40] Martin Buber defines the way in which individuals should interact as the "I-Thou" relationship. This happens when there is mutuality, openness, presence, and directness. The "I" relates to the "Thou" not as something to be studied, measured, or manipulated, but as an irreplaceable presence that responds to the "I" in its individuality. See Martin Buber, *Between Man and Man* (New York: Routledge, 2002), xii.

[41] See Roland S. Barth, *Learning by Heart* (San Francisco: Jossey-Bass, 2004), 31.

[42] See Walter Brueggemann, *A Social Reading of the Old Testament* (Minneapolis: Fortress Press, 1994), 17.

(Mk 3:14; 6:7–13). With this mission as the focus he fosters a supportive intentional community with the twelve, a community that is to be the archetypical model for all future Christian educational endeavors. They are to share his sufferings if they are to be worthy of him and his mission. Love is to bind them together (Jn 15:12).

After Christ's death and resurrection, St. Luke describes in the Acts of the Apostles how in Jerusalem the faith becomes firmly established and the first community thrives (Acts 1—5). The picture given by Luke is an idyllic one, a community that all must strive to imitate, however imperfectly.[43] People live in harmony and are deeply committed to living gospel values (Acts 1:14).[44] St. Paul describes the qualities of an intentional Christian community in these words: "Let love be genuine; hate what is evil, hold fast to what is good; love one another with mutual affection; outdo one another in showing honor" (Rom 12:9–10). Paul was a realist. He knew from bitter experience that as the number of Christian communities developed there would be difficulties, even dissension, in the communities he established.[45] Paul, who had trembled at the news of factions within the Christian community of Corinth, was devastated to discover yet more divisions (1 Cor 7:1–11; 8–10; 12–14).[46] For resolving community tensions and divisions, ongoing conversion was needed: "the fruit of the Spirit is love, joy, peace, patience, kindness, generosity, faithfulness, gentleness, and self-control" (Gal 5:22–23).

---

[43] For a description of tensions in the faith communities at the time of the Acts see N. T. Wright, *The New Testament and the People of God* (Minneapolis: Fortress Press, 1992), 452–53.

[44] For an insightful analysis of this community see Thomas Ryan, *Shame, Hope, and the Church: A Journey with Mary* (Strathfield, NSW: St. Pauls Publications, 2020), 82–84. Ryan notes that two groups represented in the community were known to be opposed to each other; "The structure of the sentence (Acts 1:14) suggests, for Mary, a role as mediator between these extremes." Ibid., 83.

[45] See Ben Witherington, *Conflict and Community in Corinth* (Grand Rapids, MI: Eerdmans, 1995); Margaret M. Mitchell, *Paul and the Rhetoric of Reconciliation* (Louisville, KY: Westminster/John Knox Press, 1991), 65–183; Raymond Collins, *First Corinthians* (Collegeville, MN: Liturgical Press, 1999), 71–73.

[46] See Jerome Murphy-O'Connor, *Paul: His Story* (Oxford: Oxford University Press, 2004), 111, 162–63.

Pastoral Strategy 2: Challenging Institutional Injustices

Pastoral Challenge

Institutional injustices, including institutional racism, residential segregation,[47] and institutional patriarchy,[48] are tragically commonplace and are being further reinforced by the pandemic and its aftermath (see chapters 4 and 5). All of us reflect the preferences and aversions of the cultures we live in, most often unconsciously (see Chapter 5). Unjust attitudes and discrimination develop and continue in society, in the church, and in parishes often because people unconsciously absorb the prejudices of their culture. Well-motivated, even kindly people just float along, unaware of their bigotries and support of unjust structures.

Pastoral Response

In practical terms, what can we do, individually and in our parishes?[49]

- Recognize that educational, economic, social, and gender inequalities breed prejudices and discrimination (see Chapters 4 and 5).
- Become aware of, and act against, racist, ethnic, and gender institutional prejudices and discriminations (see Chapter 5).[50] This task is so difficult that we need the support of our intentional

---

[47] See Cory D. Mitchell and M. Therese Lysaught, "Equally Strange Fruit: Catholic Health Care and the Appropriation of Residential Segregation," *Journal of Moral Theology* 8, no. 1 (2019): 36–62.

[48] See Gerald A. Arbuckle, *Violence, Society, and the Church: A Cultural Approach* (Collegeville, MN: Liturgical Press, 2004), 39–40, 69–71.

[49] See Gerald A. Arbuckle, *Fundamentalism at Home and Abroad: Analysis and Pastoral Responses* (Collegeville, MN: Liturgical Press, 2017), 162–84.

[50] Robert Livingston of the Harvard Kennedy School has created a five-stage process of identifying and eradicating racism in organizations: "(1) Problem awareness, (2) Root-cause analysis, (3) Empathy, or level of concern about the problem and the people it afflicts, (4) Strategies for addressing the problem, and (5) Sacrifice, or the willingness to invest the time, energy and resources necessary for strategy implementation." Robert Livingston, "How to Promote Racial Equity in the Workplace," *Harvard Business Review* 98, no. 5 (2020): 67.

faith communities. "The task of prophetic ministry is to nurture, nourish, and evoke a consciousness and perception alternative to the consciousness and perception of the dominant culture around us."[51]

- Be motivated to act (see Chapter 1). Awareness of prejudices and discrimination is not enough.[52] We must delve deep into our innermost feelings, emotions, and judgments: "For it is what comes from within, from the human heart, that evil intentions come . . . and they defile a person" (Mk 7:21, 23).[53]
- Be alert to prejudicial biases, negative stereotyping, conspiracy theories, and moral panics targeting minority groups in media (see Axioms 6 and 7, Chapter 1).
- Be vigilant to the demands of the preferential option for the poor (see Chapter 1) in decision-making in Catholic ministries.
- Do not repeat ethnic or gender jokes, which can be profoundly offensive and unjust (see Chapter 5).[54]

---

[51] Walter Brueggemann, *The Prophetic Imagination* (Philadelphia: Fortress Press, 1978), 13.

[52] In 1975 the Catholic Bishops Conference of New Zealand initiated a nationwide study of the pastoral needs of indigenous Maori and immigrant Pacific Island Catholic communities. The study revealed an overall significant unconscious bias in Catholic schools against accepting students from these communities. Following the publication of the study, the enrollment of indigenous and immigrant students significantly increased. See Gerald A. Arbuckle and John Faisandier, *The Church in a Multicultural Society: Pastoral Needs of Maoris and Polynesian Immigrants in New Zealand* (Wellington: NZCBC, 1975).

[53] See Bryan N. Massingale, *Racial Justice and the Catholic Church* (Maryknoll, NY: Orbis Books, 2018); idem, "The Systematic Erasure of the Black/Dark-Skinned Body in Catholic Ethics," in *Catholic Theological Ethics Past, Present, and Future: The Trento Conference,* ed. James F. Keenan, 116–24 (Maryknoll, NY: Orbis Books, 2011); and idem, "Conscience Formation and the Challenge of Unconscious Racial Bias," in *Conscience and Catholicism: Rights, Responsibilities, and Institutional Responses,* ed. David E. DeCosse and Kristin E. Heyer, 53–68 (Maryknoll, NY: Orbis Books, 2015).

[54] See Gerald A. Arbuckle, *Laughing with God: Humor, Culture, and Transformation* (Collegeville, MN: Liturgical Press, 2008), 17–18; and Arbuckle, *Fundamentalism at Home and Abroad*, 166.

Pastoral Strategy 3: Responding to Catholic Fundamentalism[55]

Pastoral Challenge

Pope Francis is leading the church in a rite of passage of letting go of attachments to a monarchical papacy and its theological foundations. But there is resistance in the form of religious fundamentalism. Pope Francis comments: "Fundamentalism is a sickness that is in all religions. . . . Religious fundamentalism is not religious, because it lacks God. It is idolatry, like idolatry of money. . . . We Catholics have some—and not some, many—who believe in the absolute truth and go ahead dirtying the other with calumny, with disinformation, and doing evil."[56] This form of opposition is so significant that we can speak of an implicit schism within the church, one that is even encouraged by members of hierarchies who either ignore or criticize Francis's call to preach and live the mission of Christ to the poor. Fundamentalists have become increasingly vociferous since the election of Pope Francis.[57] He warns: "Even in Catholic media, limits can be overstepped, defamation and slander can become commonplace, and all ethical standards and respect for the good name of others can be abandoned" (FT, no. 46).

Pastoral Response

We first need to understand the roots of fundamentalism. Fundamentalists find rapid mythological change extremely disturbing and dangerous (see Axioms 1, 2, and 7, Chapter 1). Cultural, religious, and personal certitudes are shaken. Consequently, fundamentalists simplistically yearn to return to a utopian past or golden age, purified of dangerous ideas and practices. History must be reversed. Here are some signs of this fundamentalism among Catholics: nostalgia for a

---

[55] See Arbuckle, *Fundamentalism at Home and Abroad*, 97–124.

[56] Pope Francis, comments to journalists on plane returning from Africa, November 30, 2015.

[57] See Mike Lewis, "The Reactionary Rift," *America: The Jesuit Review of Faith and Culture* (October 2020): 46–49.

pre–Vatican II golden age, when it is assumed that the church never changed; a spirituality in which Jesus Christ is portrayed as an unforgiving and punishing God; and a highly selective approach to what fundamentalists think pertains to the church's teaching. Well-respected theologians, bishops, and even popes can be accused of heresy. They hold rigidly to chosen doctrines, for example, the evils of abortion, and ignore the other social justice imperatives. To achieve their aims they are prepared to ally themselves with governments and powerful citizens who encourage injustices, including institutional racism and the oppression of the poor.

Because fundamentalism is an emotional reaction to the disorienting experience of change, fundamentalists are not readily open to rational discussion. In relating to fundamentalists we need to avoid being drawn into hostile or heated arguments. Expressions of anger and vigorous disagreement only affirm people in the rightness of their belief. As Pope Francis advises: "We must accompany them gently."[58] Our best witness to the truths of our Catholic beliefs will be our inner peace built on faith, charity, and concern for justice, especially among the most marginalized. At the same time, however, we expect hierarchies and pastors to support Pope Francis explicitly by clearly publicizing and explaining his statements in pastoral letters and homilies. Their silence is assumed to be supportive of fundamentalists.

The reactions of Catholic fundamentalists, however, can teach us an important lesson. As I noted in 2010, I am forever grateful to Vatican II, but "as an anthropologist I believe it was culturally naive. Interfering with a symbol and myth without involving the people concerned leads inevitably to unnecessary pain, and grief or chaos."[59] Too often people were told that changes were to be made, such as in the liturgy, without any consultation or dialogue (see Axiom 2, Chapter 1). Many people were traumatized by this and the speed

---

[58] Pope Francis, cited in Christopher Lamb, "A Schism in All But Name," *Tablet* (September 21, 2020), 5.

[59] Gerald A. Arbuckle, *Culture, Inculturation, and Theologians: A Postmodern Critique* (Collegeville, MN: Liturgical Press, 2010), 36. See Mary Douglas, *Natural Symbols: Explorations in Cosmology* (London: Routledge, 1966), 42.

with which the changes were introduced. Remember! We are to be a listening and a synodal church.

Pastoral Strategy 4: Forming Mission-Driven Ministries

Pastoral Challenge

In 2016 the trustees of the Presbyterian Church in Australia dismissed the entire ruling council of a college because "the application of the governing model being pursued by the council was resulting in corporate objectives outweighing the educational mission."[60] The trustees were concerned that myth drift was taking place in the college, that is, important decisions were being based on corporate values, not according to the values of the church's educational mission. In the tension between the mission and the business aspects of the college, the business side was winning.

The action of the trustees highlights a similar and grave threat confronting the Catholic Church's involvement in key ministries in dioceses and parishes.[61] Especially because financial resources have been severely reduced since the pandemic began, the church is in constant danger of "forgetting that the most important measure of success is the achievement of mission-related objectives, not financial wealth or stability."[62] Market mythology can become a substitute for the Christ-centered mission in *all* pastoral activities.[63] Pope Francis forthrightly expresses his concern about the dangers of myth drift (see Axiom 2, Chapter 1) in ministries. In a Sistine Chapel mass on his first day as pope, he said: "If we do not confess to Christ, what would we be? We would end up a compassionate NGO (Non-Governmental Organisations). What would happen

---

[60] Eryk Bagshaw, "Scots College: Church Takes Over Top Private School," *Sydney Morning Herald*, February 23, 2016.

[61] See Lucy Grindon, "Catholic Colleges Face Financial Strain," *National Catholic Reporter* (August 10, 2020).

[62] J. Gregory Dees, "Enterprising Nonprofits," *Harvard Business Review on Nonprofits* (Boston: Harvard Business School Publishing, 1999), 164.

[63] See Gerald Grace, *Catholic Schools: Mission, Markets, and Morality* (London: RoutledgeFalmer, 2002), 181.

would be like when children make sand castles and then it all falls down."[64] Without our focus on Christ and his values our ministries lose their uniqueness.

To summarize the pastoral challenge:

- The tension between the mission of our ministries, the proclamation of the kingdom of God, and maintaining their financial viability is very real, more so now that resources are severely stretched in the pandemic aftermath. We must heed this warning: "Business people often think nonprofit organizations spend too much time agonizing about their mission. But in fact, its time well spent, because that's how a nonprofit builds a sense of community and shared values."[65]
- A central supposition in this book is that "one can neither work nor play nor theorize with chaos. Pure chaos is pure terror. One must find forms and frames within which to contain it"[66] (see Axiom 1, Chapter 1). The process of "splitting" is one frequent method of containing the chaos, but in a way that is not life-giving and transformative. For example, when "the mission" and "the business" are split apart in ministries, positive interaction ceases. Splitting is a *cultural and psychodynamic process in which individuals and groups, in an effort to cope with doubts, anxieties, and conflicting feelings caused by difficult or anxiety-provoking work, isolate different elements of experience, often to protect the perceived good from the bad.*[67]
- It is not *either* "the mission" *or* "the business." It is *both*, but the gospel mission is the senior partner that must motivate decision-making. Unless intentional action is taken, however,

---

[64] "Pope Francis Warns Church Could Become 'Compassionate NGO,'" *BBC News* (March 14, 2013).

[65] F. Warren McFarlane, "Working on Nonprofit Boards: Don't Assume the Shoe Fits," *Harvard Business Review* 77, no. 6 (November 1999): 78.

[66] C. Fred Alford, "The Group as a Whole or Acting Out the Missing Leader," *International Journal of Group Psychotherapy* 45, no. 1 (1995): 133.

[67] See Isabel Menzies Lyth, *Containing Anxieties in Institutions: Selected Essays* (London: Free Press, 1998), 43–85; Gareth Morgan, *Images of Organization* (Newbury Park, CA: Sage, 1986), 206; Edgar H. Schein, *Organizational Culture and Leadership* (San Francisco: Jossey-Bass, 1992), 177–79.

myth drift will continue in favor of the business side of the tension.

Isabel M. Lyth explains what *splitting* means. In her pioneering study of nursing staff in British hospitals, nurses are daily confronted with two overwhelming pressures: managing the physical problems of patients (the "disease") and their emotional needs (the "illness") (see Chapter 1). Lyth found that the division of patient care into discrete tasks delegated to different nurses reduced their awareness of feelings of responsibility toward patients as whole persons. Sick people became "the cancer cases in room 3" instead of patients with personal names (people whose suffering might cause nurses emotional distress). Nurses could concentrate on the mechanical problems of disease, the "good" pole, while avoiding involvement with patients' feelings, the "bad" pole. Thus, while splitting strategies protected nurses from the anxiety-creating issues of life, sickness, and death, they did so at great cost to the holistic healing of the patients.[68]

I have also found in my research into public and faith-based hospitals that there is a great potential for dangerous splitting, to the detriment of the welfare of patients, not only between the mission and business aspects of these institutions. Detrimental splits can also occur between acute and community care; federal and state government control; physicians and nurses; and clinicians and management.[69] One side is seen as "good" and the other as "bad," or vice versa. Scapegoating accompanies the splitting (see Axiom 7, Chapter 1). Clinicians blame management and vice versa.[70] This division forms a social defense, that is, a system of relationships that people feel protects them from being overwhelmed by the chaotic

---

[68] See Lyth, *Containing Anxieties in Institutions,* 43–85.

[69] See Gerald A. Arbuckle, *Healthcare Ministry: Refounding the Mission in Tumultuous Times* (Collegeville, MN: Liturgical Press, 2000), 141–47; and idem, *Humanizing Healthcare Reforms* (London/Philadelphia: Jessica Kingsley, 2013), 120–22.

[70] Anthropologist Claude Lévi-Strauss asserts that the primary quality of the human mind is its propensity to think in binary opposites and act accordingly, for example, sacred *or* profane, man *or* woman, us *or* them. See Claude Lévi-Strauss, *Totemism,* trans. Rodney Needham (Boston: Beacon Press, 1963).

pressures of their work. There is the yearning for simple causes for their problems, especially outside themselves, in ways that pass the responsibility on to others. In other words, splitting involves scapegoating.

Similarly, in the church today, under the pressures of change and pandemic crises, there are all kinds of potential splits. Ministries may dogmatically opt for the mission *or* the business, with an inflexible refusal to integrate both poles of the tension. One pole is seen as good, the other as bad, depending on which pole one favors. There are numerous other dangers of splitting, such as pope *or* hierarchies; bishop *or* priests; school principal *or* staff; pastor *or* parish manager; management board *or* trustees; CEO *or* management board. A split can develop between the two roles, and one role will be exalted over the other. Ecclesiastical institutions, including pastoral ministries and parish pastoral councils, cannot survive or effectively function unless *both* roles are kept in creative tension. Here are two case studies:

- Tensions developed in a Catholic college between the board of trustees and board of management, with the latter claiming the former kept interfering in decisions. On the other hand, the trustees insisted that they had the right to decide on policies that the management had to implement. Mutual scapegoating intensified over time, so much so that the teaching faculty also mirrored the split into oppositional camps. Morale sank so low that a significant number of staff left the college.
- A Catholic school had been financially sponsoring several students from low-income families, but when the pandemic came the rector unilaterally decided that the school was unable to continue the support, despite the fact that the option for the poor was an integral quality of its mission. The rector reasoned that financial viability was more important than the mission in this case. Five teachers objected to this decision: "Our educational integrity has been violated! By delaying the rebuilding of several classrooms we can maintain the sponsorships." Tensions intensified so much that conversations between the parties ceased.

Pastoral Response

Since many of the church's key ministries are now led by laypeople,[71] it is essential, if a new culture of church is to emerge, be sustained, and the process of splitting avoided, that laypeople, together with clergy, be not only professionally competent, but also profoundly formed in the founding mythologies of their ministries according to the Catholic tradition.[72] This will involve inter alia formation in the meaning of Catholic identities and clarification of operational roles in ministries.

In discussing the term *Catholic identity,* there is significant confusion on two issues. The first relates to the meaning of identity. We do not personally have only one identity, but rather many identities.[73] I am an anthropologist when researching and lecturing, a New Zealander when in New Zealand where I was born, an Australian when I use this nation's passport. In other words, the context determines which particular identity I choose at any particular moment. The second confusion is the failure to distinguish between *normative* and *dynamic* identities. A mission statement should contain a set of *normative* identities. It is an ideal expression of institutional identities; it sets standards to measure behavior.[74] *Dynamic* identities, however, are identities that institutions and individuals actually craft or mold for themselves *in light of their normative identities.* Dynamic identities are identities in the process of becoming, that is

---

[71] For example, since the early 1990s an increasing number of healthcare and educational ministries in Australia and North America are governed by lay trustees who head newly formed Public Juridic Persons (PJPs) that are accountable to local bishops or the Holy See. See Gabrielle McMullen and Martin Laverty, "Learnings from the Development of New Lay-Led Church Entities in Australia," *Australasian Catholic Record* 97, no. 2 (2020): 131–43.

[72] See Arbuckle, *Abuse and Cover-up*, 203–5.

[73] This theme is more fully explained in Gerald A. Arbuckle, *Catholic Identity or Identities?*

[74] See William E. Stempsey, "Institutional Identity and Roman Catholic Hospitals," *Christian Bioethics* 7, no. 1 (2001): 3; and Etienne Wenger, *Communities of Practice: Learning, Meaning, and Identity* (New York: Cambridge University Press, 1998), 149–63.

"the-institutions-engaging-with-context."[75] Far from being forever fixed in some essentialized past, they are subject to the incessant interplay of history, culture, and power.[76]

Likewise, there is not *one* Catholic identity but many, depending on context. Peter Steinfels sensibly reminds us that we should "stop thinking about Catholic identity as though this were something univocal. . . . There may be some overarching principles . . . but there is no single way of embodying them, and it might be wiser to speak of Catholic identities in the plural."[77] By way of summary, several guidelines help to expand our understanding of what is meant by the term *Catholic identities* and the ways they are to be formed.

Guideline 1: There are seven founding normative pillars of Catholic identities, but the primary pillar is Jesus Christ.[78]

There are seven broad pillars as sources of normative Catholic identities: scripture, Jesus Christ, the magisterium, sacramental symbols/rituals, Catholic social teaching, inclusivity, and the witness of faith-filled people. All seven are foundational pillars, but the pillar that is the primary, ultimate source of our identities is scripture. The primary normative pillar, the ultimate source of our Catholic identities, is Jesus Christ. He is the one who ennobles us, gives meaning to human life; he is *the* model that pastors offer parishioners, a Catholic school offers its pupils, and a Catholic healthcare facility offers its staff and patients. As Pope Francis repeatedly reminds us: "The center is Jesus Christ, who calls us and sends us."[79] Without our relationship to Christ, our ministries have no reason to exist. Yes, it is difficult today to explain that Jesus Christ is the primary founder of our ministries

---

[75] Thomas K. Fitzgerald, *Metaphors of Identity: A Culture-Communication Dialogue* (Albany: State University of New York Press, 1993), ix.

[76] See Stuart Hall, "Cultural Identity and Diaspora," in *Identity*, ed. Jonathan Rutherford (London: Lawrence and Wishart, 1990), 225.

[77] Peter Steinfels, *A People Adrift: The Crisis of the Roman Catholic Church in America* (New York: Simon and Schuster, 2003), 147–48. See also Neil Ormerod, "Identity and Mission in Catholic Organisations," *Australasian Catholic Record* 84, no. 4 (2010): 430–39.

[78] See Arbuckle, *Catholic Identity or Identities?*, 74–75.

[79] Pope Francis cited by Thomas Reese, "Pope Francis' Ecclesiology Rooted in Emmaus Story," *National Catholic Reporter* (August 6, 2013).

and that they are accountable to the Catholic Church. But we must find a way.

Guideline 2: The cultural/economic context in which a ministry resides influences the aspects of the seven normative pillars that are emphasized in its mission statement.

Catholic identities do not exist in a vacuum but within particular environmental contexts. For example, if a Catholic hospital or school is situated in the heart of an economically poor suburb, it will certainly emphasize the mission of Jesus Christ the Healer or Liberator to people who are disadvantaged. If a social environment happens to be racist, the school will emphasize the equality of all in Christ.

Guideline 3: People entering ministry—especially members of boards of trustees and management, CEOs, senior management/ executives, and middle management officials—must undertake an initiation rite of passage. Without this initiation and ongoing formation our Catholic ministries have a doubtful future.[80]

The didactic method of ministry teaching/learning was widely accepted in the church in the centuries after the Reformation (and it still remains popular in various circles).[81] People were instructed "from above," often in great detail, about what should identify Catholics; the norms defining Catholic identities were presented as rigidly static. Theology became highly rational. There was no need to listen to, and even learn from, the experiences of people being taught. The task of teachers and preachers was to pass on dogmatic statements to members of the church, whose task was to assent without question. If learning does happen, it usually does so solely at the cognitive level.[82]

---

[80] See Arbuckle, *Intentional Faith Communities*, 167–213; Angelo Belmonte and Richard Rymarz, *Leading Catholic Schools* (Melbourne: Garratt, 2020).

[81] This is sometimes referred to as the "jug to mug" theory or, as Paulo Freire says, the "banking theory of education." Paulo Freire, *Pedagogy of the Oppressed* (Harmondsworth: Penguin, 1972), 46. See also Arbuckle, *Catholic Identity or Identities?*, xiii.

[82] See Thomas H. Groome, *Will There Be Faith? A New Vision for Educating and Growing Disciples* (New York: HarperOne, 2011), 284.

Vatican II, however, called us back to the inductive teaching/learning method of ministry formation. Catholic identities today need to be implanted by persuasion and sustained ultimately by love.[83] The method aims to involve as many different dimensions of the learner as possible; its purpose is to foster integrated learning at the spiritual, cognitive, imaginative, affective, and behavioral levels. For example, through storytelling people are inspired to make real attitudinal and behavioral changes in their lives, because they recognize and accept for themselves the relevance and importance of what they are learning.[84] That is, it nurtures participants' inner resources and awareness as much as their knowledge and skills.

Jesus Christ used the inductive method (see Chapters 1 and 3),[85] for example, in his use of parables.[86] The parables of Jesus Christ and incidents in his life and/or in the Old Testament can again be discussion starters or springboards for people to craft their own meaning systems and discover that they can contribute to a new culture in the church no matter the obstacles. Pope Francis's encyclical *Fratelli Tutti* is a fine example of inductive formation. The first chapter describes the contemporary social, economic, and political context of evangelization, with which readers can reflectively identify, followed by a chapter devoted to the parable of the Good Samaritan. In subsequent chapters Francis invites readers to ponder the lessons of the parable in seeking solutions to contemporary problems.

---

[83] See Peter Steinfels, "Catholic Identity: Emerging Consensus," *Origins* 25, no. 11 (1995): 176.

[84] See Arbuckle, *Catholic Identity or Identities?*, 5–6, 10, 70; Stephen Denning, *The Springboard: How Storytelling Ignites Action in Knowledge-Era Organizations* (Boston: Butterworth-Heinemann, 2001), 41–54; Robert J. Shiller, *Narrative Economics: How Should Stories Go Viral and Drive Major Economic Events* (Princeton, NJ: Princeton University Press, 2019), 12–40; Laurence J. O'Connell and John Shea, eds., *Tradition on the Move: Leadership Formation in Catholic Health Care* (Sacramento, CA: MLC Press, 2013); Catholic Health Australia, *Formation for Mission* (Canberra: CHA, 2015).

[85] See Arbuckle, *Catholic Identity or Identities?*, 121–42, 173–225.

[86] About one-third of the documented sayings of Jesus in the Synoptic Gospels are in the form of parables. See Brad H. Young, *The Parables: Jewish Tradition and Christian Interpretation* (Peabody, MA: Hendrickson, 1998), 7.

Guideline 4: Those who collaborate in ministries but do not belong to the Catholic tradition are expected to respect the mission of ministries.

Melanie Morey writes: "Being Catholic is not a requirement for understanding the Catholic approach to education. However, having a grasp of how Catholics think is. And what Catholics think is shaped by specific religious beliefs."[87] Thus collaborators who are not of the Catholic tradition should be challenged to develop a grasp of how Catholics think and believe. And their public behavior is expected to be shaped by these beliefs. Our Catholic institutions, if they are to maintain their Catholic identities, have the right to require their staffs to behave in accordance with the gospel values and the ethical and social principles of the Catholic Church.[88] For this to happen there must be appropriate staff formation, as described in Guideline 3.

Guideline 5: The different roles in ministries need to be clarified.

One of the major problems in ministries is the failure to clarify roles and adhere to the principle of subsidiarity. *Role* means a prescribed or expected behavior associated with a particular position or status in a group. In ministries roles must be clearly defined, for example, between ministry leader and management, between board of trustees and management, and between pastor and parish council. If the boundaries of respective competencies are blurred, all kinds of quite unnecessary tensions and splitting will emerge, draining energy inward that should be directed outward to the realization of the ministry's mission. It is only once roles are clarified that it is possible to define levels of accountability.[89]

---

[87] Melanie M. Morey, "Education in a Catholic Framework," in *Teaching the Tradition: Catholic Themes in Academic Disciplines,* ed. John J. Piderit and Melanie M. Morey (Oxford: Oxford University Press, 2012), 399.

[88] For example, Pope Benedict XVI issued an apostolic letter, "The Services of Charity," November 11, 2012. The document set out new rules to strengthen the religious identities of Catholic charities and ensure that their activities conform to church teaching.

[89] See Brian Dive, *The Accountable Leader: Developing Effective Leadership through Managerial Accountability* (London: Kogan Press, 2008), 32.

Ministry Leaders

Ministry leaders, such as a bishop, a pastor, or a CEO of a faith-based hospital, must know what the role of leading demands. A *transforming* leader, most suited to the contemporary chaotic change, is one who collaboratively molds and communicates a task-oriented mission for community growth, providing transforming focus to the actions of others so that they are able to foster within themselves their potential for change.[90] Ministry leaders must keep their eye firmly on the mission of Jesus Christ and see that it permeates all decision-making.

Boards of Trustees and Management[91]

The history of boards of trustees and management is not good. Peter Drucker bluntly comments: "There is one thing all boards have in common. . . . They do not function."[92] The basic problem is the failure to clarify roles in light of mission. In the above case study of the destructive tension between the board of trustees and management in a Catholic college, the problem is that the different roles of the board had never been clarified and implemented. Trustees in a non-profit institution, such as a Catholic college or hospital, are entrusted with a twofold responsibility: first, to articulate the mission and to formulate policies based on the mission; second, to call the CEO and management to be accountable for implementing the policies based on the mission. David Smith, reflecting on the need for discernment for effective decision-making in boards, insists "the board must be a *community*. It must have developed the habit of and procedures for

---

[90] The definition is based on J. M. Burns's insights into transforming leadership. See James MacGregor Burns, *Leadership* (New York: Harper Torch, 1978).

[91] See Arbuckle, *Healthcare Ministry*, 222–30. A two-tiered governance structure is common in Catholic ministries, that is, separate boards of trustees and management.

[92] Peter Drucker, cited in James E. Orlikoff and Mary K. Totten, "Board Job Descriptions," *Trustee* (January 1997): 1. Others are equally direct. See Barbara E. Taylor, Richard P. Chait, and Thomas P. Holland, "Effective Governance by the Board of a Non-profit Organization Is a Rare and Unnatural Act," *Harvard Business Review* 74, no. 3 (1996): 36.

talking together about issues of institutional mission and purpose."[93] Catholic ministries, including boards of trustees and management, must become intentional faith-based communities in which decision-making is grounded in discernment.

Scriptural Reflection: Discernment in Difficult Times

Daily in our pastoral ministries we are confronted with stark either/or decisions. How, for instance, can we resolve the tension between our desire in these pandemic times to assist people in poverty, on the one hand, and our limited financial resources, on the other? The scriptures offer no simple answer to polar tensions. In fact, the tension between divine mercy and justice is one of the most profound impasses of our belief in God. Almighty God is the

> God merciful and gracious, . . .
> forgiving iniquity and transgression and sin,
> yet by no means clearing the guilty,
> but visiting the iniquity of the parents
> upon the children. (Ex 34:6–7)

The paradox of a merciful God who is at the same time ultimately just remains unresolved. Biblical writers return to the dilemma many times, especially in prayer.

> If you, O LORD, should mark iniquities,
> Lord, who could stand?
> But there is forgiveness with you,
> so that you may be revered. (Ps 130:3–4)

So also in our ministries. We need to ponder and discuss contradictory pastoral tensions that seem to have no immediate resolution. In a trusting and faith-motivated atmosphere we begin to discern how best

---

[93] David Smith, *Entrusted: The Moral Responsibilities of Trusteeship* (Bloomington: Indiana University Press, 1995), 27.

to balance the poles in tension—for example, between "the mission" and "the business." Creative action results.

Mary's rite of passage to become the mother of God has here special contemporary relevance (Lk 1:26–56). In the annunciation Mary passes from being a young unknown Jewish virgin to being the mother-to-be of the savior of humankind. Since this is to be a dramatic change of status for Mary with astonishing consequences for herself and the universe, the ritual is filled with deep theological symbolism.[94] Watch what happens when Mary must make an either/or decision.

The separation stage in her rite of passage is brief (Lk 1:26–27). The initiation is to be led by God with the angel Gabriel as the go-between. The salutation, "Greetings, favored one! The Lord is with you" (Lk 1:28) is not a standard greeting, but it is messianic in structure and aim (see Zeph 3:14–17), an invitation to celebrate the coming of the messianic age. The words "favored one" refer not just to Mary's personal holiness but focus on the definitive origin of her blessedness, namely, that she is to be the mother of God.[95] The mythology that is to pervade the initiation ritual is being stated from the outset.

Now the traumatic liminality stage. The greeting causes Mary anxiety. Her orderly life is much disturbed: "she was much perplexed by his words and pondered what sort of greeting this might be" (Lk 1:29). The key words are "perplexed" and "pondered"—two words with which we can identify as we struggle to make the right pastoral decisions in worrying times. The angel seeks to comfort Mary: "Do not be afraid, Mary, for you have found favor with God" (Lk 1:30). The angel then reveals to Mary the meaning of her rite of passage: the child is to be the Davidic Messiah earlier foretold in history (2 Sam 7:9, 13, 14, 16).

At this point Mary is profoundly troubled because she is a virgin (Lk 1:34). What does Mary do? She pauses in this chaotic moment. She moves to the level of faith. Then the angel discloses something unimagined in the past, namely, that the child is to be the unique Son of God through the power of the Holy Spirit.[96] The paradox at

---

[94] See François Bovon, *Luke 1* (Minneapolis: Fortress Press, 2002), 49–65.

[95] See Wilfrid J. Harrington, "St. Luke," in *A New Catholic Commentary on Holy Scripture*, ed. Reginald C. Fuller et al., 987–88 (London: Nelson, 1969).

[96] See Raymond E. Brown, *An Introduction to the New Testament* (New York: Doubleday, 1997), 229.

the heart of Mary's liminal experience is resolved—God is to be the father. Humanly speaking this makes no sense at all, but from God's perspective "nothing will be impossible" (Lk 1:37). How is Mary to react to this awesome reality? After prayer, she accepts in faith what appears to be humanly impossible. "Then Mary said, 'Here am I, the servant of the Lord: let it be done to me according to your word'" (Lk 1:38). While remaining a virgin and through divine initiative, Mary is to be simultaneously both the mother of Jesus and his first disciple. Faith triumphs over distress.

The visitation of Mary's cousin Elizabeth (Lk 1:39–45) is the reentry stage in the ritual of initiation into her new role: Mary is fulfilling her first duty of sharing the good news with others. The fact that she so willingly and speedily is prepared to risk the physical dangers of a four-day journey confirms her profound conversion to her new role. In her song of praise in response to Elizabeth's there is further validation that she understands the culturally radical nature of her Son's future role. He is to turn the world's view of power and prestige based on wealth and authoritarianism upside down, for his message of hope is for the lowly and hungry. The toppling of the powerful is not to happen through violent riots of the weak, but through the appearance of a child who would be born not in a palace but in a stable that is exposed to marauding thieves. The reentry stage ends with Mary's taking leave of Elizabeth three months later (Lk 1:56).

In my introduction to this book I noted that no single crisis since the Second World War has left so many people dead and countless millions traumatized, overwhelmed by grief, and stunned by the chaotic cultural and economic consequences as COVID-19. There is a massive escalation of world poverty and inequalities. Tensions within and between nations have deepened. The solution? Vaccines alone will not resolve the national and global chaos. Efforts by individuals and governments to respond to these crises must be built on the values inherent in the parable of the Good Samaritan: solidarity, compassion, and justice. But the obstacles to implementing these values are so daunting that we can fall into paralyzing despair.

Take heart! In *Fratelli Tutti* Pope Francis reminds us that

> God continues to sow abundant seeds of goodness in our human family. The recent pandemic enabled us to recognize and appreciate once more all those around us who, in the midst

of fear, responded by putting their lives on the line. We begin to realize that our lives are interwoven with and sustained by ordinary people valiantly shaping the decisive events of our shared history: doctors, nurses, pharmacists, storekeepers and supermarket workers, cleaning personnel, caretakers, transport workers, men and women working to provide essential services and public safety, volunteers, priests and religious . . . They understood that no one is saved alone. . . .

"Hope speaks to us of a thirst, an aspiration, a longing for a life of fulfillment, a desire to achieve great things. . . . Hope is bold" [St. Irenaeus]. . . . Let us continue, then, to advance along the paths of hope. (FT, nos. 54-55)

Summary

- Pope Francis, speaking of the pandemic, tells us: "Like the disciples in the Gospel we were caught off guard by an unexpected, turbulent storm and we find ourselves afraid and lost. . . . The storm exposes our vulnerability and uncovers those false and superfluous certainties. . . . [A] propitious time to find the courage for a new imagination of the possible, with the realism that only the Gospel can offer us."[97]
- Pastoral imagination and creativity call us
  - To relive the founding experience of the early church, that is, evangelizing through intentional faith communities.
  - To struggle against injustices in all its forms, including institutional racism.
  - To understand the origins of Catholic fundamentalism. Membership in fundamentalist groups is not a question of logic, but generally of a sincere but misguided search for meaning and belonging.
  - To recognize that in ministries the dangers of "splitting" are real and have harmful pastoral consequences. Tensions are resolved through dialogue and discernment in a faith atmosphere.

---

[97] Pope Francis, quoted in Spadaro, "A New Imagination of the Possible."

Reflection Questions

1. Reread the section "Pope Francis: Pastoral Advice" at the beginning of the chapter. Do any particular points strike you? Why?
2. This chapter highlights three community models: enmeshed, disengaged, and intentional. Which model describes your situation? Why should we foster intentional faith communities?
3. Are there endangering polar tensions in your faith community? What steps can be taken to resolve them?

Index